211 Things A
Clever Girl Can Do

211 Things A Clever Girl Can Do

Bunty Cutler

A Perigee Book

A PERIGEE BOOK
Published by the Penguin Group
Penguin Group (USA) Inc.
375 Hudson Street, New York, New York 10014, USA
Penguin Group (Canada), 90 Eglinton Avenue East, Suite 700, Toronto, Ontario M4P 2Y3, Canada (a division of Pearson Penguin Canada Inc.) • Penguin Books Ltd., 80 Strand, London WC2R 0RL, England • Penguin Group Ireland, 25 St. Stephen's Green, Dublin 2, Ireland (a division of Penguin Books Ltd.) • Penguin Group (Australia), 250 Camberwell Road, Camberwell, Victoria 3124, Australia (a division of Pearson Australia Group Pty. Ltd.) • Penguin Books India Pvt. Ltd., 11 Community Centre, Panchsheel Park, New Delhi—110 017, India • Penguin Group (NZ), 67 Apollo Drive, Rosedale, North Shore 0632, New Zealand (a division of Pearson New Zealand Ltd.) • Penguin Books (South Africa) (Pty.) Ltd., 24 Sturdee Avenue, Rosebank, Johannesburg 2196, South Africa

Penguin Books Ltd., Registered Offices: 80 Strand, London WC2R 0RL, England

While the author has made every effort to provide accurate telephone numbers and Internet addresses at the time of publication, neither the publisher nor the author assumes any responsibility for errors, or for changes that occur after publication. Further, the publisher does not have any control over and does not assume any responsibility for author or third-party websites or their content.

211 THINGS A CLEVER GIRL CAN DO

First American edition: May 2008
Originally published in Great Britain in 2007 by HarperCollins.

Perigee trade paperback ISBN: 978-0-399-53441-6

PRINTED IN THE UNITED STATES OF AMERICA

10 9 8 7 6 5 4 3 2 1

PUBLISHER'S NOTE: The recipes contained in this book are to be followed exactly as written. The publisher is not responsible for your specific health or allergy needs that may require medical supervision. The publisher is not responsible for any adverse reactions to the recipes contained in this book.

Outdoor recreational activities are by their very nature potentially hazardous. All participants in such activities must assume the responsibility for their own actions and safety. If you have any health problems or medical conditions, consult with your physician before undertaking any outdoor activities. The information contained in this guide book cannot replace sound judgment and good decision making, which can help reduce risk exposure, nor does the scope of this book allow for disclosure of all the potential hazards and risks involved in such activities. Learn as much as possible about the outdoor recreational activities in which you participate, prepare for the unexpected, and be cautious. The reward will be a safer and more enjoyable experience.

Most Perigee books are available at special quantity discounts for bulk purchases for sales promotions, premiums, fund-raising, or educational use. Special books, or book excerpts, can also be created to fit specific needs. For details, write: Special Markets, Penguin Group (USA) Inc., 375 Hudson Street, New York, New York 10014.

This book is dedicated to the memory of Peter "Flobbadob" Hawkins, who provided the background voices to my girlhood; Edward Ardizzone, who drew the pictures; and Elizabeth Cotten, who supplied the music—not only upside down but back to front.

Contents

II Be Handy

III Life of the Party

IV Fun and Games
A Robust Guide to Leisure and Pleasure

V Knock 'Em Dead

VI Alpha Woman

Acknowledgments

Writing a book is a collaborative process that involves all sorts of people you never hear about or see mentioned in the acknowledgments. There's Mr. and Mrs. Evans who deliver my milk. Without them it would be impossible for me to make a comforting cup of hot chocolate after a hard day's authoring, yet they are never shortlisted for the Pulitzer Prize. And what about the index at the back? It goes on for pages. Who was lumbered with that soul-destroying chore? Not me of course; I'm far too important. No, it was done by an excellent gentleman called Ben Murphy who is a professional indexer—yes of course there's such a job. Then there are the illustrations that so charmingly illuminate the text. Nicolette Caven did those, and thank goodness she did; my own rudimentary scratchings would have disfigured every page on which they appeared. Three cheers also to my editors at HarperCollins, Chris Smith, Kate Latham, and Natalie Jerome, who encouraged me throughout, crossed out all the rubbishy bits, and made sure I spelled *necrotizing fasciitis* right. Please also raise your glasses to the charming Marian Lizzi, my editor at Perigee, and her alarmingly efficient assistant Katie Wasilewski. My agent Laura Morris deserves honorable mention for cheerfully bringing me back to reality when I insisted that it would have been better if I had become a nun, as does my mother-in-law Joan, who (apart from being a really good and nice mother-in-law) sent me helpful recipes and things. My sister-in-law Marianne Saabye read the text with a discerning eye and supplied valuable criticism, for which I am very grateful, while her son Jed improvised blues tunes on the guitar in a cool way. My brother Tom Cutler deserves a crouching ovation for his terse input when I was trying to get a grip on manly things. His own book, *211 Things a Bright Boy Can Do*, first gave me the idea for this one.

Last but really foremost I thank my Auntie Sarah for digging out interesting facts, clippings, and whatnot, and for generally steering me safely between a rock and a hard place. Others who should be mentioned in research dispatches are my good friend Jo Uttley and her cohort: Siobhan Collis, Susie Ireland, and Charlotte Wolff, all of whom gave me helpful ideas. Thank you, girls.

How to Use This Book

W hen I asked my brother what he was doing on Saturday he told me, "Going to bed with a trollop named Marion Fay!" I realized at once, being the literate person that I am, that he was referring to Anthony Trollope's *novel* of that name, one which I had myself only recently hurled aside, repelled by the long and mind-hammeringly boring introduction by Dr. somebody or other.

When I'm reading a book, I don't want to wade through a great big fatuous prolegomenon; I want to get straight to the juicy bits. My copy of *Don Quixote* starts with such a turgid introduction—by the unfortunately named Marcus Cock—that just one glance had me violently falling asleep, the 752-page masterpiece slipping from my nerveless grasp.

Anyhow, this is all by roundabout way of apology for my own preamble. You don't have to read it of course, you could skip straight to the juicy bits, but you might like to know that instead of twenty-nine pages of po-faced blather, this introduction is a concise exegesis designed not only to help you get a feel for the book but also to stop you setting yourself on fire.

211 Things a Clever Girl Can Do is unlike other how-to books for girls—particularly the ancient ones full of pictures of Girl Scouts holding saucepans. Cheerless volumes of the sort I have in mind include *Our Girls' Holiday Book*, which contains among its mottled cardboard pages an illustrated essay called *How to grow taller*, as well as the prize-winningly dull *Posters for school functions*. My *How to pass gas with grace and charm* is one of a number of articles in which I have striven to give advice to the modern girl in a style more exciting and lively than those musty treatises of bygone times.

I have also sought to avoid the feebleness of those dreary story-albums of yesteryear, such as (my favorite) *Gay Stories For Girls*, published in the 1950s—somewhat startlingly by Beaver Books. The pedestrian quality of the narratives in that encyclopedia may be gleaned from their not very bracing titles, like *Olive and Peggy have ideas* (how shocking!) and *Vera in the Stone Age*. They really seemed to do little back then but knit, bake cakes, darn socks, and polish their menfolk; the word *feminism* would have left them looking as vacant as the term *carpet bumping* probably does your grandma. I have concentrated instead on vital lifestyle topics most useful to the busy young lady of today such as *How to lose six pounds in six hours* and *Eighteen uses for a spare fishnet stocking*. The reader I have in mind is, you may deduce, more your typical Calamity Jane than drippy Shirley Temple.

Trying to read this book all in one sitting will cause you to go mad. You would do better to approach it like one of those big boxes of Belgian chocolates. Consult the contents; home in on a selected morsel; and consume it. If you were to eat the whole lot in one sitting you would be sick in comprehensive shades of umber, and it's the same with this book. So once you've taken in an elegant sufficiency—say half a dozen pages—go and do your nails with a glass of Champagne, or something (I don't mean do your nails with the Champagne, I mean do your nails with nail varnish and drink the Champagne—*obviously*).

If you follow my instructions carefully, safety shouldn't be a problem (pay no attention to the mix-up in the previous paragraph). You can do yourself a favor by using the tools I recommend; there's a big difference between a pair of *sharp* scissors and the rusty fluff-covered things you found down the back of the sofa. Blunt blades are no use unless you're cutting up custard.

The recipes in *211 Things a Clever Girl Can Do* specify particular ingredients. You are welcome to vary these according to what's in your kitchen but don't blame me if your Turkish delight turns to concrete because you doubled the cornstarch or something.

Finally, I know what you're still wondering: why is this book called *211 Things a Clever Girl Can Do* instead of something sensible, like *200 Things*? Well, this is a companion volume to my brother Tom's *211 Things a Bright Boy Can Do*. Don't ask me to explain what was going through his head when he came up with the number. When I talked to my publishers about changing it to something more intelligent, the marketing people suggested I shouldn't interfere with an already successful brand. I haven't got the faintest idea what they're talking about—they have a language all their own, those people. But there again I'm just the author—what do I know about anything?

Anyway, now for the juicy bits.

I

Staying Alive

Survival Skills for the Modern Everywoman

*Whatever women do they must do twice
as well as men to be thought half as good.
Luckily, this is not difficult.*

CHARLOTTE WHITTON

How to
Escape a Vicious Swarm of Bees

Instructions

* Bees normally attack only when threatened—take care if you are around a nest or a hive. Once they do sting, a pheromone is released that rouses other healthy, grown-up busy, busy bees, who then go into defense mode, stinging away merrily. The first thing to do is get out of there. Kick off high heels or other unsuitable footwear and run as fast as you can. Probably, the best place to head for is the inside of a building. But don't forget to shut the door behind you. Your common or garden honeybee will probably give up chasing you after about 150 feet (1½ times the length of a basketball court), but African honeybees will go three times this far—4½ basketball courts.

* Bees will instinctively go for your head so, as you flee, try to cover your face with whatever you have on hand (not molasses, obviously, I mean something like a blanket or a jacket).

* Running through bushes is a good way to slow down swarming bees, and a wind will make it harder for them, too. Switching on a leaf blower and blasting them with it is worth a try, but one tends to be too preoccupied with running and screaming to do much else in these bee escapades. If you must scream, keep your mouth closed. Being stung on or in the mouth may cause a swelling that can block your airway.

* *Important warning*: Never jump into water, because although bees are rotten swimmers they are excellent hoverers and will probably be waiting for you when you come up, gasping for air.

* If (when) you do get stung, remove the sting as quickly as you can by raking your finger nail or your credit card across it. Unlike wasps, bees commit suicide when they sting, releasing a poison sac

3

that continues its muscular pumping action outside the bee's body for as long as ten minutes. Unless you are seriously allergic to bee venom (in which case you might go into anaphylactic shock, a life-threatening medical emergency causing rapid constriction of the airway) you are unlikely to suffer serious harm, even if you are stung several times.

* Ice, antihistamine pills, and calamine lotion all work pretty well on a non-allergic sting. In most cases, the pain will disappear within a couple of hours, though the swelling may only become visible the next day. Also recommended is a glass of wine and a day at the spa.

❁ *Pristine honey has been found alongside the ancient mummies of the pharaohs.* ❁

How to
Survive a Plane Crash

When I was young and living in England, an entrée was a dish you were served between the fish and meat courses. This caused me all kinds of confusion when I first went to America, where an entrée is the *main* dish. It didn't bother me for long because I became more interested in other things, having met a tall, dark, handsome cowboy who rapidly became my main dish. Unfortunately there were problems; there always are.

I remember it started when we were sitting in an airplane one day and he began to wobble like a jellyfish on a spin dryer. He was, it emerged, scared of flying. This was all right by me and I was solicitous and kind, but it rapidly became plain that he was also scared of small spaces, high places, open spaces, spiders, stairs, top hats, electricity, doorways, doctors, strong smells, mailboxes, fishing with a net on a pole, pianos, and *nuns*. I'm afraid my psychotherapeutic powers fell far short of what was necessary for the treatment of this cornucopia of phobias and it all ended in tears when he refused, one day, to cross the threshold of a hotel because it had a blue carpet. He maintained that blue carpets made his hair stand on end. I told him he made *my* hair stand on end and that was that.

Anyway, the point is he knew everything there is to know about surviving a plane crash, and I've never forgotten it. Here it is, in all its compulsive neuroticism:

* Count the rows as you first approach your seat and remember exactly how far you are from the nearest exit.
* Book seats no more than seven rows from an emergency exit and preferably in an aisle or on an exit row. Best of all, sit right next to the exit.
* Practice undoing your seat belt with your eyes closed. It's quite tricky if you are in a panic and haven't had a few practice runs.
* Peruse the safety card in detail and check which brace position you are going to adopt as the plane starts to plummet toward the ground.
* Feel under your seat for the cushion, which can allegedly be used as a flotation device in a "landing on water" (unsurvivable crash into concrete-hard freezing liquid that will drown you). I wonder whether anyone has *ever* done this.
* Crashes happen most often during climb, descent, landing, and takeoff, so be alert. In a crash you may have just seconds so don't drink or sleep.
* Take off your stilettos before leaping on to the inflatable slide. Tears in the fabric are unsightly—and there's no need for carelessness.
* Survivors are the ones who don't stop for family or friends. Just walk all over other people, screaming loudly.

HOW TO SURVIVE A HELICOPTER CRASH
Very few people get out of a helicopter that's crashed from more than a few feet above the ground. My advice? Go by plane.

❋ *The pilot in the first fatal plane crash (1908) was Orville Wright.* ❋

How to
Manage an Umbrella in the Wind

*H*andling an umbrella in the wind is as hazardous today as it looks as if it was in Edwardian times, though the modern instrument is different. When I was small, umbrellas were still beautiful things and a pleasure to use, though just as today you couldn't buy one that started shrieking if you left it on a train. My grandfather used to get his from a supplier near the British Museum. Black, sleek, and pointed they were, with a yellow cane handle like the knobbly finger of an arthritic wizard. The modern equivalent is a collapsible plastic article that only lasts through a couple of rainstorms.

Opening an umbrella in the wind demands skill. If you are not careful you are likely to put somebody's eye out with one of those little blobs on the end of the spokes. People often leap away in alarm, sometimes bumping other passers-by or jumping into the road, causing mayhem and car crashes. But you mustn't worry about them because you will have your hands full, fighting something like a cross between an angry black swan and a kite. Here are a few tips.

INSTRUCTIONS

1   For a start, always open the umbrella with the wind blowing toward you. If the wind is behind you it will simply blow the thing inside out with an enormous whoof! Not only is this hard to recover from but you also look ridiculous.

2   Once it's open keep the umbrella facing into the wind. In a gale this will mean pushing it before you like a shield, with its umbrellorial axis near the horizontal. You are now effectively blind and will run into people with the sharp point (if it has a sharp point). The worst thing is two blind horizontal-umbrella holders meeting each other going in opposite directions. Let us draw a veil over the scene.

3 A sudden sharp change in wind direction can catch you off guard. A lady of my acquaintance was once picked up and carried over a low wall as she clung desperately on to what had become, effectively, a parasail. If you find the wind suddenly behind you, simply fling the umbrella down into the gutter. Better safe than sorry.

4 After a rainstorm, never stand with your umbrella open, dripping dry. I once saw a humorist drop Ping Pong balls and cotton into a lady's open umbrella at a bus stop, followed by a lighted match. Seeing the smoke, she flailed the thing around, thus fanning the fire enough to ignite the umbrella's skin. It was quite a show, I can tell you.

5   If all this sounds too much like hard work, get yourself one of those see-through folded-up rain hats that tie under the chin. Very aging but easier.

❀ *The scent from dry earth following a shower is petrichor, a plant oil.* ❀

How to
Dig a Latrine

Rather like the ability to speak Swahili or walk on stilts (see page 252) digging a latrine is one of those skills possessed by few among us these days. As such, it can score you points in any number of outdoor situations.

A latrine is a trench in the ground suitable for accommodating volume. It's environmentally friendly, too, if you follow the simple rules, and a real business opportunity. Think about India, where they have to handle some 230 million gallons of liquid matter and 297 million pounds of solid matter every day with only a dicey system of collection and disposal. Just imagine the opportunities there are for the clever entrepreneur. YouTube nothing, here comes YouTrench.

I'm getting carried away.

I know of little more rewarding than digging a latrine. It provides vigorous arm, back, and hip-and-thigh exercise as well as a sense of accomplishment once finished. And it's free. So, without more ado, here are the essential steps to the perfect latrine.

REQUIRED
*   *A pickax*
*   *A spade*

You need to dig deep and the ground will probably have too many stones and gnarly roots for a spade to be much use, so get out your pickax. This tool is ideal for excavating deep trenches, and it will cut through all manner of subterranean obstructions. Don't try this in a ball gown, though, because it's tough work and you are going to be grunting and perspiring more than a little. The best gear is jeans and a T-shirt, maybe along with a paisley bandana at the throat for a little color. But no pearls, girls.

RULES

1   Latrines should be more than 150 feet from open water or springs, and always *downhill* of a water source.
2   The position should be clearly signposted with bright ribbon hung along the trail leading to the excavation.

METHOD

1   Using your spade, cut out and save the topsoil for later replacement.
2   Now dig a narrow pit with your pickax at least the length of a man, about 1 foot wide and 4 feet deep, keeping the soil in a mound nearby.
3   When you regain consciousness the next day, dismiss the concerned friends who are feeding you sips of tea and get someone handy to help you make a solid cover that fits creepy-crawly tight, with a lid or two (why should *you* do all the hard work?).
4   Having conquered the hole, you can now properly delegate the final task of *daily trench check* to an assistant. He or she must report when the 50 percent level has been achieved (rather like the *Do not load above this line* mark in the supermarket freezer). Get your assistant to fill in and top up with remaining earth. Then you can dig another latrine, singing as you go because the fun never stops.

Along with earth from your mound, campfire ash stored in a box makes a useful post-sprinkle. Well, *it's important*. And by the way, latrines should be dug only in the wilderness. They are inappropriate for behind your motel room alongside the motorway service station.

Happy digging.

❀ *The first iron spades were made by the Sumerians c. 4000 BCE.* ❀

How to
Get a Spider Out
of the Bathtub

O ne glorious spring day last March, when the blackbirds were whistling in the magnolia, I got an email—it would once have been a letter—from somebody called sam.woodyard. It was a name I immediately recognized as that of an old school friend about whom I'd heard nothing for more than a thousand years—or several decades anyway. Samantha's father had started as an assistant in a small locksmith's shop (small shop, not small locksmith) and worked his way up, turning the business into a multimillion-dollar security corporation and becoming CEO. This was the time when everybody didn't keep changing job, school, house, country, husband, and haircut—a time when starting at the bottom and working your way up was a good way to get on.

Anyway, as I recalled his daughter, I remembered a svelte, sparkling, lithe, and willowy beauty who was going to become an actress. We arranged to meet at Penn station, but when she turned up she was a huge fat woman quite unlike the sylph of remembrance, her waddling toes swathed in carpet slippers, her blotty yellow sausage legs telling of a life spoiled by malady and defeat. She greeted me with "It's Howdy Doody time!," possibly the most meaningless and annoying catchphrase ever. She had changed.

The only reason I'm going into all this is that Samantha was one of the few girls I knew who would happily dispose of the horrible, huge, brown, hairy-legged spiders that skulked rebarbatively in the school bathrooms. These are a few of her methods:

* *Violence*: Use a tennis racket, towel, or other object to whack or smash the thing into oblivion. But mind the glass bottles.
* *Gadget*: Spider-catcher gizmos are available. But don't then wash the creature down the drain; it will shake itself dry and be out the hole again before you can say octopod.

* *Spray*: Use an aerosol insecticide (aracnicide). Failing that, hairspray will "freeze" its legs into position so it can't scuttle up the side of the tub.
* *Washcloth method*: Squash the thing. If you don't like getting up close, throw the washcloth at it first to stun it and finish it off with the loofah.

❀ *The loofah is a tropical vine fruit, not a kind of sponge.* ❀

How to
Change a Tire

One foul day, I remember, I was driving to a wedding. Squinting between the furiously swishing windshield wipers, I drove over a huge bump just as a flash of blue lighting lit up the sky. And then the car's steering seemed to go a bit weird.

Stopping beside some sheep, I craned my neck out and spotted at once that I had a flat tire. Of course, I was dressed in a new, lovely, and expensive LRD (little red dress) and now had to change a tire in a tempestuous rainstorm. I am going to draw a veil over the remainder of that morning, which contained, I am ashamed to confess, an extravagance of profane rhetoric that would have frozen the marrow of Blackbeard's most fescennine brigand and caused his blood to run yellow.

In case you ever find yourself in a "flat-tire situation" here are a few tips so you can drive away in no time. Let's just hope you never have to do it in the rain.

REQUIRED
* *Car (obviously)*
* *Wheel brace (This is a lever, sometimes in a cross formation, with a spanner-type cup at the end for putting over the wheel nuts.)*
* *A jack*
* *A rag*
* *Alcohol hand wipes*

* *Vaseline*
* *Gloves (vital)*

INSTRUCTIONS

1   As soon as you are aware of the flat, drive to a safe place, as slowly as you dare on the punctured tire. If you're on the highway avoid changing the wheel on the shoulder. Instead, use an emergency phone and call for help. On a main road, find a rest stop or parking lot. But even here, be aware of the traffic. I was once nearly hit by a flying scaffolding pole that came off a truck.

2   Having stopped on a well-lit, level surface, turn off and put the car into reverse. Put on the emergency brake and hazard lights.

3   Now, remove any heavy luggage or dead bodies from the trunk.

4   Take off your shoes if they are fancy. *You shouldn't have been driving in those.*

5   Smear your hands with a light coating of Vaseline and put on the gloves. These can be wool, leather, or whatever. I keep a pair of

suede gardening gloves in the trunk. If you need to protect your dress, try putting your coat on back-to-front.

6 Take the spare tire out/off. Now is often the time that you notice: (A) there is no spare, or (B) it's flat. Jump up and down with rage, screaming at the top of your voice. There's little else you can do. If you're lucky enough to find the spare, be careful lifting it out—it's extremely heavy.

7 Remove the tools. No jack? No wheel brace? Time for more bloodcurdling screams and a mental note to have a polite word with a mechanic.

8 Consult your handbook for detailed instructions and locate the correct lifting point nearest the wheel you are to replace. Don't jack at any other point; the car may collapse, seriously damaging the bodywork and taking your foot off.

9 If the hubcap is covering the wheel nuts, lever it off with the wheel brace.

10 Loosen the nuts by half a turn. Be aware that the nuts are often tightened in the garage by a machine. If they are really stiff, stand on the brace to shift them. If this doesn't work, try jumping up and down on it.

11 Use the jack to lift the car. Once the body is up, but before the wheel is off the ground, push the spare underneath to provide a safety cushion in case the car slips off the jack. A car can easily do this, even on a flat surface, so *never get under a car that is jacked up.*

12 Keep lifting and once the wheel is just clear of the road unscrew the nuts in diagonal pairs. I use my *rubber* gloves for this, otherwise I can't feel what I'm doing. Put the nuts in your handbag or hat so they don't roll away or fall down a drain. Wrap them in a bit of old paper or tissue so they don't make your stuff filthy. Keep wiping everything with the rag as you go—it helps *you* to stay clean.

13 Remove the wheel. Three little words that sound so simple. This is a hell of a job on your own because the wheel is enormously heavy, and also filthy. It was hard enough getting the spare out of the car;

this is much more difficult. Once it's off, heave it beside the new one, under the car.

14   Now wrestle the spare into place. More grunting, groaning, and quiet cursing under your breath. Is it on the right way? If not take it off and do it again. (This is awful, isn't it?) Replace the wheel nuts in diagonal pairs and finger-tighten them.

15   Jack the car down until the new tire just touches the road. Then tighten the nuts a little more with the brace.

16   Drag the flat from underneath and finish lowering the car. Remove the jack and fully tighten the wheel nuts, jumping on the brace if you like. Put the damaged wheel in the trunk: more heaving, finger pinching, and medical-student-type swearing. Replace the filthy tools and pop the hubcap or plastic cover back on the wheel.

17   Throw the gloves into the trunk and remove the Vaseline from your hands with a couple of alcohol wipes. They should come up clean, and no broken nails. OK, your hair's a mess, your dress is ruined, and your face is black. But your nails are perfect.

18   Get the tire replaced as soon as you can.

❀ *Tires lose air at a rate of about a pound a month.* ❀

How to
Build a Pioneer Log Cabin

*A*braham Lincoln was born in a one-room log cabin in 1809; if it was good enough for him it ought to be good enough for anyone. Of course, building your own log cabin is not exactly quick or easy, but it *is* rewarding. Just imagine how proud you'll feel as you finally step back to admire your completed work—in three years' time. Remember, though, that this is a two-person business; indeed, the more people you can rope in, the merrier.

REQUIRED

* *A broadax for tree felling and chopping*
* *An adze (an ax with its blade on sideways) for shaping and working*

Your pioneer's log cabin will be based on the traditional kind, which was generally just one story high and one log long. Depending on log size, each long wall was made typically of, say, five thick logs up to where the roof started, and on the short ends, those five logs plus about five more, forming the tapering top half of the gable, up to the roof apex. Like the inside of the traditional cabin, yours will consist of just one room, which will be big enough to accommodate a small family.

INSTRUCTIONS

1   *Cut your nails short and dress in something robust.*

2   *Select your site*: You are looking for a sunny spot that requires little clearing and offers good drainage. An earth floor requires no foundations, although the latter have the advantage of keeping the damp out. If you can rest your cabin corners on rock, so much the better.

3   *Cut down about twenty-five trees with your broadax*: There's not much to say about this except, *get someone to help you.* The best trees for the purpose are old and very straight, with few branches (less to chop off and fewer knots).

4   *Lay the logs at right angles one on top of the next, making four corners*: You are building using round logs with the bark still on, and if you've picked the best trees, very little hewing should be required. Secure the corners with notches in the form of half-moon grooves hacked with your adze into the ends of the lower of each pair of interlocking logs. Lay the upper log like a finger into a curled palm, where it will be securely held by the notch. Then make a notch in the top of that one, and so on until you have the basic hut shape, about five logs high.

5   *Hack out your doorway* in one of the gable ends. Make it a sensible size; you don't want tall uncles to keep banging their heads every

time they come into the room with a bundle of bear skins. A clap-board door secured by battens and hung from wooden hinges is a must.

6   *Cut your window*: Do this by hacking horizontally into the lower (top of the window) and upper (bottom of the window) halves of two logs in one of the long sides of your cabin, then join the hori-zontal cuts with two vertical cuts to make a rectangular hole. Cover this with greased paper. I think I first saw paper windows in Richard Sparrow's 1640 house in Plymouth, Massachusetts, but I might be wrong.

7   *Make the shutters*: Use long clapboards fastened to frames of split-wood. Fashion hinges from the same material. A wooden latch may be made for the inside. In the old days, a leather latch string was a signal of hospitality.

8   *Fill any gaps between the logs with chinking*: "Chinking" is a mortar mixture of woodchips and plaster. It may include moss, grass, mud, and sand, depending on whatever is locally available. Careful notching in step 4 will minimize the chinks between the logs. Cracks are common as the wood dries, but they are harmless and will only add to the charm of your rustic dwelling.

9   *Put on the roof*: The easiest to make is a "purlin" roof of stout poles notched at each end into the uppermost logs of the gable walls. Each of the logs making up the top half of the gable end is a little shorter than the one below it, this "staircase" forming the character-istic pointy tip of the wall. It is this angle that determines the pitch of your roof. The purlins run from one gable end right across the room to the opposite gable end. Once you've got them all on, make your roof by splitting enough 4-foot-long oak clapboards to cover the area and lay them on top of the purlin supports, keeping them in place under weighty timber poles on the outside.

10 *Furnish your log cabin*: A wood stove, two or three beds, a table and chairs are essential items, along with your exercise bike, TV, wash-ing machine, microwave, computer, and so forth. All the vital equipment of the simple life.

11   *Take it easy:* Alternatively you could get yourself a tin of Lincoln Logs and put the whole thing together in about twenty minutes on the kitchen table.

❀ *The world's largest log cabin, built in 1930, is now a Quebec hotel.* ❀

How to
Cope with Football in the Home

He's six inches from the screen (remote control clutched tightly) either leaping ceilingward with cries of, "Yeeeeeeeeeesaa!," or writhing about the furniture in despair, giving out low primeval moans like a bear in a pit. Yes, it's football.

How are you going to cope with it? This is no trivial question if you've set up home with a man, because it will become a routine feature of your weekends. There are, happily, a number of methods at your disposal—not cures so much as symptomatic treatments, since the condition is hopeless.

The first idea—a preventive or prophylactic one—is to attach yourself to a fellow who doesn't like sports. My friend Liz thought she'd solved the problem when she married Graham, a quiet and studious graphic designer. Unfortunately, it became rapidly clear that he was little different from the rest of them, expressing his masculine side by obsessively watching unsubtitled French films every Saturday, six inches from the screen, remote control clenched tightly. Liz told me, "I am as sick as any human being could be of *A Bout de Souffle!* I have sat through it hundreds of times, and I never liked it in the first place." So be warned.

Perhaps the most useful ruse is the if-you-can't-beat-'em-join-'em one. My friend Siobhan says she lets out knowledgeable-sounding phrases such as, "They're really 'asking questions of the other side,' aren't they," as she surreptitiously flips through a magazine. She adopted this tactic after her remarks like, "What's on the Discovery Channel, darling?"

and "Whoa—look at his legs; I wouldn't mind peeking up *his* shorts," were met with snarls of hate.

If you are not going to go out for hours, then the generally preferred strategy seems to be grin and bear it, and it's the same for poker evenings. My friend Lola returned early to find a boys' night still in full swing, with a thousand beer bottles strewn about the carpet, chips everywhere, and four men sitting six inches from the screen (remote control clutched tightly), watching two ladies dressed in unlikely nurses uniforms pouting, moaning, and bending. "What did you do?" I asked her. "I spent two hours shopping on the Internet," she said. "Using his card." Excellent idea.

❋ *A football's distinctive shape is the prolate spheroid.* ❋

Correct Toilet Seat Procedure in a Shared Dwelling Place

On the wonderful wooden trains of long ago there used to be a notice in the bathroom that said, in the terse prose of the time, "Gentlemen lift the seat." Was this a philosophical premise, a bald statement of fact, or maybe a suggestion that any man who didn't was not a gentleman? What it really was, of course, was a forlorn request disguised as an imperative.

Although we are certainly glad when the gentleman does lift the seat, the main problem really comes, of course, when he doesn't put it back down again. If you live somewhere with a lot of men—or even just one man—the raised-seat problem can move beyond the forlorn-request stage to become a daily botheration that may, with the cumulative power of water dripping on a gray stone, wear you down over months, years, or even decades. I've never heard of anyone divorcing her husband just because of careless, or even willfully improper, toilet seat procedure but it wouldn't surprise me.

Let us examine the arguments. I am for the moment excluding the lid from the discussion because things are quite complicated enough without that.

FUNCTION

* There is only one way that ladies can use the toilet and that is with the seat down. If you've ever wandered into a dark bathroom in a shared student flat in the middle of the night and sat down, forgetting to check first, then you will know just how startling it can be to find yourself suddenly with your knees against your chin, your lower legs sticking out horizontally in front of you, and the cold hand of the vitreous china against your privates.

* Men, on the other hand, have the luxury of choice. And since, most of the time, they can go standing up, it makes sense for them to lift the seat and replace it after use. Some of the time, down will be right for them anyway (point 1).

* *Note*: For reasons best known to himself, the actor Kenneth Williams always insisted on sitting on the porcelain. Not surprisingly, a seat one day fell against him, causing nasty scratches to his back. This only confirms, I think, that down is the sole reliable seat position.

STATISTICS

* Statistics show that women are more frequent users of the lavatory than are men, even once you allow for things like men availing themselves of the rosebushes, going behind fences, or signing their names in the snow. The argument for down is, therefore, further inclined in our favor (point 2).

AESTHETICS

* A bit like opinions about *The Scream, Mona Lisa,* or something by Mark Rothko, the aesthetics of toilet seat position are what you might call a gray area, a sort of backwater of the art criticism racket. Who, after all, is to say whether up is more pleasing than down?

* Although the argument is likely to end in fisticuffs, I think a very good case can be made for down being the natural, normal, and most pleasing TSP (toilet seat position), as well as the safest. There is a wholeness, an authority, a Dutch-Masters-landscapeness to down. Up is much more angular, unhappy-diagonal-Cubist, with out-of-

tune-Stravinsky musical overtones. It's Expressionist-Russian rather than Dutch Masters. I don't know about you, but I definitely don't want to sit on a Wassily Kandinsky, thank you very much (point 3).

The final position is clear. Down is the proper default position for the toilet seat in a shared dwelling place, with up an acceptable temporary position only. So please, gentlemen, lift the seat, but put it down again afterward.

❦ *In August 2004* The Scream *was stolen from Oslo's Munch Museum.* ❦

How to
Tell When a Man Likes You

W omen are so far ahead of men in the field of understanding and using body language that they are already at a distinct advantage. Men, bless them, are about as clever in this department as a gibbon trying to get a fistful of raisins out of a narrow jam jar. That is to say, not very. Men are also simpler than women, fancying almost all of them almost all of the time and giving out fairly obvious signals. If you can spot these signals you will be ahead of the blonde, blue-eyed, air-headed competition—always a good thing. You should therefore start from the assumption that Man A *does*, in fact, like you. Your problem will be the common female one of Man A passing *your* acceptability tests. How complicated it all is. Anyway, let's not go into that but get straight on with things.

WHAT TO LOOK OUT FOR

* *Erect posture*: The first sign that a man is taking an interest in you is that he will pull in his gut, stand or sit up more erect, and puff out his chest. He will do these things without realizing.
* *Preening*: Just like those birds on the Discovery Channel, men go in for preening. Tie straightening is a giveaway, as is hair smoothing, cuff-link tinkering, clothes brushing, and so forth.
* *Body position*: If he turns his body toward you that's a positive sign.

A more subtle sign is if he points his foot or feet toward you. Sometimes when trying to conceal his interest in you from someone (his wife?) he will not turn toward you but will subconsciously point his foot in your direction. If you spot this, you will notice that every now and then he also glances at you. If he does, smile warmly or wink—depending on what you think you can get away with. This should cause steam to rise from his trousers.

* *Present buying*: If he buys you a drink or presents you with a trivial gift of some sort, that is a sign he is interested in you.
* *Gaze*: When you are talking to a man in a meeting he will look at your eyes and forehead. In a social encounter he will look at your eyes and mouth. If he likes you, he will subconsciously use a more intimate look in which his gaze focuses on your eyes but also takes in what I shall call your chest and/or what I shall call your lap. He will also be holding your gaze a smidgin longer than normal. Dilated pupils are further cues. When you are attracted to someone your pupils open wide, so if his pupils are large this is a clear sign he likes the look of you—either that or the lightbulbs need to be changed.
* *Eyebrows flash*: A lightning-quick and subtle signal is when he opens his eyes wide and raises his eyebrows. Blink and you'll miss it.
* *Hands on hips*: This is the equivalent of one of those toads inflating his neck. It makes him look bigger. If his thumbs are in his belt and his legs are spread in the cowboy posture, this is a frank courtship cluster, his thumbs pointing to and accentuating what I shall call his trouser region.
* *Crotch display*: If he spreads his legs it's rather like the market trader setting out his stall. I've

seen a seated man exhibiting the crotch display slide his heels either side of the legs of the woman opposite. A very aggressive move. If this happens to you, you're definitely in business.

* *"Would you like to see my etchings?"*: He may be lacking in originality but not in clarity. Best of luck!

⚘ *The first etchings were printed by Daniel Hopfer (c. 1470–1536).* ⚘

How to
Descend a Staircase in High Heels

*T*here was this woman I used to know who wore high heels every day in the office. You could hear her coming down the corridor like a ticking bomb. She always looked perfect and you just knew she wasn't wearing control-top hose, either. She was that kind of a woman.

It's true that high heels do something for a woman, causing the buttocks to tense, emphasising the calf muscles, adding height (always good), and making you walk in that quintessentially poised, feminine way, as if stepping along a ribbon with a book on your head.

But, *gawd*, they can be a nightmare to wear. Your center of gravity is higher and you have to learn to balance with your bottom and boobs pushed out and your hips jiggling to compensate. Coming down a curly staircase in a ball gown and stilettos is an activity simply fraught with hazard. But here, along with some other high-heel know-how, is the way to do it, so that next time you find yourself at the Palace with a prince on your arm you can come downstairs like Kim Novak in *Vertigo* instead of like Bozo the Clown.

PRACTICE
It is logarithmically harder to walk in six-inch heels than it is in five-inch heels; a bit like stilts. Indeed, six-inch heels are for the experienced

only, so start with a nice low heel, moving up in half-inch increments—it's not going to happen overnight. *Note*: Heel height is the distance from floor to the sole of the shoe.

Buy good shoes that fit properly. Wedge heels are easier than stilettos and better for the linoleum, and strappy ones can feel more secure. To begin, stand in front of a full-length mirror to get used to the feel, and examine your new posture, then walk a few steps toward the mirror and back again, building up slowly.

Take shorter steps than usual, coming down heel first in the usual way but with most of the weight on the ball of your foot. Stand erect, don't lean forward. The reinforced heel will prevent you falling backward. Before you go out wear your heels around the house for a while as you watch TV and go about your business. But look out for loose rugs and slippery parquet. Point your toes straight ahead, with each new step coming down directly in front of the last, as if you were walking a narrow plank. Once you can gracefully carry a tray of full wineglasses across a carpet like this you will know you have mastered the basics.

The staircase

OK, so you can walk around. But now you are faced with the staircase, and all the eyes are on you. How are you going to handle it? Only the most brazen would slide down the banister. No, take hold of the rail, a man in a tux, or even better, both, and begin your descent. The technique is slightly different to walking on the floor, in that the whole foot should come down flat on the step instead of heel first. To add stability, turn your body—and feet, obviously, or you'll look like a human corkscrew—so that you are coming down at a slight sideways angle to the stairs. Your feet should strike each step off the perpendicular. Not only is this the fitting way for a lady to descend the stairs, it reduces the possibility of her toppling forward in a shower of pearls and tumbling down the stairs like Buster Keaton. Grip that banister but do it nicely. *Note*: If you're wearing a long gown, take pains not to tread on the hem or the gallery will echo to the sound of rending satin, and you might trip.

Don't walk on snow, mud, lawns, beaches, or long gravel drives. You'll either sink like a candleholder into a birthday cake or just topple over in the old-fashioned way. Instead, do like the Bond girls do and go barefoot, with your precious high heels cradled safely in your arms.

❀ *"Whoever invented high heels, women owe him a lot."—Marilyn Monroe* ❀

How to
Dance with a Shorter Man

*D*on't look down your nose at short men if you are a lady of stature; it's possible to be *short*, dark, and handsome. Alexander the Great and Napoleon were both small, after all, but that didn't top them being powerful and attractive, while Tom Cruise is diminutive (five-foot-seven), rich, *and* good-looking. Finally, think of the famous English variety comedian Jimmy Clitheroe, who was only four-foot-three and had a squeaky voice and looked ridiculous and wasn't funny. Well, OK, let's forget Jimmy Clitheroe. But the others are all right.

So while it's true that more children are fathered by tall men than short ones, and that short men are more likely to be poor, fat, cigar-smoking heart attacks waiting to happen, there's no reason you shouldn't be able to dance with a Toulouse-Lautrec-size chap even if you're lofty, elegant, and poised like Tom Cruise's ex-wife Nicole Kidman (just short of 6 feet), who managed OK.

When it comes down to it, you can deal with the problem of dancing with a man who is shorter than you by two methods, known as *go with it* and *even out the difference.*

The *go with it* camp is probably more likely to contain cheerful normal ladies, while the *even out the differencers* are never going to be really happy—a bit like Prince Charles when they made him stand on that crate for the royal photograph of him and his wife. No wonder he had that funny look on his face.

GO WITH IT

Going with it is so much easier than evening out the difference because there's only so much leaning and flat-shoe-wearing you want to be doing if you're statuesque. Why hide your height under a bushel? If you've got it, *flaunt it.* So remember:

* Never take your shoes off; perhaps wear a low heel but only if this doesn't compromise your own looks—if you don't make much of the difference, neither will others.
* Concentrate on each other, not what other people may be thinking.
* If he is a lot shorter than you, be sure your bodice is in good order; it will be up for very close and extended scrutiny.

EVEN OUT THE DIFFERENCE

Here are a few tips:

* Use perspective to your advantage by keeping a distance between yourselves. This greatly reduces the possibility of a slow smooch, though.
* Flat shoes for you, built-up shoes for him.
* Hair down.
* Tangos are good because of all that bending over backward.
* Train him to wear stilts under his trousers (you're getting desperate).

❈ *General Tom Thumb was 3 feet 4 inches tall.* ❈

Eighteen Uses for a Spare Fishnet Stocking

How many times have you been woken by the click of your bedroom door closing the morning after the night before only to find you're a fishnet stocking short? That was a rhetorical question; please don't send me autobiographical postcards. Unless you are a one-legged lady, there isn't a lot of use for a single stocking. Or so you'd think. But think again, because here are a few ideas.

1 *Used plastic bag holder*: Cut a small toe hole and stuff your used shopping bags in the top of the leg. When you need a bag for drowning some kittens or something, just pull one from the toe.

2 *Salad spinner*: This works great. Carefully drop your lettuce, radish, and wet legumes into the toe and go outside. Spin the stocking around your head like a sling, holding the fat end. But don't let it go or one of your neighbors is going to get the surprise of his life.

3 *Hammock for soft toy in car window*: If you are sad enough to want one of these, then get yourself some of those window suction caps and you're golden.

4 *Drain cover*: Tired of bits and pieces going down the sink? Scrunch stocking, stuff into drain, and *presto!* it's an instant straining device.

5 *Flour sifter*: Measure the flour, stand on a chair, and sift as normal.

6 *Tennis ball holder*: What could be simpler?

7 *Hairnet*: They may be a bit out of fashion but you could start a new trend. Use the middle of the stocking and sew closed.

8 *Dog ball sling*: Drop in a tennis ball and tie off directly above the ball. Swing it around your head and release across the park like the Hale–Bopp comet. Rover will retrieve it for you.

9 *Clam bar–style interior décor*: Cut down side of stocking, pin out flat on wall, and decorate with lobster pot, crab, starfish, and glass buoy. True '70s chic. Lovely!

10 *Claustrophobic bank robber's face mask*: For the more neurotic rapscallion.

11 *Smalls bag*: Pop your underpants, socks, etc., into the stocking and tie loosely, then wash as usual. And *bingo!* no more lost-sock misery.

12 *Plant support*: Stretch the stocking leg over a wigwam of three canes in a flowerpot. Black-eyed Susans and morning glory seeds will gallop away.

13 *Draft excluder*: Pack the stocking with old rags and a heavy chain. Lay against the door (not *you*, the *stocking*) to stop the wind whistling under like a knife.

14 *Onion and ham nets*: Hang onions, salamis, and ham joints from the beams of your kitchen ceiling. Perfectly rustic.

15 *Butterfly net*: Straighten out a wire coat hanger and thread through top of close-weave fishnet stocking. Bend hanger into rough circle, twist wire ends together, and poke into cane handle. Tie off and cut surplus netting.

16   *Magical bubble wand*: Dip your butterfly net in a solution of dish-washing liquid and water, and wave it around. *Oooh.*

17   *Animal feeder*: Fill stocking with dandelion leaves and hang in corner of bunny cage.

18   *Bird feeder*: Cram stocking with stale bread and bacon scraps and hang from a branch near a window.

And if you locate the other stocking behind the sofa after doing any of the above, don't blame me.

There's no reason you can't do things of a similar kind with an ordinary nylon stocking or even an old sock. Here are a few more ideas in a nutshell.

* *Luggage marker*: Tired of watching all those identical-looking suitcases and bags going past on the airport carousel? Mark yours by tying a stocking containing a fluorescent ball to the handle. Clever and unmistakeable.

* *Trunk tie*: Got the corpse of your murdered mother-in-law or something else bulky in the trunk of your car? Tie down the lid with your spare stocking. It's elastic *and* tight.

* *Cheese strainer*: Never made your own cheese? Now's the time to start. Stuff the curds into the foot and hang in the shower overnight. Delicious!

* *Lumpy-paint strainer*: This is the item the professionals use. Works well with lumpy soup, too.

* *Back-soaper*: Tie a bar of soap into the middle of the stocking. With an end in each hand, you can now soap your shoulder blades, just where you can't usually reach.

* *Garbage bag holder*: Keep your garbage bag in place in the container by stretching a stocking top (cut it off first) around the circumference. Good for bundling newspapers, too.

* *Idle gardener's irrigation device*: Tired of watering houseplants? Trail a stocking from the plant to the water source to capitalize on the "wick" effect.

* *Contact lens finder*: Dropped a lens on the sheepskin rug? Stretch a nylon over the vacuum nozzle and "scan" the floor from ½ inch above the surface. The lens will adhere to the stocking.
* *Scent-release device*: Tuck some lavender into a stocking, rinse under water, and tie off. Throw into your dryer and your sheets will smell divine.

❀ *Fishing nets are made of synthetic polyamides.* ❀

What to Do with a Snoring Man

*J*ust imagine the picture: you lay aside *Pride and Prejudice* with a sympathetic sigh, switch off the light, and start dozing dreamily, thinking lovely thoughts. The next thing you know, you are brutally awakened by a spectacular noise like a gigantic walrus roaring through a didgeridoo into a tank full of blancmange. Yes, once again the man next to you is snoring. Amazing how the hunky guy who once seemed so darkly handsome and mysterious can turn like Dr. Jekyll into a snoring, belching, guffing ape creature who nightly tears the duvet off you and rolls himself up in it, utterly oblivious.

You *must* act. The following are a few snoring causes, along with their remedies.

* *Booze*: Everything relaxes including the throat muscles. Tell him that his floppiness is leaving you *unfulfilled*.
* *Smoking*: This bad habit causes all kinds of problems such as super-mucus, inflamed naso-pharyngeal passages, and scratchy throat. Get him to stop by explaining that smoking causes permanent impotence, which it can. Milk is a mucus maker, too, so watch out if he's a milkshake-aholic.
* *He's overweight*: Fatty tissue around the neck can block his airway. Get him to cut down on the pizzas, burgers, and beer, and do more exercise.

* *Sleeping position*: When he sleeps on his back the root of his tongue is more likely to fall back and cover the airway (see "sleep apnea" below). Try giving him more pillows to sleep on or get him to sleep on his side. Tennis balls sewn into his pajamas was a remedy recommended by my milkman. It worked for him—apparently. In a pinch, you could try rolling him over, or calling his name and telling him to roll over. Works best with a non-drunk guy.

* *Allergies*: Replace his feather pillows with something synthetic. Don't let him take antihistamines before he drops off. They can do more harm than good snorewise.

* *Sleep apnea*: This is a serious—indeed life-threatening—condition in which the subject stops breathing for short periods. It also results in low-quality sleep, causing the poor fellow to walk round all day like a zombie. Get him to the doctor; it's treatable, in severe cases, by surgery.

One young man I used to know once told me that he snored so loudly he actually woke himself up. He cured it, he said, by going to sleep in the spare room. Our relationship foundered on such allegedly witty remarks. But the spare room is indeed an effective measure of last resort. Either him or you, it doesn't matter. So remember: laugh and the world laughs with you; snore and you sleep alone.

SOME OTHER TIME-TESTED REMEDIES

1   Hit him.
2   Hit his pillow.
3   Earplugs (for *you*, obviously).
4   Nasal strips and a variety of masks that are designed to keep the nose passages open. There is also some kind of dental appliance that is meant to pull his lower jaw and tongue forward so there's more room at the back of the throat. These all sound a bit freaky to sleep next to, though.
5   Go to bed first so that you are asleep by the time the snoring starts. (You're entering the desperate zone because this works only if his

decibel level is low enough that it bothers you only while you're trying to nod off.)

6   Exercise all day so that you are exhausted and impossible to wake.
    (You've clearly lost it.)

I can't promise success with any of the above, I'm afraid, but they are all
worth a try even if the suspense ends up killing you, because it's such a
relief when one night, after months of insomnia and recrimination, you
sense triumph.

Hooray!

❀ *Loudest recorded snore: 87 decibels. Typical vacuum cleaner: 70 decibels.* ❀

How to
Get Out of a Car Without Flashing Your Skivvies

W hen you're a student and you find yourself with a pizza in your arms
being unceremoniously forced backward out of an old Volkswagen
Beetle in jeans and a smelly old parka, it doesn't really matter. But when
you emerge slinkily from a throbbing red Ferrari or a purring black Rolls-
Royce to the popping of flash bulbs you'd better do it right and look the
part. The move should be smooth, practiced, swift, and elegant.

Here are the essentials, so that next time you get out of a car—as a
passenger—you will look more like the svelte Jennifer Lopez than the
lumpen Britney Spears.

CLOTHES

For starters, you'd better wear the right undies, just in case it all gets bared.
So not your favorite great big belly-hugging Grandma Moses bloomers in a
tasteful grayish-white, nor the old faves with the holes, that you wear because they're nice 'n' comfy. These had better be pretty to look at.

While it's fine to wear a miniskirt, it's going to make the job that much trickier. So do yourself a favor and pull it down as far as you can before you open the door. If you try to leave the car with the skirt snarled round your hips, I'm afraid it's not going to be pretty.

If your skirt or dress is longish and flowing, make sure your knees are covered before you turn (see below) so that your legs will pull the material after you in a controlled way, without it riding up or snagging your feet. And mind that gear stick.

THE BUSINESS

1   Once you are sartorially fixed up and ready to go, open the door as far as you can. Ideally a gentleman should do this for you from the outside. Don't stretch out all undignified into the street. Keep your body as erect as possible.

2   Whatever you do from now on, imagine that your knees have been stuck together with a piece of tight elastic. The cardinal rule is to keep those knees touching whenever you possibly can. Place your left leg out and step on to the ground. The right leg should follow quickly, closely, and smoothly.

3   Swivel your body toward the exit, keeping your knees together. Both feet should be firmly planted on the ground in front of you. Keep them still.

4   If you can support yourself on the hand of a gentleman outside the car as you exit, do so. Place your left hand on the seat beside you and push down firmly. Rest your right hand on his and pull yourself gracefully up. He will take your weight and help you out. Don't loose hold and fall backward, smacking your head against the car in an unladylike way. If there is nobody to assist, place both hands on either side of your bottom and push up. It is more dignified to keep you hands low, rather than grab desperately at the door frame. It should all look smooth and easy. Any strenuous grunting and wriggling is to be avoided.

5   Bob your head gracefully as you leave the car to avoid banging it painfully on the sharp surround.

6   At no time should you swear.

7   Stand effortlessly, making certain that you have a secure footing,

and either allow someone else to shut the door or do it yourself—
nicely, not like you're in a mood. It is only too easy, having left the
car gracefully, to spoil it all by losing your balance and staggering
around on your high heels with a desperate look on your face. Either that or bending an
ankle agonizingly as you
step out and going
down like a felled
antelope.

Work hard and do as the professionals do by practicing in private
before daring to perform your exit
in public. Then if you do happen to flash your thigh and
panties, you'll do it sexily
so that you receive admiring wolf
whistles, not flatulent raspberries,
from the ugly scrum on the red carpet.

How to ride a bicycle without flashing your undies
You thought getting out of a car with decorum was difficult? You try riding a bicycle without giving the world and his wife a laundry show.
Goodness only knows how they survived in the nineteenth century,
when the bicycle was the latest thing and all the Boston bluestockings
whizzed up and down Court Street in their long frocks. How they
avoided snarling the chain I simply can't guess.

Nowadays, of course, the problem is rather the reverse: how to get a
skirt that stops well above the knee, from riding up as you cycle about
town. Like most problems in life, the solution is easy: make sure you
have a robust pair of panties on. Then you'll have all the bases covered
even if you find yourself obliged to dismount in a high wind.

❀ *Victoria's Secret headquarters is in Columbus, Ohio, hometown of Jack Nicklaus.* ❀

How to
Pass Gas with Grace and Charm

Since Chaucer, people have been writing funny things about passing gas, but the subject must surely have been amusing the masses long before *The Miller's Tale* (1386). I bet cavemen and -women without number sat around the fire farting like gooduns and roaring with laughter whenever somebody let one go.

Certainly the language of farting is centuries old. The word "fart" comes from the Old English *feortan*, derived from the Old High German *ferzan*, and is related to the Old Norse *freta*, from the Germanic *fertan*. So now you know.

Letting one fly in public can be problematic in our modern—civilized—world. Loud traffic, music, and general hubbub can all provide a useful cover if timing is nicely judged, but they are not infallible. Thinking himself adequately shielded by the climax of a boisterous Strauss march during a brass band concert in Orpington, my Uncle Bob told me he let off a sneaky one against the rough surface of his canvas chair but was caught out by the abrupt ending of the music. The mayor, I'm told, was visibly shaken by the undisguised ferocity of it in the sudden silence of the reverberant chamber.

At an ambassadorial function, things are trickier because you are more exposed; indeed, you have nowhere to hide. There is therefore a need for general caution, to avoid frightening the horses, and you wouldn't want to send a plate of those Italian chocolates flying with a mistimed venting. But get your timing right and things should be OK. Here are a few ideas.

* *The string quartet*: The cello's *con brio* passages are the ones to look out for.
* *The opportunist*: Waiter noisily dropped a tray of wineglasses? Now's your chance.

* *The cigarette manoeuver*: Go on to the balcony to light a cigarette.
* *The dissembler*: Just say, "Good gracious, Mr. Ambassador, your hinges need oiling."
* *Trumpets and drums*: My friend Ingeborg (we used to call her "ironing board") was once involved with the Nobel Prize ceremony. She suspected from the faraway look on their faces that many nervous recipients were timing their emissions to coincide with the trumpet fanfare. If you ever receive the Nobel Prize take a leaf from their book.
* *The applause ruse*: Are they clapping for a speech? What better coverage?
* *Brazen it out*: If push comes to shove, simply smile and *dare* anyone to challenge you.

❊ *Alfred Nobel invented dynamite in 1867: U.S. patent 78,317.* ❊

How to
Send Back a Meal at a Restaurant

You know how some dining experiences are so crappy they cross the border into farce? Well, I remember eating out at an official function once in a bleak red cube of a hotel in the middle of nowheresville. The dining room, grandly called The Boardroom, was gloomy because the strip lighting had been turned off, but there was still enough light to see the cheap cutlery and the nasty paper napkins folded into a special decorative feature on everybody's plate.

The main course included: Minted Lamb Shacks (*sic*), and Risotto of Wild Mushroon and Goats With Nuts (*sic*). I kept the menu. Starters were huge plates covered in whitebait, squid, bright orange ribs, and some tomatoes with things sticking out of them. "You got to 'elp yerself," said the staggeringly ill-trained waiter—one of a bunch, including a man who, presenting the main course, demanded, "Who ordered this?," waving it around under our noses, and striking me hard on the back of the head with the plate. I remember the lady next to me exclaiming, "Oerugh!" as a dish piled high with mashed potatoes surrounded by a moat of chocolate-brown gravy with a lump of lamb on top and sprinkled with bright green fluorescent mint was plopped down in front of her. The woman on my left was asked, "Is this yours?" It was—she assured me—risotto but her lip curled at the sight of it: a basin of gray sludge, with black leechlike things lurking in it. Examining one on her fork's end she exclaimed, "I think they're shitake." Well, yes. As diners stared at their plates in disbelief, a waiter dropped a serving dish of steaming broccoli into the lap of a guest, who jumped up with a sudden "Whooaurgha!" This was at once followed by a shout of alarm from the company's managing director himself as scalding gravy was liberally poured into his collar by another waiter distracted by the kerfuffle.

I declined dessert and was chatting to the lady on my left when I felt a sharp jab under my arm caused by the poking index finger of charmless waiter number 1. "Hey!" he remarked, wiping my nose roughly with his sleeve as he reached in front of my face to collect a plate. "You want coffee or what?" *I'm not making this up.*

Nobody complained, because we were all guests, but we could and maybe should have refused to accept this fiasco, at the expense of embarrassing our host. Here's the way to tactfully reject a restaurant meal without shame.

METHOD

* *Don't be embarrassed*: This is like any other arrangement where you exchange money for a service or goods. If it isn't what it says it is, if it is not of decent quality, or the service is incompetent, you shouldn't accept it or pay for it.

* *Rejecting the meal*: Say why you are doing so. For example, "This casserole is frozen solid in the middle. Please take it away; I don't want it." You do not have to accept a replacement, nor does it matter if you've eaten nearly all your ice cream before noticing the frozen Band-Aid on the plate, or whatever it is. Don't send back a meal for trivial reasons, though, such as it's not like your mom makes.

* *Refusing to pay for the meal*: You can pay a portion if you feel, say, that one course was no good, and you can deduct a service charge that has been included, if service was poor. You can legally refuse to pay anything at all, if, for example, the food was late and wrong and cold, the leg came off your chair, and the waiter had poked you in the eye with a stick. Be clear why you feel justified in doing so and leave your name and a contact address.

* *Training yourself*: If you feel nervous, start by politely returning cold coffee and bad food before you move on to sending back something at Le Perigord.

TURNING A NEGATIVE INTO A POSITIVE

We've all seen what should have been an enjoyable meal turned into an awful experience, all because something went wrong with the food or the service. Barring psychotic waiters or poisonous food full of broken glass, a sent-back meal needn't spell disaster. Indeed, it's an opportunity, especially if you're the host, to snatch success from the jaws of defeat. Here's how.

Why not get a round of free drinks? Smile at the waiter and say, "While we all wait here for your mistake to be remedied, perhaps we could have a drink on the house." Not *drinks*, you'll notice. Put as an implied question, this non-threatening suggestion allows the waiter to turn *your demand* into *his offer.* This is known as "psychology." Remember, you are in a strong negotiating position because you could cause trouble.

Now you can fill the time and save the day with a few entertaining tricks.

The magic candle: In a candlelit restaurant, draw attention to the candle and blow it out with a staccato puff. Allow the smoke to rise, then quickly strike a match. Hold the flame steadily against the smoke plume, a few inches above the wick. Candles differ in their properties, but, with a healthy wisp of smoke, a good one will suddenly relight with a pop. In dark rooms where the smoke is almost invisible the effect appears truly magical.

Spoon "photography": Hand a spoon to someone and say, "I'm going to turn away and I want you to take a spoonograph of one of the others. Just point it at their face, and say, 'Click.'" When the picture has been taken, you turn back and examine the spoon closely, in due course naming the right person. The trick can even be repeated throughout the evening, with different spoonographers and subjects. You need a confederate to secretly transmit the subject's identity by mimicking the position in which she is sitting.

The magnetic bottle: Rub an empty (small) beer bottle rapidly up and down against the corner walls of the restaurant. With any luck, it will "stick" in the junction when you remove your hand. Without any luck, you've created a bit of a clatter.

Antigravity salt: Pour some salt on the table and put a glass of beer over it, then pick up the saltshaker and say, "This is a funny thing—the salt comes up from the bottom." Tap the saltshaker sharply on the rim of the glass and bubbles will rise from the bottom as if the salt is floating up through the drink.

The napkin ghost: Drape a napkin carefully over your hand, which is palm up. As you are doing so, quickly close your middle finger. This will be hidden by the moving napkin. Leave the napkin draped over your hand and it should all look quite innocent if you keep your middle finger still.

Gradually raise the finger from your palm and it will appear that something is weirdly materializing under the cloth. As soon as your finger is fully extended, remove the napkin with a flourish and, as everyone sees that it's just your finger, say, "Well, what did you expect, ectoplasm?"

The magic shoe: This makes a terrific finale. Prepare by slipping off one of your shoes and hiding it in your lap. At the right moment attract everyone's attention and hold your left forearm in front of you, as if checking your watch. Drape a napkin over it so that the bottom edge is resting on the table. As your right hand comes down behind the napkin, grasp the shoe from your lap and, as you move your left arm forward, simply place the shoe on the table, where it will be hidden behind the napkin. Remove the napkin with an elegant flourish to reveal your strappy footwear on the beautiful napery.

And then hope that your replacement meal arrives before everyone's had a few too many cocktails.

❀ *Famed chef Auguste Escoffier trained Ho Chi Minh as a pastry cook.* ❀

How to
Remember Absolutely Anything

My brother-in-law once suggested I should go shopping at the Mall of America, which is in his hometown. He said it would be the experience of a lifetime, and he wasn't wrong, because, let me tell you, that is some *huge* place. After wandering around for an hour, I got completely lost and discovered I'd been going up and down the same two escalators for ten minutes, trying to get out of there. A variety of mild panic descended upon me, but some kindly people, noticing my distress, pointed me the right way and I found myself finally back in the parking ramp, grateful to have escaped with my life.

Being enormous, the Mall of America has some 13,000 spaces in two identical seven-story parking structures, and I suddenly realized that I couldn't remember where my car was. Fortunately, a lady in plaid pants recognized my plight and said she would be pleased to help me look for the car, having once done the same thing herself. "Oh thank you," I said. "It's a little silver Hyundai and there's a copy of *Anne of Green Gables* on the seat."

For half an hour we hunted, high and low, but we couldn't find it. Then I suddenly remembered I'd been driving my brother-in-law's huge pickup truck, with a white fridge and some Christmas trees in the rear bed. "Oh, it's not a little silver Hyundai," I said brightly. "It's a red Ford pickup with trees and a fridge on the back."

A sickly smile leaked onto the woman's face as she cautiously backed away, putting several vehicles between us, before sprinting off into the darkness. She must have thought I was crazy and waiting to pounce, with a deadly salami or something concealed in my shopping bags. Because you aren't thinking about it, things like where you left the car, or even that you're driving *someone else's* car, are difficult to remember, unless you *do something* to help yourself. For example, I now turn around to look at my car whenever I've just parked it—so as to plant it in my memory. Then I take in a few noteworthy landmarks. I haven't reached the Hansel and Gretel breadcrumb stage, but it might come to that. It's the same on the subway: I always look behind me as I get up to leave, and this has saved me lost umbrellas without number.

That's all very well, I hear you cry, but what about those things that seem *impossible* to remember, such as all the state capitals, or the order of the planets, or the presidents? Well, it's easy; here's how.

INSTRUCTIONS
Let's start with the presidents. Like other lists, the names are difficult to remember unless you can turn them into arresting, rude, or silly pictures. Some, such as Washington and Lincoln, are easier to remember than others, but who today remembers presidents Millard Fillmore or William Henry Harrison, anyway?

Here are the forty-three (*so far*) in proper order. In italics beside each name I've jotted down my own memorable picture for each president. Actually, the ones I use are a lot ruder than this but I didn't want to offend your sensibilities so I've substituted more innocent ones. These are a guide only, and you may not immediately see the connection—but I do, that's the important thing. When you come to do this yourself you should invent your own.

1   George Washington—*Sitting in cherry tree*
2   John Adams—*Morticia Addams*
3   Thomas Jefferson—*Jiffy baking mix*
4   James Madison—*The Flatiron Building*
5   James Monroe—*Marilyn Monroe*
6   John Quincy Adams—*TV medical examiner Quincy*
7   Andrew Jackson—*Pop star Michael Jackson*
8   Martin Van Buren—*A burning van*
9   William Henry Harrison—*Harrison Ford as Indiana Jones*
10   John Tyler—*A roof tiler with a hammer*
11   James Knox Polk—*A polka-dot suit jacket*
12   Zachary Taylor—*A tailor with a tape measure*
13   Millard Fillmore—*A dentist*
14   Franklin Pierce—*Body piercings*
15   James Buchanan—*A blue cannon*
16   Abraham Lincoln—*Lincoln in his famous hat*
17   Andrew Johnson—*A convenient (handy) john*
18   Ulysses S. Grant—*A grand piano*
19   Rutherford Birchard Hayes—*A haystack*
20   James Abram Garfield—*Garfield the cat*
21   Chester Alan Arthur—*Chess-playing King Arthur*
22   Grover Cleveland—*Grover from the Muppets*
23   Benjamin Harrison—*A hairy banjo*
24   Grover Cleveland (*again*)—*A meat cleaver*
25   William McKinley—*King Macbeth*
26   Theodore Roosevelt—*A teddy bear*
27   William Howard Taft—*Daffy (Daft) Duck*
28   Woodrow Wilson—*A Wilson brand basketball*
29   Warren Gamaliel Harding—*A bell with a "hard ding"*
30   (John) Calvin Coolidge—*A cool fridge*
31   Herbert Clark Hoover—*A vacuum cleaner*

32   Franklin Delano Roosevelt (FDR)—*A fedora*
33   Harry S. Truman—*Charles Atlas*
34   Dwight David Eisenhower—*An ice-cold shower*
35   John Fitzgerald Kennedy (JFK)—*JFK airport*
36   Lyndon Baines Johnson (LBJ)—*An elbow joint*
37   Richard Milhouse Nixon—*Golf knickers*
38   Gerald Rudolph Ford—*A Ford truck*
39   James Earl Carter Jr.—*A cart full of peanuts*
40   Ronald Wilson Reagan—*A ray gun*
41   George Herbert Walker Bush—*An old gnarled bush*
42   William Jefferson Clinton—*Clint Eastwood in a poncho*
43   George Walker Bush—*A young shrub*

The Ancient Greeks developed a memory system that required placing memorized images at various numbered positions on a well-known journey, but the method I am going to describe here, to enable you to memorize the presidents in order, is the "link" system. What you have to do is link one of your memorable images/people to the next in as striking a way as you can. Here are the links I've devised for the presidents. Ruder ones work even better—this is the perfect time and place for political incorrectness—but I'll leave those to your imagination.

1   George Washington puts a bunch of cherries into the hair of
2   Morticia Addams, who mixes the cherries in with her
3   Jiffy baking mix, and spreads it all over the outside of the
4   Flat Iron Building opposite Madison Square, where
5   Marilyn Monroe is singing. She drops dead and
6   Quincy, the medical examiner, tells
7   Michael Jackson to stop dancing and drive her to hospital in a
8   Burning van, which is whipped to a halt by
9   Indiana Jones, who then whips the hammer out of the hand of
10   A roof tiler who has been trying to nail tiles to the
11   Polka-dot jacket of a
12   Tailor, who then has to rush off to his dentist, who

13   Fills more of his teeth and removes his body

14   Piercings, which he throws into a

15   Blue cannon beside the chair. He fires and shoots

16   Abraham Lincoln's hat off into a

17   Handy john that is being used as a stool for a

18   Grand piano, under the open lid of which is a

19   Haystack with

20   Garfield the cat on top playing

21   Chess with King Arthur, who throws the taken pieces at

22   Grover, who bats them away with his

23   Hairy banjo, which is suddenly cut in half by a

24   Cleaver being wielded by

25   King Macbeth, whose

26   Teddy bear is sitting in his crown being pecked by

27   Daffy Duck, who is having to bounce up and down on a

28   Wilson basketball, which bounces away, making a

29   Hard ding on a bell.

30   At the sound a cool fridge is opened to reveal a

31   Hoover, which is emptied into a

32   Fedora belonging to

33   Charles Atlas, who has to take it off to take an

34   Icy shower, before going to

35   JFK airport to meet an

36   Elbow-joint surgeon who wears golf

37   Knickers as he drives them off in a

38   Ford pickup, which crashes into a

39   Cart of peanuts driven by a man with dyed hair, holding a

40   Ray gun with which he sets fire to a

41   Gnarled old bush behind which

42   Clint Eastwood has been changing his poncho. He has to get behind

43   A smaller shrub.

Rehearse you story once or twice during the day, replacing the harder to remember images with stronger ones. I guarantee that it won't take you more than two or three attempts to remember the presidents in order, possibly for the first time in your life. Indeed, you can recite them backward or forward or identify the number of any president by going through the list. Once you've mastered it, you'll find you can remember the list for a long time, and if you get rusty, a quick revision will polish everything up very nicely.

By the way, don't worry: I found my brother-in-law's pickup pretty quickly.

❀ *Presidents Adams, Jefferson, and Monroe all died on the fourth of July.* ❀

How to
Bluff Your Way in Classical Music

W hen I was at school there were a number of music staff who managed to give us a bit of the history, a dollop of theory, and plenty of practice, while making the whole subject seem delightfully fun. I remember Mr. George in particular. He was a short, white-haired Scot with stubby fingers and a tweed suit, who had pushed a piano over the Cairngorms and claimed it was this, rather than his twenty-a-day cigarette habit, that had given him heart disease. You could make up a tune, hum it to him at the keyboard, and he would immediately harmonize it in whatever style you chose from Brahms to boogie-woogie. He was a *real* musician so he had no need to bluff his way. But if you're not much of a music buff, you can *seem* terribly clever just by airily regurgitating a few of these key facts.

SOME USEFUL MUSIC BLUFFING FACTS AND FIGURES

* *The Middle Ages*: 400s–1500s. Music first begins to be written down in the 800s. Medieval monks develop "plainsong," an unaccompanied liturgical chant. No electric guitars yet. Hildegard of Bingen, German monastic mystic and musician, writes oratorios for her nuns.

* *Late Medieval to Renaissance*: 1300–1600. The age of out-of-tuneness with croaky polyphonic harmony. Lizards, shawms, sackbutts, racketts, crumhorns, 7-foot-long trumpets marine, and other wacky instruments accompany a lot of chicken legs being thrown over shoulders. The funniest instrument ever—the serpent: a cross between a huge blood sausage, a vacuum cleaner, and a saxophone—is invented in 1590 by Canon Edmé Guillaume in Auxerre, France. Loads of church music is produced, with Palestrina leading the field. Plenty of women composers, too, including the snazzy-sounding Lucrezia Orsina Vizzana. The first opera—Dafne—is composed by Jacopo Peri in 1597. Lutenist Bálint Bakfark (1507–1576) has a really good name.

* *Baroque*: 1600s. Music becomes curlier and cleverer. Britain can boast Henry Purcell, Lady Mary Dering, and Giles Farnaby (a whiz on the virginals), but two Germans, J. S. Bach and G. F. Handel, lead an international field. Then Herr Handel becomes a British subject and moves into number 25 Upper Brook Street, London, as Mr. Handel, next door to Jimi Hendrix, at number 23.

* *The Classical period*: 1750–1820. First symphonies appear. Some really good silly names, too, including Florian Leopold Gassmann, August Carl Ditters von Dittersdorf, and the exotic-sounding Anna Amalia, Duchess of Saxe-Weimar-Eisenach, and Fanny Krumpholtz Pittar. A great deal of deeply boring music is churned out. A time of dumbing down really, but with some golden nuggets among the slag: Mozart, Schubert, Haydn, Beethoven. And women, too, I'm delighted to say, including Maria Anna Walburga Ignatia "Nannerl" Mozart: Wolfi's long-winded sister.

* *Romantic era*: 1820s–1910. Self-conscious emotionalism and the drama of storytelling. Ludwig Spohr, Franz Liszt, and Frédéric Chopin are early Romantics, and Tchaikovsky is typical of the late school, as is Master of the King's Musick, Edward Elgar in Britain. There's Mahler, *Richard* Strauss (not the Waltz man, A different chap), and loads of women again, including the super-sounding Constance Faunt Le Roy Runcie. First photographs of musicians

45

appear, as does Engelbert Humperdinck (1854–1921): not the chap with the microphone but the one with the high forehead and the fantastic curly moustache. Excellent!

* *The Modern era*: 1900s till now. Mood, atmosphere, self-consciousness, and a calculated upsetting of the musical apple cart. Here are just some of them, in no particular order: Berg, Bartók, Britten, Boulez, Ives, Debussy, Stravinsky, Ravel, Prokofiev, and loads more. And they're still at it, including the women, of whom my favorite for a good name is the terse Meredith Monk. She says: "I work between the cracks." Excellent, Meredith. My favorite of the squeaky-gate-and-broken-glass school is Elliot Carter. I think he's really got something. Have a listen.

❀ *J. S. Bach had twenty children, of whom ten died in infancy.* ❀

How to
Tell a Colleague She Smells

O nce I worked in an office near the Smithsonian. One of the women I had to manage there was—how shall I put it?—strange. She had a sort of obsessive-compulsive disorder that caused her endlessly to repeat various actions. Thresholds were a big thing for her so that if you asked her into your room she would have to step in and out thirty or forty times before finally coming in. It was like watching a hokey-pokey DVD that got stuck. She kept putting her left leg in, left leg out, in/out, in/out—never getting to the point where she was able to wave it all about, or do the hokey-pokey, or turn around. For her, that was *not* what it was all about.

Because she was otherwise very good at her job, we all put up with her behavior until, that is, somebody complained about her BO. I advised an understanding and tolerant approach and did nothing myself until one day she set off the fire alarms so smelly had she become, and we finally had to get rid of her (she had also been stealing Liquid Paper by the gallon). I remember it took two burly security men to wrestle her off the premises, what with her in/out, in/out, in/out . . .

Telling a colleague about her BO is a tough one, and you may just have to make a full-frontal approach. Before you do, try a few of these options:

* The occasional comment to the room in general: "What is that curious scent, ladies?"
* Open a window near her.
* Leave deodorant prominently in the ladies' room or near her desk or bag.
* Buy strongly scented flowers and put them near her desk.
* Offer the occasional squirt of air freshener or perfume in her direction and ask if she likes the fragrance.
* Introduce a policy that stipulates clean clothes and individual responsibility for personal hygiene.
* Ping her an anonymous email. The IT department might be able to prevent it from being traced back to you.
* If all else fails, then now is time to find out what you are made of. Tell your colleague in private that you've noticed there may be problems with her personal hygiene—be kind because BO can be the sign of underlying problems, medical or emotional.
* If you have no luck, it's time to get your own back. Leave a bag of sardines in her desk drawer. If this has no effect, drag her outside, take the fire extinguisher off the wall, and hose her down. Even if it doesn't work, you'll feel better.

Here are a few variations on the theme. You'd be surprised how often they'll come in handy.

Bad breath: Before a kissing scene, actor Michael Caine says he always takes a tiny breath-freshener aerosol from his pocket. Apparently the actress always asks, "What's that?" to which he replies, "Breath freshener. Do you want some?," and before she has time to demur he squirts it liberally into her mouth. Not subtle, but doubtless effective. If you find yourself recoiling from the halitotic dragon's-breath blast from a friend or acquaintance, why not try the same thing? A related alternative is to offer one of those fierce mint-flavored candies, or simply say, "Bruce, you smell like a dog!" and hand him a large bottle of mouthwash.

The odoriferous boss: This is a tough one. It really depends on the nature of your relationship, and also on whether the boss in question is female or male (see below). If it's a he, try the remedies below; if a she, try going over her head. A quiet word with the boss's boss puts the ball in someone else's court and keeps you out of the firing line. If the malodor continues, just breathe through your mouth as you continue to build your resume or resign. Life is full of these little dilemmas.

Smelly male friends: In one way it's easier with men. First, their egos don't bruise so easily, and second, they often imagine that your polite criticism is the start of something so they are amenable to persuasion. It matters not that you know it isn't the start of *anything*; just push ahead with subtle remarks such as, "Did it ever occur to you to change your shirt?" or "You dress like a scarecrow and smell like a pig. Take a shower before you set the burglar alarms off you sickening fleabag." He will think you are being simply charming. Failing these subtle approaches, three of your friends should join you in spraying him all over with the most ferocious industrial-strength all-purpose deodorant you can lay your hands on.

The ghastly boyfriend: Related to this tortured subject is what to say when your friend of many years asks you what you think of her unspeakable new boyfriend. Ambiguity and ellipsis (leaving things out) are old favorites here. Try these on for size:

* You've done it again, haven't you! (Big smile required.)
* He seems like a real nice guy! (But is actually horrible.)
* What a hunk! (But an utter dimwit.)
* What a brilliant guy! (But fat, ugly, old, bald, short, and humorless.)
* What fantastic teeth. (Shame about those feet, the beer belly, and the crossed eyes.)
* Oh, he's so cute, clever, sensitive, charming, tall, dark, handsome,

rich, artistic, and brainy. And he loves his mom, too. (Are you blind? He's obviously gay!)

❀ *Coco Chanel was the illegitimate daughter of a traveling salesman.* ❀

How to
Deal with Telemarketers

W hat is it about telemarketers that makes them think you want to listen to them? They are an odd bunch, often young, I suppose because the burn-out rate is rather high. I mean, could *you* do that job? I was called recently by one of them, who got my name a bit wrong, therefore tipping me off about his sinister purpose. He said he was Dave from some exciting-sounding company or other and started off on his script about how I'd been specially selected to win a free prize. I wanted to ask him what other kind of prize there is than a free one, but I didn't. What I said was, "I'm so glad you called, Dave, because *you've* been specially selected by *me* to win a prize." He hesitated for a moment but recovered himself and continued, "Are you the homeowner?" to which my riposte was, "Are *you* a homeowner, Dave? Because I'm here to tell you that this is *your* chance to win a fantastic bag full of my kitchen garbage—hefty, not wimpy. All you have to do is . . ." But he'd hung up. Their managers have these guys under the gun in their cubicles and as soon as they realize they are talking to a no-hoper they are calling the next computer-generated number on their list.

But what about those callers who won't give up? Here are a few ideas that really work for dealing with them, from the plain to the baroque. Try a few and see which suit you best. Good luck.

INSTRUCTIONS

1   *Hang up*: Easy but unrewarding.
2   *Ignore them*: Don't hang up but put the phone down and walk away. This leaves the caller in some suspense. After five minutes he will have given up and you can hang up.
3   *The offstage prospect*: Say, "Oh, just a moment, you need to speak to

Jolene." Put the phone down and go back to your business, occasionally calling out, "Jolene!" at the top of your voice. This really annoys them because they feel they must hold on in case Jolene is a tasty prospect, but they are unable to hurry you or her up.

4   *Pass the parcel*: If there is a group of you, pass the phone from one to the next, with a comment such as, "Oh, I've got a friend here who might be interested."

5   *Customer feedback*: Get hold of one of those toy karaoke machines, the kind that have a microphone and a mini amp connected to a speaker, switch it on, and put the microphone next to the earpiece and the speaker next to the mouthpiece. Your telemarketer will suddenly hear herself talking, as the phone's output is amplified back to itself, until a hideous shrieking howl builds up, and she is forced to hang up or go deaf.

6   *The interested but exasperating prospect*: Sound interested and engage the caller in detailed conversation (you need a bit of time on your hands). Keep asking for clarification, or say, "Can we go back to the question of the weather in the area where the time-share is?" This drives them nuts because you seem tantalizingly close to saying yes, but keep asking for clarification. Some companies have a policy of hanging up after three minutes if they perceive they are getting nowhere, while others will go on for ages.

7   *Table turning*: Now we are starting to get more creative. Adopt a character and turn the tables on the caller. A favorite of mine is the religious zealot. Have a Bible near the phone, and as soon as they give their name and ask to speak to whoever, say, "Hey, Mike, I have a question for you: Do you read the Bible?" It's then a matter of taking the ball and running with it. You can read out long passages from the Old Testament and quiz them about their beliefs. If they try to drag you back to credit cards or time-share, accuse them of being immoral or of offending your religion. This can be great fun.

The most fundamental piece of advice is *do not accept the telemarketer's premise*. For example, the woman on the other end of the phone wants to talk to you about time-share or newspaper subscription. You must get her off her subject as quickly as possible and on to yours.

A FEW TRICKS OF THE TRADE

Telemarketers are trained to hook you and keep the conversation going. They do this with various tricks including a series of innocent-sounding questions, the so-called Brooklyn Optician strategy, the use of emotion, suspense, transferred excitement, and transferred confidence. You are going to borrow some of these techniques. Let us list a few at your disposal, moving from the simple to the more elaborate.

* *Scout's motto*: Be prepared, and be ready to leap into character when the phone rings.
* *Confidence*: Take control and *sound* in control. Don't answer their questions but *respond* to them, maybe with a question of your own.
* *Emotion*: Create emotion in the caller—anxiety, curiosity, anger. Some excellent ways of doing this are the following:
  * *Adopt a position of authority*: Assume the role of an FBI officer, a customs officer, a nun, a medical examiner, etc. (see 7 above). If you claim that the person they have asked for has just been arrested by your team, or that they have called during a drug bust and where on earth did they get hold of this phone number? You'll have them quaking in their boots as you demand to know if they've ever smoked "imported cigarettes" and are they a dealer?
  * *Ask a favor*: Ask the caller to lend you money or to collect your child from school. It's amazing how quickly they will want to get off the line.
  * *Embarrassment*: Tell them you are suffering from terrible gas and ask them for remedies.
* *The Brooklyn Optician*: Start by making your story highly credible but introduce weirder and weirder elements as you go. This strategy is named after the famous Brooklyn Optician who says, "These lenses are cheap ($40), each ($80), these are the standard plastic frames ($130), but the ones you liked are more ($180)

yellow metal is a little more ($220), gold is best ($360), there is a premium for fast turnaround rather than the regular six-month wait ($410)." The original sum quickly escalates until it's ridiculous, without you noticing. So the telemarketer having accepted say, that you are a nun, will swallow each little extra salami slice of crazy information more easily until he is ready to believe that you have indeed just tried to take out Mother Superior's appendix with a kitchen knife while she was under the influence of Drambuie and he will be offering suggestions about how you might sew her up with nothing but a needle and some dental floss.

My friend Lucy is very good at leading telemarketers down the primrose path like this. She once encouraged a storm window salesman to visit her while she was on a campground. When she showed him her tent his mouth dropped open in disbelief. Another time she was being hassled by a telemarketer trying to sell her an enormous inground pool. Finally she agreed to let someone visit her at home—in her tiny third-floor apartment. She told me he was not very pleased.

More boringly, you can contact the National Do Not Call Registry at its toll-free number, 1-888-382-1222. Telemarketers covered by the National Do Not Call Registry have up to thirty-one days from the date you register to stop calling you. But where's the fun in that?

❀ *The first telephone exchange opened in 1878, in New Haven, Connecticut.* ❀

How to
Spot a Cheater

W omen, it has been alleged, use sex to get what they want whereas men are unable to do this because sex *is* what they want. It is one of those observations, like "aspirins are small" and "dusters are yellow," that seem obviously true.

The problem comes when your man is unable to confine his wants and starts spreading himself around in contravention of the 11th Commandment: "Thou Shalt Not Cheat on Thy Lady." It's a bit like the coveting your neighbor's wife one. If you are harboring a suspicion that your man might be a rumpler of other girls' sheets, now's the time to rate your date.

Some men are more likely than others to cheat on their women, and a gentleman's personality profile and attitudes can reveal the likelihood that he will do the dirty on you. Have a go at the questionnaire below and see how you get on.

THE CHEATER-PROFILE SCREEN

1   Does your man love action and thrills? Sky-diving and fast-car men look for thrills wherever they can get them. Be warned, their dangerous sports can include playing with fire and playing on the side.

2   Is he thrusting, powerful, charismatic, and ambitious (JFK syndrome)? That charismatic thrusting will not stop this side of your bedroom door.

3   Did his dad cheat? Guys often learn how to treat women from their dads.

4   Do his chums cheat on their girls? Birds of a feather flock together. As do guys.

5   Does he have a vigorous bed-history? Don't expect him to confine his vigor just because he's met you. Simple as that.

6   Does he know lots of ladies? Contacts with many women can turn into romps before you can say *bedsprings*. The more girls he's friendly with, the greater the numerical risk.

7   Is he relaxed about the male infidelity thing and has he been unfaithful to previous girlfriends? Well then, why should he rein himself in now? Cheaters remain cheaters, and a cheater never changes his spots. If you answered yes to this one, look out!

8   Does he often come home covered in blond hairs and lipstick, or

with other girls' panties in his pocket? You may be entitled to the first faint flickerings of doubt.

The more yeses you got, the more likely you've landed a cheater. What you do with him now is entirely up to you . . .

❀ *King Solomon had 700 wives and 300 concubines (and a full calendar).* ❀

II

Be Handy

Out-Martha Your Friends and Impress Your Neighbors

As a housewife, I feel that if the kids are still alive when my husband gets home from work, then hey, I've done my job.

ROSEANNE BARR

How to
Churn Butter

*Betty Botter bought some butter. "But," she said, "this butter's bitter.
If I put it in my batter, it will make my batter bitter." So she bought
a bit of butter, better than her bitter butter, and she put it in her
batter and the batter was not bitter.*

N ow, as far as I'm concerned Betty Botter was making a mountain
out of a molehill and it may well have been time for one of her
pills. If she was worried about her bit of bitter butter why didn't she just
churn some herself? I mean, it's not difficult. Here's how.

REQUIRED
* *Half-and-half*
* *Salt*
* *A whisk*
* *A bowl*
* *2 wooden butter paddles (or Ping Pong paddles)*
* *A thermometer*
* *Wax paper*
* *A glass of Champagne*

You make butter by taking some cream and giving it a good old wallop-
ing. To get this to work, you must have the cream at the right temperature: 68°F. The bacteria should have had time to turn some of the lactose
(milk sugar) into lactic acid so that it is "ripe" or slightly sour but not
"off " or completely solid.

I'm assuming you do not possess a vintage butter churn. These simple
barrel-like gizmos either turn over, flopping the contents from one end
to the other, or have a paddle that you twist around with a crank, or are
a simple lidded tube with a sort of broom handle plunger sticking out.
They all do the same thing: throw the cream around. You can do exactly
the same job on a smaller scale using a wooden spoon and a mixing

bowl, or even a whisk. Almost anything will do so long as you can give the cream a good bashing. Perhaps not boxing gloves, though.

Anyway, here we go.

INSTRUCTIONS

1   Pour your cream into the bowl and start manhandling. Butter globules will start to form rather soon—in about 2 or 3 minutes. If you are still manipulating a very liquid liquid after 10 minutes, reheat and start again.

2   After a while, the cream will begin to curdle and coagulate. What is happening is that the emulsified fat and water are separating out. Drain off the buttermilk; it's the fat you are interested in.

3   Dump the butter on to a clean draining board.

4   Wash it thoroughly by running under cold water and squeezing and pressing with your butter paddles or Ping-Pong paddles.

5   Time for a glass of bubbly.

6   Continue to squodge, removing all traces of buttermilk and water. *The secret to good butter is to squeeze out all the water and buttermilk.*

7   Add salt to taste and mix well.

8   Now shape the butter with wetted bats, squeezing out any remaining water. This is the fun part, and it sounds like two fat swimmers smacking each other with glossy magazines.

9   If you have a mold you can make your butter look neat and tidy. If not, form it into as nice a shape as you can. Mine ended up looking like the thing that crawled out of the swamp in that film, dripping and squelching with a hideous sneer on its features. But never mind, I never claimed to be Julia Child.

10   Wrap in wax paper.

Goats milk butter is really good, too. But don't run before you can walk.

❀ *Marlon Brando won an Oscar nomination for* Last Tango in Paris *(1972).* ❀

How to
Make a Compost Heap

Right then, before we start, do we know what we're talking about? What exactly is compost? The word comes from the Latin *composita* meaning "something put together," which gives you a good idea that a pile of twigs with an old settee on the top, or a heap of grass cuttings leaking a virulent brown ooze are not really compost. You need a balance of decayed organic material before you will get anything that is a good fertilizer for your rhubarb.

The best compost is made by putting vegetable matter (say hay) into one end of a compost generator (say, a horse) and collecting it at the other end not long afterward. This is the also the quickest way.

To produce the compost in a heap, you must provide air, water, and nitrogen to the aerobic (oxygen-loving) bacteria and fungi so they can break down the plant cellulose. The more nitrogen in your compost heap the quicker the rot and the greater the heat—a useful by-product that kills off the weeds.

* *Air*: Comes in from gaps in your compost heap.
* *Water*: A bit of rain or a regular dose of dishwater in hot weather will be enough.
* *Nitrogen*: Good sources are animal manure, urine, fishmeal, and blood.
* *Carbon*: Plant cellulose (say twigs, cabbage leaves, and $5 bills).

The bacteria you need are already there in the garden, but if you use animal manure, you'll be adding some extra.

THE COMPOST COMMODE
One of the niftiest compost heaps is the straw toilet.

1   Tie a load of dry straw stalks in a barrel-size bunch and stand them in the garden, upright like a trash can.

2 Whenever you need to, simply pee on top of the straw. This process is less scratchy for gentlemen. Gravity and capillary action will distribute the nitrogen and water amongst the carbon stalks, where air and time will work together with the garden bugs to decompose the plant cellulose. You'll see the steam from the reaction on cold mornings. It's odor-free and fun for visitors, too.

THE TRADITIONAL COMPOST HEAP

1 Lay several rows of bricks, leaving gaps between.
2 Overlay sticks or slim branches perpendicular to the bricks, to let air in underneath.
3 Nail together four wooden pallets to form a box. Pallets are ideal, having gaps in the side that let in the air. Leave one side as a loose "door" for easy compost removal in due time.
4 Build the heap by sprinkling a 10-inch layer of vegetable matter. Don't include too much woody material; it takes ages to rot down. You need a balance of soft and hard (peelings, fruit, grass-cuttings, last year's tax forms, a few bark chippings), followed by a couple inches of nitrogen-rich stuff—manure for preference.
5 Water regularly in dry weather.
6 Keep the layers going all season, paying attention to the balance of plant matter. Don't throw on any meat, eggs (washed shells are OK), your mother-in-law, or other animal matter that will attract foxes or vermin.
7 At the end of the season stop for the winter.
8 In February or March open your compost "door" and dig out the compost from the bottom. Lay around your runner beans and raspberries and over your delphiniums and daisies.

❀ *Rhubarb is seedless and is therefore classified as a vegetable.* ❀

How to
Re-Mortar a Wall

W hen I was a girl my mom used to tell me to say please and thank
you, always to take the smallest piece of cake, and never to stick
my tongue out at people. She also said it was rude to point. Of course
she wasn't talking about filling the joints in the brickwork of a building,
which is only rude when done by fat builders with their butt cracks
showing.

While converting your loft is probably something you want to get the
experts in for, there's no reason you shouldn't be able to do a bit of re-
pointing, or re-mortaring, yourself. Don't expect your *giornata* to match
Michelangelo's efforts, though; it's bound to look a bit rough the first
time you try it. Practice on an unobtrusive bit of wall at the back somewhere or on the home of an unliked neighbor before you dare move on
to the brick frontage of your place.

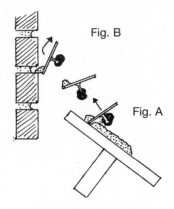

Fig. B

Fig. A

As well as smartening up a building's crumbling countenance, mortaring is a valuable weatherproofing exercise. For example, if you've noticed damp penetration in your boudoir, and the pointing's all dilapidated in the relevant place, then get out your trowel and you can kill two stones with one bird.

Anyway, here's how to go about re-mortaring a wall.

REQUIRED
* *Hammer and chisel*
* *Watering can*
* *Sand and cement*
* *Mortaring trowel*
* *Mortarboard (tasselless)*

INSTRUCTIONS
1 Whack out the old mortar to a depth of 1 inch, using a chisel. This is great fun. Better wear safety goggles though. I know they make you look silly but it can't be helped.
2 Clean the interstices with a brush, then soak the joints with water—the moisture helps your mortar to stick. A watering can works well but you might need to stand on a chair or ladder; gravity won't allow you to water upward.
3 Make the mortar on a mixing board. It's a simple compound of sand and cement. Try some experiments with different combinations.
4 You can dye mortar in different colors to match your existing mortar. This can be fun, but for gawd's sake practice first to avoid producing ugsome monstrosities.
5 You must use the mortar within a couple of hours, before it hardens. This is a chemical process that won't work at very cold temperatures, when the water will freeze, leaving you with an uncompounded mush that just falls out.
6 Shape a trowelful of mortar into a wedge on your mortarboard (Fig. A).

7   With a mortaring trowel (or a cake cutter in an emergency), scoop up a little mortar from the thin end of the wedge and push it into the wet joint. Beginners drop lots of it so put a sheet down or it will harden on the ground (Fig. B).

8   The mortaring may be finished in different ways. So-called weather mortaring projects slightly from the joint, like a little pitched roof, allowing rainwater to run off. You can accomplish this by running your trowel along the joint at an angle. If you want a concave profile, drag a piece of hose along the wet mortar. Or you can just rub it flush, which is good if the joints are especially tight.

9   Don't try to tackle large projects such as the Great Pyramid of Keops until you've got a bit of practice under your belt. Or they'll be very cross with you.

❀ *In Ancient Egypt, Nile mud was used to bond building materials.* ❀

How to
Make Sloe Gin

The blackthorn is a kind of hedge-plum (*Prunus spinosa*) used in Ireland for the manufacture of the shillelagh (a stout knotty stick with a large knob on the end). The bush's blue-black berries ripen in September and are known as sloes, or in Scotland *slaes*.

Somewhat resembling blueberries, the round fruits are easily recognizable by their light blue bloom, and are used in sloe gin, utterly transforming the spirit's distinctive taste such that even gin haters can enjoy it. You shouldn't pick the berries until the first frosts have reduced their tannin content, but don't wait until the end of October or there will be none left and the characteristic sourness that you're looking for will have been lost. (Come to think of it, if there are none left the sourness is academic.)

REQUIRED FOR 1 LITER (1¾ PINTS) OF SLOE GIN

* *1¾ pounds (350–550) sloes*
* *1 bottle of the strongest gin you can get*
* *1⅓ cups granulated sugar*
* *2 old gin bottles (cleaned)*
* *A sharp skewer*
* *A funnel*

METHOD

1   Pick the sloes. Watch out for the spikes. A long pole with a bent wire coat hanger at the end will help you to pull down the high branches. *Don't* wash them.

2   Put ⅔ cup sugar into each bottle and pour in the gin—equal amounts. If some accidentally ends up in your mouth, no harm will have been done.

3   With a skewer, pierce the skin of each sloe and drop into a bottle. The tricky part is to allow a complete intermixing of gin and juice. This is one of those soul-destroying jobs that would be considered torture if you made prisoners do it. The best way to reduce the monotony is to sit opposite a friend and each pick up two sloes at once, pierce them, and drop them into the adjacent bottles in one move. You can chat while you do it. Wear old clothes for this because sloe juice stains indelibly. Suddenly you'll notice that the level of the displaced gin has nearly reached the top. Stop, and screw on the caps.

4   Wash your hands (they will be purple) and put the bottles in a dark place, say under the stairs (see page 107). Give them a daily turnover and a gentle shake. Over time, the sugar will dissolve and the liquid will darken. Once the sugar is no longer visible, you can just give them the occasional shake as you're passing. Over the next twelve weeks or so, the liquid will take on a ruddy hue and the sloes shrivel and wizen like raisins.

5   When time's up, decant the liqueur by pouring into a new bottle through a tea strainer and funnel. The alcoholic leftover sloes can be put into cakes or you can just eat them.

Sloe gin has a complex taste with sorbet-like palate-refreshing properties. When young it is tangy, and bright in color, but it mellows rather quickly, losing its astringency, and becomes increasingly round. As it does so, it turns an attractive brownish color. Yum!

❀ *Churchill's martini: (1) pour a glass of cold gin; (2) look at the vermouth bottle.* ❀

How to
Replace an Electrical Socket

R eplacing an electrical socket is another of those things that women are not supposed to be able to do. Possibly with reason: it's certainly harder if you have long fingernails. Come to think of it, though, my brother is hopeless at it, too, and he often tells us he's a man. I remember the last time he tried it we sat there for hours, gazing in disbelief as the darkness closed in, while he fiddled and cursed and crouched and lost his balance and knocked an expensive vase off a table. Finally, with a blood-chilling scream of frenzy he snipped through the bird's nest of wire he was cradling in his arms, and snatched up the phone to call an electrician. Except he'd cut through the telephone wire...

Obviously it's important to get this right so as not to burn your home down or fry the housekeeper when she plugs in the vacuum. Fortunately, the fuse will blow in most instances when there's a problem, thus saving the day, but that doesn't mean you shouldn't be careful wiring the thing. Here are the instructions in a nutshell. They are designed for modern sockets, not the ancient ones you sometimes find in houses that look like that one in *Psycho*. Get a professional to tackle those.

INSTRUCTIONS

1   Turn off the power!
2   Unscrew the outlet cover, exposing the socket. This is often where the PG-rated cursing starts. You can spend hours fiddling with table knives, coins, and nail files before deciding on a proper screwdriver. And even then it can be a nuisance. Who designed these

nutty contraptions? To help things go a little smoother, have four or five nephews ready to act as assistants, along with a large pot of coffee and a strapping masseur on standby.

3   Carefully unscrew the socket from the wall and pull it out, minding the wires that are still attached. This will reveal the metal junction box inside the wall. It's a bit like a scene from *General Hospital* or *ER*, where someone's intestines have to be taken out, fiddled with, and put back in again. The only difference is *you* won't get any commercial breaks to allow you to powder your nose.

4   Unscrew the connector screws on the sides of the socket. This will free the old socket from the wires. It is now that you will realize if you haven't switched off the power, as, with a blinding flash, your hair stands up on end like blackened cotton candy and lightning flashes all over your body like in that movie where they open the Arc of the Covenant and horrible things come out. Only joking! Discard the old socket. A good joke is to put it inside a friend's washing machine. Next time she does the laundry she'll find this alien "thing" in there and wonder what on earth's happening.

5   Check that the bare ends of the wires are clean and sufficiently exposed. If not, use a wire stripper to remove some of the insulation. Time for some PG-13 swearing and a Band-Aid or two.

6   Wrap the exposed ends of the white wires around the silver screws on the new socket. Tighten the screws. Gosh, isn't this fun! And so *easy*.

7   Wrap the ends of the black wires around the gold screws on the opposite side of the socket. Tighten these screws as well. OK, I confess, it's all very fiddly—a few R-rated expletives will help.

8   Wind some black electrical tape around the socket a couple of times, making sure any and all screws and bare wires are covered. This will help prevent a short circuit in the future. What generally happens is that the short circuit decides to occur just as the people you are trying to impress sit down to dinner, and out go all the lights.

9   Press the whole socket gently back into the junction box and screw it back into the wall. Notice the way I put that? I was trying to make it sound as easy as sliding an encyclopedia back into position on the

bookshelf, whereas it can be more like trying to force a Tupperware-type container into another of exactly the same size.

10   Screw on the outlet cover. Sometimes the screw that does this job is just too short so that you have to squeeze the cover on while screwing, alternately punching your skin and dropping the cover. Some filthy blasphemy is what's required here. Followed by a very stiff drink.

❀ *The electric toaster was first unveiled in 1905.* ❀

How to
Polish a Good Table

*D*on't forget that tables—even good ones—are there to be used. I was once talking to Lord Linley, if you'll pardon my dropping a name, who makes lovely furniture. He said he thought tables and chairs were there to be used, which seemed hard to argue with. If they got bumped, scratched, or dented, well the sun would probably rise tomorrow nonetheless. Anyway, it's not possible to have a life *and* preserve the pristine surface of your table, without wrapping it up in carpet and storing it in a crate somewhere. On the other hand, if your favorite old table is looking a bit down on its luck and you'd like to buff it up to an optimistic shine, here's how.

PREPARATION

1   Wipe and dust your table.

2   You can deal with rings and small scratches by covering them with Vaseline and leaving overnight. Wipe off the splotch the next day. The broken edge of a walnut shell rubbed along an unsightly scratch will darken it.

3   Grease stains can be removed by mixing a paste of talcum powder and mineral spirits. (Caution: This mixture is poisonous and flammable.) Apply with a brush and allow to dry. Then brush off.

4   You can get rid of old wax with a half-and-half mixture of linseed oil and genuine turpentine: smells terrific. Wipe it on with an old rag and remove it with fine steel wool. Wear rubber gloves because it does your nails no favors.

POLISHING WITH WAX

Polishing your wooden furniture with wax will bring up an attractive lustre. It is a very simple and easy process and the key to success is to use the right products. Try to find a wax polish that comes as a cream rather than a paste. It's easier to apply and won't set rock hard. Some of the best polishes are the natural ones. Avoid those containing toluene, a malodorous poisonous solvent. It smells as if you've repainted your car in the house. Use a wax containing genuine turpentine. It is distilled from pine sap so its perfume is just wonderful.

REQUIRED

* *Beeswax furniture polish (specialist suppliers are easy to find)*
* *Clean cotton rags*
* *A soft lintless cloth*

INSTRUCTIONS

1 Put the wax on sparingly with a clean cotton rag, working with the grain of the wood. Don't apply huge dollops or smear it all over ancient coatings of hardened polish. That won't glow, it will just look thicker and browner than yesterday. See preparation 4 above.

2 Buff with a soft cloth that won't snag.

3 Invite your friends over to admire the shine and sniff the scent.

❀ *German proverb: At a round table, every seat is the head place.* ❀

How to
Boil an Egg Like a Pro

My maternal grandma used to boil eggs until they were the consistency and color of surgical gloves, and when we complained would say, "Don't blame me, I only laid the table." This was mildly amusing the first time but wore pretty thin after about twenty years. These instructions therefore reflect my subsequent research and experiment rather than her Neanderthal technique.

There are two main types of boiled egg: the soft and the hard. These methods cover both and will work a treat so long as you follow them precisely.

Size makes a difference of course, and a quail egg will be done long before one that came out of an ostrich. I'm assuming you are using medium-size chicken eggs.

HARD-BOILED

Put your eggs in a saucepan and cover them with about ½ inch cold water. Heat the pan until the water is simmering and cook like this for seven minutes, *using a timer*. As soon as the timer dings put the saucepan into the sink and turn on the cold tap, allowing the water to overspill. It doesn't need to be galloping, a steady but vigorous flow will do. After a minute turn off the tap and leave the eggs in the cold water for another couple of minutes, or until they are cold enough to hold comfortably.

When time's up your eggs will be cooked, and with no soft center remaining. Knock off a minute if you like a bit of sticky in the middle but want the white solid.

PEELING HARD-BOILED EGGS

Peeling hard-boiled eggs can be hard to do without damaging the whites. Older eggs perform best. The way to do it is to tap the eggs and then crackle the shells between your hands underwater. Start peeling at the fat end and keep them in the water until they are cold. A hot egg is still cooking even when it's off the heat, so you need to get them out of the pan and into cold water quickly.

SOFT-BOILED EGGS

Put your eggs in a pan with cold water as above. Turn up the heat to full and as soon as they start boiling reduce to a slight simmer for four minutes. This will produce a creamy yolk and a firm white. The egg will still be cooking when you take it out of the hot water so get it down your neck very smartly.

HINTS AND TIPS

* Very fresh eggs require an extra 30 seconds of cooking. The timings here are for eggs you've had knocking around for three days or more.

* There is an air pocket at the fat end of the egg. As it heats up, this air expands such that the pressure can actually crack the egg from the inside. If you want to be a real pro, prick a tiny hole in the end with a needle before cooking.

* Eggs straight from the fridge will crack if you put them into hot water. Take them out half an hour before you plan to boil them.

* Never try to guess the cooking time. Use your watch or a timer.

* Never boil eggs for too long because the yolks become tough and glaucous.

* Always boil your eggs in a *small* saucepan. Big pans cause eggs to crash into each other like bumper cars, cracking the shells.

* Don't boil eggs to death, simmer them gently. You won't get a better egg by boiling the water like a volcano.

By the way, white eggs come from hens with white feathers and white earlobes. Brown eggs come from hens with red feathers and earlobes. That's the only difference, though how you find a chicken's earlobe beats me.

❈ *U.S. hens lay some 65 billion eggs a year.* ❈

How to
Make Really Regal Royal Icing

*H*ave you ever wanted to create a Christmas cake like the ones your granny used to make, with icing just hard enough but not too hard? This is the way to do it. There are two magic ingredients in my recipe that moderate the hardening effect and produce a snow-white color.

Note: Soak bowls, spoons, and knives *as soon as you can* once you've finished or you'll be in trouble.

INGREDIENTS
* 1 *pound confectioners' sugar*
* 1 *tsp lemon juice*
* 2 *egg whites*
* *A few drops of blue food coloring*
* 2 *tsp glycerine (optional)*

INSTRUCTIONS

1   Sift the confectioners' sugar into a mixing bowl.

2   Combine the lemon juice and egg whites in another bowl and tip in the confectioners' sugar a little at a time, beating with a wooden spoon until the mixture is smooth. This usually takes about 10 minutes but seems like 1½ hours of hard labor.

3   Now for the first magic ingredient. Royal icing should be pure white (not yellow) so stir in 3–4 drops of blue food coloring. This will

71

counteract the yellowing that occurs when icing is kept for any time. Don't go mad though; you don't want to turn the icing blue.

4   Next, the second magic ingredient: the glycerine. Exactly how much you put in is up to you. Its effect is to soften the icing without making it soggy. Too brittle and your cake will be uncuttable, and you'll be getting insurance claims for expensive dental repairs from your friends. Try a little scientific experiment with different amounts the day before you make the final mixture.

5   Beat it until your spoon will stand upright. If you need to leave it for a minute, you may, but cover the bowl with a damp dish towel to stop the icing from hardening.

6   Using a broad-bladed knife dipped in hot water you should be able to apply the icing pretty smoothly. You'll never get it as ice-rink smooth as the cakes you buy in the shops, because they use machinery to produce their supernatural surfaces.

7   If you want to make snowy peaks, use a dry knife. Don't make them too sharp though, or you'll have people's eyes out.

8   You can pipe it, too. But that's another story and I need a cup of coffee.

❈ *Lübeck, Germany, is a traditional center of marzipan manufacture.* ❈

How to
Make Brandy Snaps

*F*ood scientists know that a firm or crisp outer with a soft or yielding inner is a successful combination for packaged foods. Mallomars, apple pies, and Ding Dongs all rely on these dual properties. Brandy snaps are the same. Often filled with double cream, they offer the perfect fusion of crisp and soft.

I first encountered brandy snaps—a fourteenth-century French confection—one summer when I was invited to Beryl Jellie's house in Edinburgh and we were served them at tea by a uniformed maid. I remember thinking the combination of brittle shell and melting innards were the height of sophistication although her mother told me later that they'd come out of a box. Nonetheless, I learned how to make them. Here's the way.

INGREDIENTS
* 4 *tbsp dark corn syrup*
* 1 *tsp ground ginger*
* 1 *tbsp brandy*
* 4 *tbsp all-purpose flour*
* 4 *tbsp brown sugar*
* 4 *ounces butter*
* *A bit of nutmeg*
* *The zest of ½ lemon*

INSTRUCTIONS
1   Slowly melt together the butter, sugar, and syrup, and remove from the heat.
2   Stir together the flour, nutmeg, ginger, and lemon, then add the brandy and beat thoroughly.
3   Drop teaspoonfuls of the mixture on to some greased baking sheets. Space 'em out a bit or you'll end up with one huge brandy snap per tray.
4   Bake at 350°F for 8–10 minutes or until golden.
5   Lift each flat brandy snap off the baking sheet with a palette knife and roll it up, while still malleable, over the handle of a wooden spoon. Then slip the brandy snap tube off the spoon and put it somewhere to harden.
6   Fill your brandy snaps with whipped cream, flavored, if you like, with a few drops of brandy. A piping bag is by far the easiest way to get it in there. In fact it is impossible any other way. I know; I've tried.

If your brandy snaps cool too quickly and won't bend, return them to the oven for just a few seconds to soften up. They go really well with sticky toffee ice cream. Ooh, my mouth's watering at the thought.

❀ *Kirschwasser is a fruit brandy made from cherries.* ❀

Feng Shui in a Jiffy

Feng shui is the ancient Chinese art of placement and arrangement, is pronounced "fung shway," and means "wind and water." Feng shui emphasizes balance, which, when well accomplished, causes people to feel good without noticing why. In this way it is exactly like watching the president get a pie in the face.

Feng shui compartmentalizes life into nine divisions, each of which is represented by materials: wood, water, earth, fire, metal, and polystyrene—no, not polystyrene, I made that up—and also by colors.

Here they are:

1 *Affluence*: purple; wood and water
2 *Celebrity and reputation*: red; fire and wood
3 *Relationships and love*: pink; earth and fire
4 *Family*: green, black, and blue; water
5 *Well-being*: yellow, brown, and orange; earth and fire
6 *Creativity and children*: yellow and earthy tones; metal
7 *Expertise*: black and green; earth
8 *Helpful people and travel*: black and white; metal and water
9 *Career*: blue and white; metal

To feng shui your home, decide which of the nine sections could do with a bit of help and follow the guidance below. You can give a different emphasis to each room if you wish, so that your garage, say, gets most of the well-being treatment and your career is in the toilet (well, you know what I mean).

TOP FENG SHUI INTERIOR DESIGN TIPS

1 Select those colors recommended for that part of your life you wish to improve.
2 Choose furniture and objects containing the chosen elements (wood, earth, etc.).

74

3   Allow no dark areas in any room; these block the free flow of energy. And if your energy isn't free-flowing the vacuum won't work.
4   Sofas and chairs must be arranged so as to allow sitters to see the door easily (especially important with ghastly mothers-in-law).
5   Mirrors should be placed according to the position of the objects you wish to reflect. There is no feng shui method of getting a mirror *not* to reflect your fat behind or saggy boobs. Sorry.
6   Beds should not be set right across the door. Now this one seems obvious to me, or else how do you get in the room? Ideally they should have a wall at one side as protection (don't bang your head on it, though). If you experience difficulty waking up in the morning, point your head east or south (and cut down on the Champagne a bit). Poor sleep may be ameliorated by pointing your head west or north. If you sleep badly *and* find it hard to wake up, I simply don't know what to suggest unless you try going to bed on a revolving turntable.
7   Feng shui sees relationships between the physical world and the inner world of your mind. So clear out your cupboards to allow space for the good things in life to come in. Along with the huge checks from all those eBay customers buying your old and broken trash.

OFFICE CUBICLE FENG SHUI

*   For a start, your computer screen should *always* face away from any doors or plants. I realize that in most offices this means you will be looking at the back of it, but at least your environment will be in balance.
*   Pens and pencils must be parallel at all times. Rather tricky when you're taking down a phone message, but nobody said life was going to be easy.
*   The phone itself should always be blue or purple and always out in the open, not stuck against the wall.
*   Finally, if you have one of those little squashy animals with a sucker on it stuck to your computer, make sure he always faces the elevator. If you work on the first floor, I'm afraid feng shui can't do much for you.

STUDIO APARTMENT FENG SHUI

The problem with living in a studio apartment is that you sleep in your kitchen and cook in your bedroom. Moreover, when you're cooking there's nowhere to put the saucepan lid. So feng shui in a studio is all the more important. When I lived like this, the following helped:

* Forget that stuff about sleeping facing north or south or whatever it is; you'll have enough trouble sleeping on a pull-down arrangement that doubles as the dinner table.
* Never cook with anything containing garlic, smoked fish, or strong cheese unless you like your coat, pajamas, cat, and friends to smell of it. I speak from experience.
* All male friends who "stay over" must be pointed at the coffee-making apparatus first thing in the morning, then directly at the shower, then at their clothes, and shortly thereafter at the door. Feng shui nothing, I'm talking sanity preservation.

❦ *The Chinese invented paper, printing, and gunpowder.* ❦

How to
Light a Fire in the Fireplace

So your man has announced he is going to light the fire. First he shovels up a load of ashes from the grate, knocking the fire irons over noisily with his elbow and terrifying the cat. This is just by way of an overture: a flavor of what's to come.

He decides he will carry the ash outside for disposal—a shovelful at a time. As he steps gingerly across the room, the piled shovel gripped in front of him at arm's length, hot orange smuts start to fly off, landing on the rug, on the cushions, behind the TV. As he opens the door with one hand, the full force of the breeze catches him for the first time, blowing huge gray clouds of ash into his eyes, all over him, and back into the room. *Very loud swearing and coughing.*

Finally, he's got everything cleaned up and prepared: he's piled the kindling, put in the fire starters, and artistically arranged the coals and logs over the top. Now he applies the match. One of the fire-starter logs begins to flicker slightly, and he fiddles noisily with the grate (for optimum draught). But the fire sulks. So he holds a sheet of newspaper across the opening to draw air up faster: "Don't worry," he reassures you, "I know what I'm doing." Immediately, the draught rips the paper out of his hands, sending it—a flaming ball—up the chimney.

After one or two more alarming attempts, he stands up smartly to admire his handiwork, banging his head on the mantelpiece. A single wheezy fire-starter log continues its heroic gasp-and-flicker performance.

It's not really that difficult. Here's how.

REQUIRED
* *3 fire-starter logs*
* *A bunch of kindling*
* 10 *lumps of coal*
* *4–5 small dry logs*
* *A box of matches*

INSTRUCTIONS
1 Clean the grate of ash to allow air under the fire.
2 Check that your fuel is dry.
3 Arrange three fire-starter logs on the grate amid leftover and partly burnt coals.
4 Place a bunch of kindling in a shallow wigwam over fire starters.
5 Surround with lumps of coal. These will help buttress the kindling.
6 Put some small and very dry logs over the whole arrangement, allowing huge air holes.
7 Ignite the fire starters.
8 Don't fiddle.
9 Within fifteen minutes it should have taken hold. If not, check for sufficient airflow.

10   Once the kindling is flaming nicely and the small logs have taken, start adding on more logs or coal. But don't smother.

11   And don't keep poking it. There's no point.

HINTS AND TIPS

*   *Your chimney should be swept regularly.*
*   *Coal tends to glow but produces an intense heat.*
*   *Logs afford big flames but are often not so radiantly hot.*
*   *A few drops of a woody essential oil on your logs a couple of hours before burning give off lovely aromas—cedar, pine, and sandalwood are all good.*

❀ *It is considered lucky to see a chimney sweep on your wedding day.* ❀

How to
Prune Roses

Supermarket flowers! There, now I've said it. What is it about blokes that makes them forget Valentine's Day, wedding anniversaries, you name it? Then at the last minute, they remember and think you won't notice when they present you with a box of gumdrops and a bunch of desperate-looking flowers wrapped in cellophane, with the price tag still on. Nice fresh roses is what you want, proper chocolates, and a bit of care and attention. You could grow roses yourself, of course, and then he could just snip a few off while watching football through the window.

Roses are cultivated round the world and are available in every color except black and blue. But how do you prune them? Can you just cut them anywhere or what? Here's a useful guide.

Pruning is necessary to:

* Remove old and diseased wood.
* Encourage new flowering shoots.
* Keep the plant in trim, with a center open to light and air.

The time to prune roses is during the cold weather, when the plants are dormant. Well, I say that, but there were some great big yellow ones round my front door in *January* and climate change is certainly making these things harder to judge. If it's mild you can prune in November, but once frost and snow take hold put down your pruning shears and wait for spring.

REQUIRED
* *A good pair of gardening or pruning gloves*
* *Some sharp pruning shears*
* *A small pruning saw for big hummers*
* *Garden twine for climbers and tidying up*

INSTRUCTIONS

You need to remove any shoots that are dead, weak, spindly, old, or knotty. You should also cut out shoots growing into the middle of the bush, which might produce a snarled thicket over time, along with any that are rubbing against each other.

CUTTING SHOOTS

1   Always cut just above the bud. Look for where the leaf was attached to the stem. Just above this mark is a bump. This is the bud, which will grow into a new shoot.
2   Select an outward-facing bud that will grow away from, not into, the middle of the plant.
3   Make a clean slanted cut, about ¼ inch above the bud. By cutting at an angle you will cause rain to run away from the bud, so that it isn't inundated.

Most cultivated roses are grafted on to a vigorous, wild rose root, which may send up "suckers" that can overpower and kill the cultivated rose.

Suckers are light green, thin, and fast-growing snakey shoots, the leaves of which look smaller than those of the cultivated rose. They come from below the graft—where the shoots grow from the root—so you might need to dig out some soil to reach them. Do not *cut* suckers. Instead, pull them off at the root, which will prevent them from re-growing.

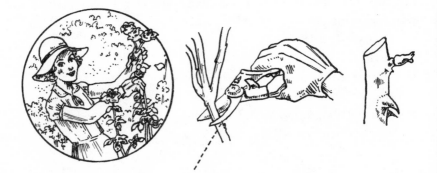

Once you have pruned your roses, give them a good feed with fertilizer and homemade compost (see page 57).

And by the way, I know they *say* you can get black roses, but they aren't really black. Not under a good lamp anyway.

❀ *Roses are often nibbled on by deer.* ❀

Pancakes Without Fuss

William Shakespeare must have *really* annoyed his English teachers, sitting there smugly knowing all those quotes. I bet they were always telling him, "Stop talking like that; you're confusing everyone." To which he probably replied, "Come, thou shalt go home, and we'll have flesh for holidays, fish for fasting-days, and moreo'er puddings and flapjacks, and thou shalt be welcome." In case you're wondering, *flapjacks* are what are better known here as "pancakes." I mention all this only to show that pancakes were popular even in Tudorbethan times. Here are a couple of tasty recipes that I bet Pericles would have loved.

Ingredients
* 4 *ounces butter*
* ¹/₂ *cup soft brown sugar*
* 4 *tbsp dark corn syrup (Use black molasses for "blackjacks.")*
* 1¹/₄ *cups rolled oats*

Instructions
This is your standard pancake. Serves 12.

1 Melt the butter, sugar, and syrup over a low heat (in a pan obviously), then stir in the oats.
2 Spoon into a greased baking tin in a ¹/₂-inch layer.
3 Bake at 350°F for about 25 minutes or until golden.
4 Allow to cool in the tin, then cut into munchable squares or strips.

Cheesyjacks are a savory alternative. Good with a fried egg. Serves 12 again.

INGREDIENTS

* 2 *ounces butter*
* 2½ *cups chopped peanuts*
* 1¼ *cups halved macadamia nuts*
* 1 *large carrot, grated*
* 4 *ounces sharp cheddar cheese, grated*
* ⅔ *cup rolled oats*
* ½ *tsp mixed herbs*
* 1 *egg, beaten*

INSTRUCTIONS

1 Melt the butter and mix with everything else.
2 Spoon into a greased cake tin and press.
3 Bake at 350°F for about ½ hour or until golden.
4 Let cool in the tin and then cut into slices.

Both these recipes produce delicious pancakes. But don't stuff your face; remember: "They are as sick that surfeit with too much, as they that starve with nothing."

Fly's graveyard: In addition to the cheesy variety, my niece Anna particularly likes what she calls, "those pancakes you make with flies in them." To accomplish this effect, simply sprinkle a handful of raisins into the batter before it goes in the pan.

Greedy boy's breakfast: Chop one apple (leave skin on) and one banana (take skin off) and throw into the batter; add a handful of blueberries and some broken walnuts. This is a clever way of making a person who lives off fast food eat something that will do him a bit of good. There's potassium, vitamin C, manganese, fiber, and all kinds of health-promoting antioxidants in them thar fruits. Decorate the pancake with an attractive dribble of maple syrup and a squirt of delicious extruded aerosol cream-type product.

Death by chocolate: Named for the well-known dessert, this one is always a winner. Get yourself a few interesting chocolate bars. Grate them, squash them, cut them up, and drop them in the mix. They smell fantastic as they melt into the cooking batter.

Puritan's pancake: Make a watery batter and pour a tiny spoonful into your pan. Burn lightly on both sides and serve with nothing. Good for dieters.

❀ *The macadamia nut is a native of eastern Australia.* ❀

How to
Cook with Edible Flowers

Some years ago I knew a rotund and avuncular cravat-wearing gourmand named PJ. Sadly, I don't know him anymore because he ate himself enthusiastically into the grave some time ago. I miss his urbanity, his cigar smoke, and his sardonic Latin translation on the hoof. But most of all I miss his delight in buying you dinner. I remember once he took me to a little restaurant tucked away in the Welsh hills. Every dish in this place contained, and was decorated with, a profusion of edible flowers. I have never seen a more lovely horticultural display than the salad that arrived at our table, bursting with the multifarious efflorescence of nasturtiums, pansies, and lavender.

A FEW TIPS

1   As well as being pretty, edible flowers are often highly nutritious; many are a good source of vitamins A and C.

2   Usually it's the petals that are the edible bit so you should remove the stems, anthers, and pistils because they are often bitter. Sometimes, though, the whole flower may be eaten.

3   Clean your flowers before use. There's nothing less appealing than a cheeky caterpillar wagging its green little head at you out of a cowslip. So before preparing your dishes, flick off any insects you can see (check underneath, too), and run the flower under a slow cold tap.

4   Flowers are delicate things and though they can be stored in the fridge for a short time they will wilt pretty fast. Better use them as fresh as you can: it's flick, pick, rinse, and serve.

THESE ARE ALL GOOD IN SALADS

* *Nasturtiums*
* *Comfrey*
* *Pansies*
* *Gladiolus*
* *Rose petals*
* *Marigolds (not the French frilly sort—the kind that look like orange daisies)*
* *Elderflower*
* *Lavender*

Though I've never seen them recommended as a food, I've been eating daisies for decades. The ones I mean are the little things that grow in your lawn. Whenever I'm sitting on the grass somewhere I will pop a whole one in my mouth, with a bit of stalk attached, and munch away. It is a distinctive taste with an "electric" edge.

The appearance of a plate of blossoming food creates a terrific impression on guests and it's not hard to conjure up an entire floral dinner using the plants in your windowbox. There are plenty of recipes out there, too, and once you've settled on the flowers you like, you can invent your own. Here are three to be going on with, beginning with a recipe for a tart that Archbishop Parker used to drool over.

INGREDIENTS FOR ARCHBISHOP PARKER'S
MARIGOLD TART (1572)

* *A ready-made 9- to 10-inch shortcrust pastry crust (who's got the time to make one?)*
* *$\frac{1}{2}$ tsp saffron strands (take out a mortgage)*
* *3 tbsp dried marigold petals (heads off)*
* *4 tbsp superfine sugar*

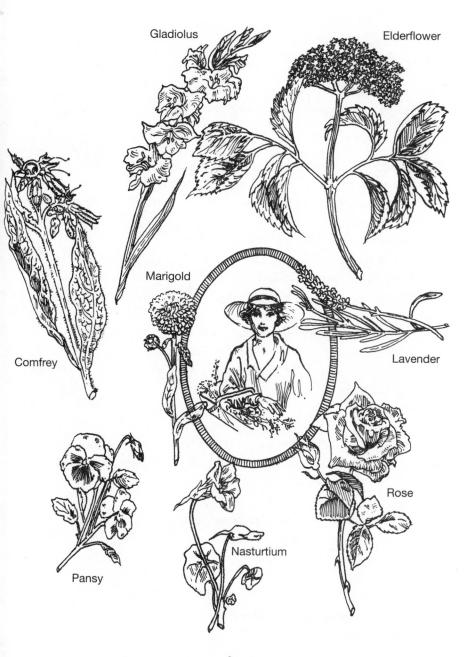

Gladiolus

Elderflower

Comfrey

Marigold

Lavender

Pansy

Nasturtium

Rose

85

* 8 *ounces cream cheese or crème fraîche*
* 2 *eggs, separated*
* 3 *tbsp half-and-half*
* *Zest of 2 oranges*
* 1 *cup all-purpose flour*
* *Crystalized borage or violet flowers to decorate (optional)*

INSTRUCTIONS

1. Bring a little water to simmering point and sprinkle in your petals. Wet them thoroughly then drain straight away and reserve.
2. Beat together the sugar and cream cheese or crème fraîche until soft and smooth.
3. Beat in the egg yolks one at a time, followed by the half-and-half.
4. Stir in the grated orange, marigold petals, saffron, and flour. Golly, doesn't this sound *delicious*.
5. Whisk the egg whites until thick. Stop as soon as they stand in peaks.
6. Fold the egg whites into the mixture.
7. Pour the resultant goo into your pastry crust and cook in the middle of the oven at 400°F for 35–40 minutes or until the center of your tart is firm to the touch.
8. Arrange your flowers on top and serve.

A friend of mine made Archbishop Parker's marigold tart for a tea the other day and she said not a crumb was left. So three cheers for His Grace.

BLOOMING LAVENDER AND HONEY ICE CREAM

This goes brilliantly with the tart above but it takes about eight hours to prepare, what with the freezing business and everything. So do it on a day when you aren't tied up with other things.

INGREDIENTS

* 2 *tbsp dried edible lavender flowers*
* 2½ *cups heavy cream*

* ²/₃ *cup whole milk*
* ²/₃ *cup honey*
* 2 *large eggs*
* *Pinch salt*

EQUIPMENT

* *Ice cream maker*

INSTRUCTIONS

1   In a large heavy saucepan, bring the cream, milk, honey, and lavender to a boil over a medium heat, stirring occasionally. Then remove from the hob, cover, and let stand for 30 minutes.

2   Finely sift the mixture into a bowl and discard the lavender flowers. Pour into a fresh saucepan and heat gently but do not boil.

3   Whisk the eggs together in a large bowl, adding a pinch of salt. Then, in a slow stream, pour in 1¼ cups of the hot mixture, whisking as you go. Pour this eggy custard into the remaining mixture in the saucepan and stir constantly over a low heat until it begins to coat the back of the spoon. Don't let it boil.

4   Now sift into a clean bowl and let the custard cool thoroughly, stirring it a bit any time you pass by. If you are impatient put the bowl into a sink containing a few inches of very cold water and stir it around.

5   Cover and chill for at least three hours. It should be good and cold.

6   Now freeze it in your ice cream maker.

7   Once frozen, transfer the ice cream to an airtight plastic container to harden in the freezer.

This ice cream makes a grand accompaniment to the Archbishop's tart above and you can adapt it on Valentine's night by using rose petals instead of lavender. Rose petal ice cream goes especially well with a generous dribble of black-pansy syrup. Delicious!

BLACK-PANSY SYRUP

I will not tell you what my Uncle Bob said to me when I mentioned the name of this syrup. Instead I will get straight on with it. It couldn't be easier.

INGREDIENTS
* *½ point black or purple pansy petals (loose, not compressed)*
* *12 ounces granulated sugar*
* *1¼ cups water*

INSTRUCTIONS
1   Blend your pansy petals together with 2 ounces of the sugar. A food processor is ideal for this because you want a smooth paste, but you could try it by hand and see how it goes.
2   In a small saucepan, mix the sugar/petal paste with the water and the rest of the sugar. Don't use aluminum pans; strange things happen.
3   Bring the mixture to a boil over a moderate heat. Stir once and turn down low. Simmer to reduce to a syrup but *do not allow it to burn.*
4   When the syrup is beginning to become sticky but will still dribble off a spoon, remove it from the heat and pour into a jug and let it cool.

Like some other flowers, pansies are actually fairly tasteless. Their chief benefit in cookery is the power they have to color things intensely. They are beautiful as a garnish too.

The pretty violet color of black-pansy syrup makes a lovely complement to any dessert but is especially effective against the lavender ice cream mentioned above. And with a pansy flower on top of the lot, it looks a picture.

❀ *Lavender is a member of the mint family.* ❀

How to
Make Authentic Turkish Delight

W ho can forget poor Edmund in *The Lion, the Witch and the Wardrobe*, the unlucky boy who is corrupted via an addictive form of "enchanted" Turkish delight by the chillingly glamorous White Witch? After snarfing a whole box of the stuff he becomes spellbound, behaving thereafter like an absolute beast. But, thank goodness, he becomes his "real old self" again on page 163 (in my 1967 Puffin edition).

There is certainly something seductive about Turkish delight, with its evocations of the mystic Orient. It's a delicious combination of perfume, taste, and texture, the best-made yielding to the tooth in a gelatinous but firm way, and glowing beguilingly like chunks of amber or some precious pink crystal. The sparkling icing sugar and starch mixture with which it is dusted not only prevents the cubes sticking together in the box but looks wonderfully pretty, too. Of course its taste is divine—owing chiefly to the presence of a secret ingredient, which I will reveal in a moment.

There are numerous formulae out there for Turkish delight, but my "Sultan's Mistress" recipe is based on a traditional one from the Middle East, where Turkish delight is known as *lokum*.

INGREDIENTS

* 4 *cups granulated sugar*
* 5 *cups water*
* $^2/_3$ *cups cornstarch*
* 1 *tsp cream of tartar*
* 1 *tbsp lemon juice*
* 1$^1/_2$ *tbsp rosewater (the magic ingredient)*
* 1 *cup confectioners' sugar*
* *Oil for the baking pan*

INSTRUCTIONS

The unique physical properties of proper Turkish delight are the result of a delicious alchemy between starch and sugar that produces a heavy sweetmeat with a density something like that of Jupiter. When you put it down on a wood floor it often burns a square hole in the surface. (Only joking.) There is no gelatin in my recipe—unlike others. Gelatin has a tendency to produce transparent, bouncy, and rather ersatz characteristics that are at odds with the opaquely viscous properties of the authentic confection. The best Turkish delight is golden of cast or just faintly pink, never the eyewateringly synthetic Barbara-Cartland-boudoir color that leers at you from some commercial products. You will not, therefore, be needing any red food coloring.

1   Grease a baking pan with vegetable oil or something, and line it with oiled wax paper.
2   Mix 1¼ cups water, the lemon juice, and the sugar in a saucepan. Turn on the heat to medium.
3   Stir all the time while watching *Days of Our Lives* or something until the sugar has dissolved. You will know this has happened as soon as the liquid clarifies.
4   Now turn up the heat and let it boil. Once it does, quickly turn it down low.
5   Simmer gently, without stirring, until the syrup reaches the softball stage. You'll know you're there when you can drop a blob off the spoon into some cold water so that it forms a ball that you can squeeze flat between your fingers. If you have a sugar thermometer, you will see that this happens at 238–245°F. Remove the pan from the heat and set it aside.
6   In a saucepan over a medium heat, mix the cream of tartar with ½ cup of cornstarch and the remaining water. Stir out all the lumps and let the mixture begin to boil. When it reaches the consistency of glue you can stop stirring.
7   Mix in the syrup and the lemon juice and keep stirring for about

five minutes. Then turn it down low and simmer for 1 hour, stirring frequently. This is when the magic change begins to happen.

8 As soon as your mixture has attained a golden color, add the rosewater and stir well. The perfume will at once conjure visions of sunkissed minarets and dusty winds wafting warmly over the Great Mosque of Kahramanmaras. Have a little taste and if you can't detect the rosewater or the minarets, add a little more until you think it's right. Don't forget, you can always add a drop more but you can't take it out.

9 Pour the delicious sludge into your paper-lined pan. Spread it around evenly and let it cool overnight.

10 Sift the powdered sugar together with the rest of the cornstarch and sprinkle a little on to a board. Then turn out the Turkish delight and cut it with an oiled knife into sensibly sized cubes.

11 Coat your Turkish delight with the rest of the cornstarch and sugar mixture. You can layer it in an airtight container with wax paper between layers. Or you can just eat it.

❁ *Demre in Turkey is the birthplace of St. Nicholas (Santa Claus).* ❁

How to
Get by at the Butcher Shop

These days, it's quite a job to find a butcher who remembers your name and seems to know what he's talking about. I'm lucky; there's one near me who does the butchering right there in front of you and it's a joy to watch. The problem is that the supermarkets have cured us of our knowledge so that it can be hard to know what to ask for when you enter a *real* butcher shop.

Here's a short glossary of some of the more interesting cuts to give you a head start.

BEEF

* *Neck*: minced for shepherd's pie or hamburgers.
* *Shoulder*: stews and casseroles.
* *Shin*: a versatile meat for shepherd's pie, etc.
* *Brisket*: needs to be cooked slowly.
* *Sirloin and fillet*: prime, marbled, juicy roasting joints and steaks. Fillet is actually part of the sirloin. Very tender but less flavorful than rump.
* *Rump*: the joint next to the sirloin. Delicious for kebabs.
* *Topside and silverside*: good for roasting.
* *Leg*: best in casseroles.

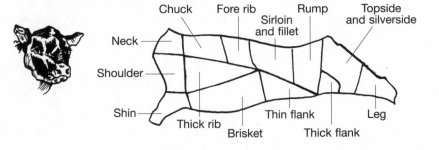

PORK

* *Neck*: the best part of the neck is used in sausage meat.
* *Shoulder*: boned and rolled makes a roasting joint. Can also be diced or minced.
* *Loin*: best for pork chops. Also cured to make back bacon.
* *Belly*: fatty but makes a superb roast or stew if well prepared.
* *Knuckle or shank end*: boned and rolled for roasting.

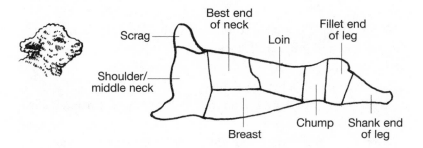

LAMB

* *Shoulder*: boned and rolled or can be cut into chops.
* *Scrag end of neck*: delicious for stewing.
* *Best end of neck*: a joint with a row of half a dozen ribs (rack of lamb). Two joined together and arranged bones-out, with little chef's hats on, are the famous crown of lamb. Also sold as chops with one rib each.
* *Loin and chump*: divided into loin end and chump end and cut into chops—chump has a round bone and loin has a T-bone—or you can roast in one piece.
* *Leg*: can be bought whole or split into two joints, fillet and shank. Lamb shank can be on or off the bone. It is a delicious succulent roasting joint and one of my favorites.

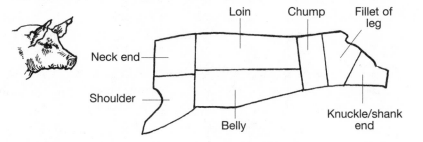

OFFAL

* *Haggis*: sheep's stomach stuffed with boiled liver, heart, lungs, rolled oats, and other stuff. Delicious!
* *Faggots*: minced pork (mainly liver and cheek), bread, herbs, and onion wrapped in a pig's caul. Ooer!
* *Brawn*: leftover pork meat from the skull. Set in gelatin and chilled. Ugh!
* *Tripe*: white honeycomb-like stuff made from the first three of a cow's four stomachs. Yikes!
* *Chitterlings*: pig's intestinal pipes. Bleurgh!

The less fashionable (cheaper) cuts are nowadays reclaiming the attention they deserve. Longer, slower cooking times for "Cinderellas" such as brisket of beef, trotters, or belly of pork produce some of the most delicious meals imaginable. If in doubt about what to go for ask your butcher—he knows.

❈ *Shari Lewis's Lamb Chop sock puppet has appeared on TV since 1957.* ❈

How to
Press an Ox Tongue

On their picnic in *The Wind in the Willows*, Ratty and Mole take along "coldtonguecoldhamcoldbeefpickledgherkinssaladfrenchrolls-cresssandwichespottedmeatgingerbeerlemonadesodawater . . . ," a diet redolent of yesteryear and, notice, it's the cold tongue that rightly heads the list.

Pressing an ox tongue has fallen out of fashion in recent years, maybe because diners don't like the idea of eating something that has been in someone else's mouth. But, let's face it, it's different with ox tongue, which is really delicious when properly cooked and prepared. Here's a simple method—courtesy of my mother-in-law, Joan—that will provide enough tongue for a fortnight's diet of nothing else.

INGREDIENTS

Go to your favorite butcher and ask him if he can give you some tongue. On second thought, don't say that. Ask instead for two ox tongues. These sometimes come in a packet, but you don't want the cooked ones; what you are after is either fresh or those preserved in brine.

METHOD

1   Place your ox tongues on the kitchen table. They are great big mean-looking things covered in bumps and are a splotchy salt-and-pepper color. Not the prettiest sight you've ever seen.

2   Put a large pan on the stove and drop them in, with just enough water to cover them. Add some chopped carrot, onion, celery, and a bay leaf. I always put in a few fennel seeds, too, along with a handful of black peppercorns and plenty of salt. However, if you are using salted tongues, don't add more salt to the water.

3   Turn on the heat and simmer your tongues. They are big hummers and will take hours to cook (one hour per pound) so open the window or your kitchen will soon resemble a Turkish bath. Do not let the pan boil dry; keep checking it and after a while your woman's intuition will tell you that it's time to test the tongues with a skewer. They should be tender all the way through.

4   Once they're cooked, remove them from the pan but keep the liquid simmering away to reduce.

5   Skin the tongues while they are still hot. If you don't do it now, you will require the help of three firemen to do the job once they are cold. During the skinning process remove the cartilaginous lumps and bony pieces from underneath, using all your surgical skills.

6   Cram the tongues into a round dish only just big enough to accommodate them, the pointy end of one touching the fat end of the other.

7   Strain your reduced broth and pour it over the dark red meat.

8   Now for the pressing business. Put a round dinner plate on top. Try to

find one just a little smaller in diameter than the dish, for maximum pressure. Now you need to use your imagination a bit. You can either ask a fat man to stand on the plate overnight or do what I do and put a huge pan full of water on top. It's up to you; anything really heavy will do.

9 The next day you can remove the plate and if your pan is circular you can slide the meat out. It slices beautifully and tastes wonderful. Serve with a few pickled gherkins and some buttered toast.

Unsuitable for vegetarians.

❀ *The ox is one of the twelve animals of Chinese astrology.* ❀

Natural Limescale Removers

W orking once, as I did, in an office at the top of a Belgravia mansion, I used to get through a lot of tea. This was provided by the ancient and longtime factotum Mrs. Treen, who kept a huge and elderly aluminium kettle constantly on the stove. One day I tried to lift it but it weighed a ton, and when I looked inside I noticed an archaeologically significant buildup of limescale from decade upon decade of hard London water. It must have been 2 inches thick.

Hard water is just an informal name for water with a high mineral content, usually metal ions: mainly calcium (Ca) and magnesium (Mg) in the form of carbonates, though it may also include other metals, as well as bicarbonates and sulfates. But you don't need to know this very dull information, because you can discover your water's hardness by lathering some soap. If it produces a meager foam, your water's hard, but if the merest scintilla makes enough froth for a movie snowstorm, then you have soft water (good for making Scotch whisky with).

Calcium carbonate (limescale) deposited on your taps is unsightly, but you can get rid of it laboriously with elbow grease, or much more easily using an entirely natural limescale remover, which I'll tell you about in a moment. It's best to do this regularly because by the time it becomes as thick as the kettle I mentioned, removing it is less a housekeeping job than a major civil engineering project.

KETTLE METHOD

Perhaps the most obvious testament to hard water is the buildup in your kettle. If you lift the lid, look inside, and see a cavern of stalactitic crusts and what appear to be huge brittle ice sheets that break off and end up in your tea, then it's time to act.

1   Empty the kettle.
2   Pour in 2 inches of water and a couple of capfuls of your magic natural limescale destroyer: vinegar.
3   Now for the witchcraft: boil. You *must* keep a watch, and as soon as it starts to boil switch it off. If you don't do this the vinegar will cause a noisome Vesuvian eruption, covering your worktop with an eye-watering scalding brown froth and filling the kitchen with a mephitic effluvium.

A weekly boiling of this water-vinegar mixture in your kettle will keep it in tip-top condition. Don't forget to rinse it out afterward, though!

TAP METHOD

1   Half fill a sandwich bag with vinegar and slide it over your tap, snapping a rubber band over the lot. Leave overnight with the tap immersed in the vinegar and next morning it will be bright and shiny. Pour the vinegar down the drain.

BATH AND SHOWER METHOD

1   Mix ¼ cup vinegar and 1 cup water in a spray bottle.

2   Spray bath and shower. Make sure there's nobody in there first.
3   Lounge in sunshine for an hour, reading romantic novel.
4   Wipe off with wet sponge—the bath and shower, not you.

You need to do this regularly to make an impact. Or even better, get *someone else* to do it and go skiing instead.

❁ *More than 90 percent of the world's freshwater is in Antarctica.* ❁

How to
Remove Tricky Stains from Almost Anywhere

There's nothing quite so time-consuming for the compleat housewife as clearing up after other people. Guests come around and drip cof-fee on your carpet, grind ballpoint pens into your sofa, and ruin your best shag rugs by squashing chewing gum all over the place. Then there's clothes washing and all the muck on the walls. If only you were rich enough to buy a party space . . . Well, until that time comes, why not try some of these ingenious cleaning agents.

* *Coffee*: On carpets, apply a mixture of egg yolk and glycerin, then sponge with warm water; on clothes, wash after sponging with the eggy glycerin.
* *Bird droppings on your windows*: These disappear like magic with a rag dipped in hot vinegar.
* *Sweat*: Spray the dress or shirt with clear vinegar (after you've taken it off). Then wash the garment with a couple of soluble aspirins dissolved in water.
* *Ring around the collar*: Try using the shampoo that's advertised as being for oily hair, and give it a good scrub with the nail brush.
* *Horribly filthy mechanic's overalls*: Soak the overalls in a can of generic cola, then wash in detergent as usual.

* *Ballpoint pen*: Easy one if you catch it fresh. Rub the ink gently with some dishsoap, then scrape the stain with a knife, and repeat.
* *Fun-Tak adhesive on walls*: This is a weird one. Apply a blob of toothpaste and leave it to harden. Next day (or once it's hard) wash off the toothpaste and the Fun-Tak will come with it. I do not understand how or why this works, but it seems to.
* *Scratches on a wooden table*: OK, not really a stain but can be unsightly. Rub the edges of a broken walnut shell on to the scratch. I think there's tannin in there, which darkens the wood. But don't quote me.
* *Chewing gum*: This can be a real bear. Freeze the gum with a bag of ice or frozen peas. Once it's solid, strike the gum sharply with a hammer and pick off the fractured pieces. Use a rag soaked in mineral spirits on any bits left over. Not infallible but better than nothing.
* *Residue of sticky labels on jars*: Sometimes you want the jar but not the label. Peel off what you can and then use a lump of smooth peanut butter on a cotton ball, rubbing in circles. Or if you want to be boringly utilitarian, use mineral spirits.
* *Dust on silk flowers*: My Auntie Sarah told me about this one and it's brilliant. Put the flowers in a large paper bag and season well with plenty of salt. Now shake, and presto! the dust is gone. A bit like Shake and Bake. Oh dear, I'm showing my age.

❀ *Staines was the major producer of linoleum until the 1960s.* ❀

How to
Test Pearls for Genuineness

Genuine pearls are classed as "natural" or "cultured." Natural pearls are formed when a small foreign object becomes embedded in an oyster. The mollusk secretes a mixture of crystalline and organic substances called nacre, which builds in protective layers around the irritant, eventually forming a pearl. Cultured pearls are natural in all respects except their inception, whereby a foreign object is deliberately introduced to provoke the pearl-forming process. Nowadays, more than 95 percent of the world's pearls are cultured.

Fake pearls, in contrast, are made by coating a plastic or mother-of-pearl core with a paint containing ground fish scales or pearly-looking plastic.

Even these paste gewgaws will take people's minds off your wrinkles in a low light, but if you want to find out the true worth of a pearl necklace some gentleman has just given you, then, girls, you gotta test 'em. Good fakes can be hard to spot these days but you can try the following.

* *Tooth test*: Rub the pearl delicately along the biting edge of your top front teeth. Pearls are made mostly of calcium carbonate ($CaCO_3$) and the genuine article will feel gritty or sandy, whereas a synthetic pearl will feel smooth. This is the easiest way to test a pearl but it's rather rough and ready so don't rely on it if you are a newcomer to the world of pearl chewing.

* *Magnification test*: Examine the pearl's surface with a strong magnifying glass. Real pearls look smooth and finely granulated while imitations appear more coarsely grainy.

* *Necklace-hole test*: Examine the hole with a lens. The edges of the hole will be sharp and crisp in a genuine pearl and may even be chipped. The hole will be blobby and irregular in an imitation.

* *Weight test*: Gently bounce the pearls in your hand. They will feel dense and heavy if real, and light and insubstantial if fake—unless they are made of glass.

* *Blemish test*: Look closely for flaws in the surface. Real pearls will have a variety of natural irregularities in their surface. If your pearls are flawless and look too good to be true they probably are.

PEARLY NAMES

The name Margarita means "pearl" as do Margaret, Peggy, Marjorie, Margot, Maggie, Gretchen, Greta, Gretel, and Rita. They signify purity, humility, innocence, and sweetness.

Most notably, of course, the name Pearl means "pearl." I think it's time for one of my tablets.

❀ *80 percent of thatch used in Britain is imported.* ❀

How to
Make Natural Yogurt in a Thermos

When I was a girl I went with my school orchestra on a band trip to what was then called West Germany. I used to hold on to a cello in that ensemble and scrape away so supernaturally badly that the kindly music teacher who conducted us used to ask me to please mime. This is not hard to do in the fast bits of the *William Tell Overture* because things are going like the clappers, but it can be a hell of a job to fake something lyrical such as the slow movement of Mozart's clarinet concerto. My bow always seemed to be going in the opposite direction to that of all the other cellists and at a different speed. It was, frankly, embarrassing.

I was staying during our visit with a lovely German family who one day took me down to their huge Aladdin's cave of a basement—bigger and better stocked than a modern Wal-Mart—to get a pot of something they wanted me to try. They told me in perfect English that it was called *quark*, which turned out to be a sour, yogurty, pus-colored, and in all other ways uniquely repellant, liquid cheese that, once tasted, was never again to be touched by me even with barge poles. And they made me eat it with pumpernickel, too.

When we were back in England I fell with longing upon my Auntie Sarah's delicious homemade yogurt, which she always kept brewing in a thermos flask in her kitchen. It was like imbibing nectar after the loathsome filthy-old-sockness of the unspeakable quark.

Here's Auntie Sarah's yummy recipe.

INGREDIENTS

* 1 *pint whole milk*
* 1 *huge tbsp live yogurt*
* *Your favorite flavoring*

INSTRUCTIONS

1 Warm the pint of milk just short of boiling on the stove. You can test this by dipping your finger in; it doesn't take long, but warm it slowly.

2 Add a good dollop—about 1 tablespoon—of natural live yogurt and stir it all in.

3 Pour the mixture into a thermos. The best ones are those with a tartan on them. Then go away for a few hours (6–12 recommended).

4 Next morning you will have a pint of delicious yogurt waiting for you. The longer you leave it, the more tart it gets so if you prefer it mild eat it straight away and if you like it more sour wait a few days.

Once it's brewed, of course, you can flavor your thermos yogurt with whatever you fancy, from chocolate—just shave it in—to vanilla extract to crushed-up raspberries or blueberries or strawberries or sardines. No, not sardines; I was getting carried away.

The wonderful energy- and money-saving thing is that after you've brewed the first batch you needn't buy live or "active" yogurt ever again because you can use your own to start a new lot.

And if anyone ever asks you if you'd care to try a product called quark, pretend to be dead or something.

❀ *The vacuum flask was dubbed "thermos" by a resident of Munich.* ❀

How to
Get the Top Off
a Pickle Jar

*H*ow many times have you opened the cupboard and taken down a handsome-looking jar of pickled onions, mayonnaise, or whatever, and then spent ten minutes trying—and failing—to get the top off the wretched thing?

And how peculiar it is that one's desire for something should increase in direct proportion to one's inability to get it. I'm not a huge fan of cocktail onions as a rule but when I tried rather idly to open a jar of them one Christmas, and couldn't, I felt suddenly as if I would simply never rest until I had eaten two or three jars of them. My whole life seemed quite meaningless without a cocktail onion. It's a problem that results in an awful lot of trying everything you can think of as well as a fair bit of storming off in disgust, which is a shame really, as there is not one solution to this puzzle but several.

First, it helps to understand a bit of the science. The problem is caused during the bottling process. After the gherkins, onions, or whatever go into the jar, hot vinegar follows and the lid is screwed on by a powerful machine before anything has had time to cool. As the air and liquid cool, they shrink. This means that the pressure of the air outside the jar is now greater than that inside, effectively forcing the lid on very tightly. Together with the machine closure and the shrinkage of the metal lid itself, this makes it a mammoth job to get the top off again.

In the old days you would just ask a man to help, but some of these jars are now so huge and so ludicrously tight that even the men end up staggering around red-faced and gasping. The following tips are ones I've tried, and they've all worked for me, though you sometimes need to try more than one on a particularly contumacious container.

1   Break the vacuum seal by tapping the lid against a work surface. Not infallible, but sometimes works.

2   Invert the jar
     and "smack its
     bottom" hard a
     couple of times,
     just as one would a
     newborn baby. Hit
     and miss, this one,
     and more effective with narrow jars of
     capers and that kind of thing.

3   Put the triangular tip of an old-fashioned
     bottle opener underneath the lid and lever it
     away from the glass until the vacuum is broken. You'll hear a sigh as
     the air escapes.

4   Use a flat screwdriver to do a similar thing. Insert it under the lid
     but *twist* the screwdriver to pull the lid away and release the pres-
     sure.

5   Hold the top of the jar under very hot running water for a couple
     of minutes, turning it so that the lid is evenly heated. This will ex-
     pand the metal, and to some extent the air at the top of the jar, too,
     allowing you to open it more easily. Just heat the lid, not the whole
     jar. Then try 6, 7, and 8 below.

6   Rub your hand on your thigh (or someone else's thigh if you like) for
     about twenty seconds. You need to be wearing jeans or something
     similar. Your hand will become hot and you'll get a superb grip.

7   Wrap the lid in a tea towel to give your hands more traction as you
     twist.

8   Wear rubber gloves to do the same job. This often helps after you've
     put into place a preliminary measure such as number 5, above.

9   Take a short pointy kitchen knife and in classic right-hand *Macbeth*
     position, with the handle gripped firmly and the blade protruding
     from under your fist, bring it down with a short sharp stab on the
     middle of the lid. Keep your other hand out of the way. You will
     pierce a small hole and you'll hear a pop as the air escapes. Now
     twist it off: nice 'n' easy.

10   If all else fails, undo your top button and go and ask the nice man next door. Maybe he can do it and maybe he can't but what have you got to lose? *Don't* answer that.

❀ *Americans consume more than 20 billion pickles a year.* ❀

How to
Make Rosehip Syrup

When I was a tot, I used to look up at the world from my perambulator admiringly. All the pillar boxes were brightly painted and ladies in hats, with baskets on their arms, shopped for cauliflower, mackerel, and chitterlings at the markets, while all around the smack of spring was in the air. Things seemed better then than they do now and among the best of those better things was stamina-promoting rosehip syrup. All of us babies drank it then—by the imperial gallon. Bursting with vitamin C, it did us good like school milk, sunshine, and red meat—all those things that are now bad for us. Children carried on drinking it throughout the groovy '60s and into the ungroovy early '70s. But then it all sort of petered out.

So here is a recipe for wonderful old-school rosehip syrup that you can knock together yourself in a twinkling. Diluted with about five parts water, hot or cold, it makes a delicious autumn cordial, suitable for children and grown-ups alike. Or you can dribble it undiluted on ice cream or toast. The ingredients couldn't be simpler and you can gather the rosehips yourself. They are the seed pods of the plant and are rather heavy, which is fortunate, because you will need two pounds. They look like little pinky-red zeppelins and are hard to mistake. But do your homework first.

INGREDIENTS
*   *2 pounds rosehips*
*   *1 pound sugar*
*   *A large pan*

* *A jelly-straining bag or some muslin*
* *A measuring jug*
* *A few small bottles*

INSTRUCTIONS

1. Gather the rosehips on a sunny day. It's best to have too many.
2. Come home again and give them a good wash.
3. Crush them up in a bowl (get help, it's boring) and drop them into three pints of boiling water.
4. Return to the boil and remove from the heat. Allow the mush to stand for about 10 minutes. That's just enough time to pluck your eyebrows.
5. Now strain the mixture through the jelly bag. In case you've never met a jelly bag before, they are simple cloth affairs used for straining, well, jelly. If you are straining through muslin, get someone to help you; it's all a bit fiddlesome.
6. Once it stops dripping, reserve the juice and return the pulp to the pan with a further 3½ cups of boiling water. Bring the mixture back to the boil and remove from the heat to let stand again.
7. After 10 minutes, strain as before and combine the juice of both strainings.
8. Pour this liquid into a clean pan and boil down until you have 3½ cups of juice.
9. Add 1 pound sugar and stir over a low heat until it dissolves.
10. Boil for five minutes but do not allow it to burn.
11. Decant your hot rosehip syrup into very clean small bottles. If they look medicinal, so much the better. Seal them tightly and give away to your undernourished-looking friends.

❀ *Rosehip soup is popular in Sweden.* ❀

Best Use of the Closet Under the Stairs

*J*udging which of my embarrassing experiences has been the most embarrassing ever is a tricky one. There are so many to choose from. There was the shameful time I drank the finger bowl in front of a boy I was trying to impress at a fancy restaurant; or the time I came out of a job interview and the young, pretty, coifed, and icy secretary pointed out that my skirt was tucked into my underwear.

But neither of these vexations quite matches for total skin-prickling discomfiture the time I was about to give a talk at school and felt a giant sneeze coming on. Deciding to suppress it at the moment of climax, I clamped my lips, eyes, and nostrils closed, my face taking on a kind of gurning leer. Unable to exit through my nose, the pent-up energy found egress instead in the guise of a sudden, gruff, and barking fart—somewhat akin to a mezzo forte blast on the tuba. This was met by a roar of laughter from my classmates, mortifying me to such an extent that the incident was thereupon seared into my long-term memory like the brand on a calf's behind.

So instead of forgetting this shameful thing, as I have all the Greek I ever learned, I love to take the memory out often to polish and fondle so that it remains as bright and fresh as the day it happened. Why hide your embarrassing moments, girls? Why not keep them in the closet under the stairs and fetch them out now and again for buffing like trophies?

Or you could use the closet space for a few of the following ideas:

1   The obvious one: storage space for vacuum, shopping bags, ironing board, and unopened boxes of things that have moved house with you time after time.
2   Storage space for home-brewed beer or wine. My brother used to brew his own beer and occasionally a bottle would pop its cork under the stairs with a muffled *bloop*.
3   Cozy home office.
4   The Naughty Hole for nephews and boyfriends who misbehave.

5   Storage space for sale-bargain mistakes that are to be worn "someday."

6   Excess-shoe hole.

7   A halfway house between home and charity shop, for huge garbage bags of old clothes, baby toys, artificial limbs, and so on.

8   Home mushroom farm. Very suitable conditions. *Not on the floor—use kits.*

9   Boyfriend bundle-hole for when parents return home unexpectedly. No smoking!

❀ *Severe blushing is called idiopathic cranio-facial erythema.* ❀

Life of the Party

Be a Hostess with the Mostest

*Serve dinner backwards, do anything, but for goodness' sake,
do something weird.*
ELSA MAXWELL

How to
Make a Proper Cup of Tea

*M*aking a proper cup of tea is one of those black arts that they don't teach you in school or at the Girl Scouts; you are just supposed to know how to do it by some sort of tannic osmosis. This is unfortunate, since getting it wrong can result in a sinister mahogany-brown beverage so eye-crossingly strong that it has to be served in slices, or a feeble and pallid infusion that tastes like dishwater that has had a tea leaf waved at it. So it's important to get the process right. In the words of the old Chinese proverb: look after your tea and your tea will look after you.

The British are famous for their tea-making proclivities, though they almost always drink it with *milk*. This may sound weird but once you've tried it you'll discover its seductive potential. British tea is often quite strong and it's interesting to note that British teabags contain 50 percent more tea than U.S. string-and-tag teabags. Anyway, I've borrowed one or two British ideas, adapted for the American tea drinker.

There are two main methods of tea making: (A) teacup, and (B) pot. I hasten to point out that this doesn't mean you use tea leaves in the first and illegal "substances" in the second. It's just a choice between spout and saucer. Unless you like it fantastically strong, tea brewed in a cup requires a shorter infusion time. The instructions here are for the pot method—a more elaborate routine—and are much the same for loose tea and teabags.

INSTRUCTIONS

1   *Use good-quality tea.* The most deliciously aromatic and tasty results come from coarsely cut loose tea brewed in a teapot. If you have the moral resources to track down some loose tea, the improvement in flavor will be dramatic.

2   *The best way* to make tea is to boil *freshly drawn* water in an electric kettle. This is one of the keys to success. Microwaved water or water boiled in a pan is not the same. Someone told me it was something to do with the oxygen, but I couldn't understand what he was

saying. Never reboil the water or reheat the tea once made. Both these crimes produce foul-tasting tea (especially the second).

3   *Warm the pot.* As soon as the kettle boils, pour a little of the water into the pot, swirl, and tip out (*no, not on the floor*). This helps keep the water hotter for longer so that more flavor is extracted from the tea.

4   *Put your tea or teabags into the pot.* Remember: the recipe is one teaspoon or teabag per person, and *one for the pot.*

5   *Quickly bring the kettle back to the boil* (takes only seconds) and pour over the tea, filling the pot about three-quarters full. *Always use boiling water.* It should be on a rolling boil as you pour it. Nonboiling water will simply kill your tea: it just won't brew.

6   *Cover the pot* with a tea cozy and allow to steep for three to five minutes, depending on pot size. Experiment a little. Shorter than this and the flavor will probably not have developed, longer and too much tannin will be released, giving the tea a stewed and bitter taste. It is the tannin that is largely responsible for tea being such a healthy drink (as long as you avoid stirring in half a pound of sugar).

7   *Pour your tea.* Use a tea strainer when pouring tea from loose tea leaves or you'll end up with a cup of black sludge; not harmful, just unpleasant. Mugs are OK for work and when you're sipping solo, but use a nice cup and saucer if you are entertaining.

8   *The milk question.* Whole evenings have been squandered in arguments over milk in tea. If you prefer lemon or nothing, then just go ahead and drink. If you'd like to try milk, you must decide whether you want whole milk, skim, or whatever. There is no love lost between the MIFs and the MILs. (MIF stands for "Milk in First" and MIL is for "Milk in Last.") Milk in first is more easily scalded, which can give the tea a boiled-milk flavor (unappealing), but it results in a much better fat distribution. Take your pick, I'm staying out of it.

❀ *A 1999 study found tea drinkers have a 44 percent lower risk of heart attack.* ❀

How to
Mix a Harvey Wallbanger

W hy must cocktails have such ridiculous names? I feel silly enough asking for a Screwdriver, but the epithets attached to some recent drinks are simply unspeakable in polite company. Then there's "cocktail" itself; where on earth did that come from? I'll tell you: it first appeared in the May 13, 1806, issue of *Balance and Columbia Repository* where, in response to a reader's query, it was defined as "a potent concoction of spirits, bitters, water, and sugar." Did the editor of *Balance and Columbia Repository*, I wonder, make it up?

My favorite story about the origins of the Harvey Wallbanger is this one. A Californian surfer called Harvey liked his Screwdrivers enlivened with Galliano—a delicious liqueur containing anise, lavender, and mint as well as vanilla, cinnamon, and coriander. (You can get it in most supermarkets.) One unhappy night, after losing a big surfing competition, Harvey drowned his sorrows so comprehensively that his several abortive attempts to find the bar's exit resulted in his head making repeated contact with the wall. And a name was born.

My least favorite, probably true, story is that bartender Bill Doner just invented it. Anyway, here's the way to make it.

INGREDIENTS

* 1 *part vodka*
* 4 *parts orange juice*
* 2 *tsp Galliano liqueur*
* 6 *ice cubes*
* 1 *orange slice*

INSTRUCTIONS

There are five main methods for mixing cocktails: layering, building, blending, shaking, and stirring. You will recall that James Bond prefers his Martini cocktails shaken not stirred. This is because you get a different blend, temperature, and appearance with methods of different sorts. This procedure for mixing a Harvey Wallbanger is a combination of layering and shaking. Shaking ensures that the drink is chilled and diluted to the proper degree, and of course it's entertaining to watch.

1   Put three ice cubes, the vodka, and the orange juice into a cocktail shaker.
2   Shake well for 30 seconds. Try to look the part.
3   Strain into a tall glass over the rest of the ice, leaving the shaken ice in the shaker.
4   Float the Galliano over the top. This looks very cool and is not hard to accomplish. What you do is carefully pour the Galliano over the back of a spoon that is touching the surface of the drink.
5   Decorate with slices of orange.
6   Serve to the lounge lizard in the white tux. No cocktail umbrellas please.

❋ *November 8 is Harvey Wallbanger Day.* ❋

How to
Perfume a Room in Ten Seconds

Once upon a time I was looking around at houses in search of a suitable one to buy. This can be a demoralizing process at the best of times because (A) you realize that what you can afford is smaller and nastier than you'd at first imagined, and (B) many of the places you are shown are dumps. I remember one house where there were hideous specimens of a man's pants scattered all over a bedroom, and another where a jelly doughnut adhered mysteriously to the ceiling of an otherwise charming and well-kept property. Further places smelled of dogs or damp—which leads me on to the subject of today's life-coaching seminar.

There can be many reasons why you wish to perfume a room in a hurry, from the desire to create a welcoming aroma for sudden visitors, to the need to cloak the odor of yesterday's kitchen misadventures, or the requirement that your feculent studio be swiftly converted into a cozy concubine's lair.

Let us forget for the moment the nose-cauterizingly pungent commercial preparations that you can nowadays plug into the wall, and those aerosol products that "neutralize odors." These will conjure up for any visitor a baleful redolence of the eye-watering pong you get from those plastic things that turn the water blue in your toilet, or the noisome miasmatic stink of fake pineapple that lurks over a sewage farm on a hot day.

For olfactory cheerfulness, try some of these quick fixes.

* Spray a few lightbulbs with perfume and switch them on. Instantaneous and strong in effect.

* Drop essential oil on to a cotton ball and tuck it behind a radiator.

* Mix about twenty drops of lemongrass or lavender oil with water in a plant mister and spray it around. A subtle effect, best on hot days.

* Lilies, freesias, hyacinths, and other flowers give off a powerful aroma. But unless you've got them in the place already, they're hardly quick.

* If a fire is burning, drop woody oils like cedar or sandalwood on to a log before burning. Alternatively drop oils on the hot tiles around the fire.

* If you are a bit of a hippie, just light some incense.

* In an emergency, set light to a spill of brown paper. This will successfully mask even the mashing of a stinkhorn.

* Cut or peel oranges, tangerines, or other citrus fruit for a subtler effect.

* Fry onions or garlic. This is good for concealing old cooking smells and giving guests an appetite.
* Light a huge cigar and blow it around. Very fast effect but rather lacking in femininity.
* Open the Camembert.

❀ *Synthetic-odor compound "Who-me?" smells like rotting carcasses.* ❀

How to
Organize a Rip-Roaring Block Party

*H*ardly a day went by in the '50s and '60s without a block party of some kind or another taking place in neighborhoods across the land. And what jolly occasions they were, too, featuring rosy-cheeked children, dressed impeccably (like adults), sitting up straight and chuckling with fun as they listened to *Nellie the Elephant* and *The Bee Song* on a wind-up gramophone: boys in shirts, shorts, and ties; girls in pink frocks, pigtails, and pretty shoes. Moms sporting quilted housecoats and headscarves would pass around jelly and ice cream, while Brylcreemed dads—smoking cigarettes—leaned ladders against hot stink pipes to adjust the bunting, in tweed jackets with leather buttons.

I suppose the last block party bearing any resemblance to this idyll must have happened in 1977. If you visited one today, you'd more likely find an ugly mob of surly children dressed in trainers, hoodies, and shell suits, with iPods stuck in their ears, slouching over PSPs as a smattering of their single parents, rudely dressed (like children) in baseball caps and phys-ed uniforms, sent foul-mouthed text messages to each other across an ill-kept stretch of disfigured tarmac to the sound of some screaming punk or heavy metal band.

Well, in case you'd like to conjure up the block parties of yesteryear, here are a few hints and tips.

PLANNING AND ORGANIZATION

Start planning in spring with a few enthusiastic neighbors and choose a date early on. A Sunday in early August is good. Set a sensible schedule, say: cars away by 11 a.m., lunch by 2 p.m., coffee at 5 p.m. with children retiring at a sensible time and adults carousing into the early hours, as they clear up. Keep it simple and it should be a terrific day.

INVOLVE EVERYONE

Invite every household (and business) on the street, and consult them about the road closure. Apply three months in advance to your local town council for permission to close the road.

You'll get a more positive response by knocking on doors than you will with a note through the mailbox and you won't have to work around several grumpy old men. Your town council may want to see evidence that you have consulted everyone so send written invitations nearer the time. Follow up with a reminder to people the day before, and ask them to move their cars in good time.

Involve people by asking them to contribute their special skills: Miss Smiley does the door-to-door invitations while Mrs. Cook masterminds the food and Mr. Jolly entertains the children during the lulls. Mr. Sharpe can be in charge of discipline.

SAFETY

Most block parties should not need special insurance but your town council may insist on it. However, it will come in at a manageable sum, usually between $100 and $250. Make sure that everyone agrees to be sensible and take responsibility for themselves.

THINGS TO DO

* If you are running the party, remain visibly in charge and all will go smoothly.
* Put up your decorations ahead of time to create a sense of expectation.
* Music really puts people in the mood and it's best if it's live. Most

parts of town have a few amateur musicians lurking. Not too loud, though.

* Sit-down meals at fixed times lend the event a proper sense of occasion.
* Have a few well-run party games in the middle of the street but don't go on too long.
* If you have a fire-eater in the neighborhood, you're well away.
* Work around uncooperative neighbors. Just throw a tarp over them and tow their cars around the corner.

Summer thunderstorms and tornados are, I'm afraid, an occupational hazard in some areas. Bad luck.

If all this seems like a lot more work than you need, why not crash somebody else's party? I know what you're thinking: how do I pretend to be a neighbor when everyone knows everyone else? Well, you can relax, there's no requirement for a *Mission: Impossible* makeup job to disguise you as Mr. Smith from the big house at the end of the street. Just take it easy and act confident.

What you do is turn up after things are already under way. The general confusion will do a lot to distract attention, and anyone who doesn't recognize you will be unwilling to spoil things by asking, "Who on earth are you, lady?" If you can make balloon animals, then for the price of a pack of balloons, you can feast yourself silly on all the food and drink, while offering high-visibility entertainment value. If challenged, claim to be somebody's sister from out of town. It they still give you a hard time, just say, "Good gracious! I'm on the *wrong block!*"

❧ *The most common U.S. street name is "2nd" or "Second."* ❧

How to
Be the Hostess with the Mostest

*H*ardly anyone I know has time to entertain in the way people used to, once upon a long time ago. These days we are constantly flying around the home picking up after other people, or flying out of the door at 6:30 to earn a crust and flying home again at 9:30 to gobble takeout in front of the TV with a bottle of wine. Our children are raised by nannies, our dogs walked by walkers, and we hardly have time for our friends, who seem almost as busy as ourselves. So the idea of a dinner party or a cocktail party or any kind of ghastly entertainment in our own home seems like more trouble than it's worth. But don't despair, because I have some top tips to make entertaining easy. It's rather like making a film.

* *Actor/director*: Don't just direct the action, you should be part of the story, too. Although gourmet food is delicious, you want to enjoy the company of your guests, and they have no desire to see you in rubber gloves and an apron ferrying dishes to and fro all night. So take time to talk to your guests, join in the fun, and relax a bit. Most of the hard work should be over once they arrive (see "Catering" below).

* *Assistant directors*: Your assistant directors can be close friends or family. They can take coats, order cabs, hand around bowls of nuts, show people where the loo is, shoo smokers on to the patio, and so on.

* *Cast*: Cast your guests as if for a blockbuster. This means a mix of people, with a good sprinkling of extroverts. Not boors—extroverts. If it's sit-down don't put couples together, divide them up. And don't invite people you despise.

* *Catering*: Preparation is the single most important element of a successful do. Plan ahead and prepare as much food as you can so you're not stuck in the kitchen all night. Here's a secret: guests don't

really care what they eat so long as it isn't actually poisonous. They've come to see you and to relax a bit. Remember that Bridget Jones girl making blue soup by mistake? We've all done that sort of thing and guests don't mind so long as you can turn it into an entertainment. Keep some emergency stuff in the freezer and in the cupboard in case of disaster. It needs to be instantly doable, though.

Canned consommé is a fantastic starter that's easy to keep at serving temperature in a big pot until you're ready. Just pour in a capful of sherry two minutes before serving and they will swear the soup's homemade. Beef stew is a real winner for gentlemen, whether it's sit-down or buffet. It's easy to cook in advance and keeps hot for absolutely ages. The smell is delicious wafting from the kitchen as your guests arrive. You can also fry some garlic in butter if you like—not for eating, it just smells good. Vegetarians can be catered for with a good spinach quiche, which you can make or buy. But if you buy it, remove it from its wrappings and surround it with a load of fresh arugula and chopped sweet cherry tomatoes as a disguise.

For dessert, I suggest buying some fancy cakes, or a big pie and slicing it up in advance. Put it on plates and microwave for thirty seconds before serving, with some decent ice cream. Vast pots of coffee are easy, and you can serve it with some of those fancy cookies. They always go over well. Get the idea? Very little messing around in the kitchen, good food that people imagine you made yourself, and therefore plenty of time to spend with your guests. Don't give guests anything you haven't tested on yourself first, though. They don't like to be guinea pigs.

* *Plot and dialogue*: Seat poets next to accountants and introduce women to men. An introvert will blossom if put next to a warm and friendly person. Don't dump two shy people together or they will stare at their shoes with a rictus of shame, and the frost will spread round the whole room. When you do introduce two people, help them to get talking by saying something such as: "Susie, this is

Malcolm who is an expert on the flesh-eating disease, necrotizing fasciitis. Malcolm, Susie collects glass spiders." Then circulate. I knew a *hostess with the mostest* who used to run dinner parties with a theme, or where people had to guess what the name was on the sticker on their head as soon as they arrived. I never enjoyed her dos very much.

* *Set*: Parties in offices are horrible for lots of reasons: the bottom photocopying, the stock cupboard groping, the large numbers of people you loathe. But they are certainly not helped by the buzzing fluorescent lights. Keep your own lighting at a level where people can see their food and each other's faces but not so low they are searching for doorways with their outstretched hands. Christmas lights can turn a dull patio into an intimate twinkling fairyland: especially if your guests have had a couple of drinks.

Flowers are always a winner. A restaurant with flowers on the table can get away with an extra $10 on the menu, it is said. Put fresh flowers all over. Unless you are entertaining the National Hayfever Convention, of course.

A small gift for each guest at the dinner table, such as a wooden toy, modelling balloons, a mouth organ, a book of poems is a nice touch. Suit your gifts to the guests. If you know them well you can really please people by providing something inexpensive but personal, whether it be a guitar pick, some chocolates, a packet of sparklers, or a cigar.

* *Wrap*: The best guests will leave at a decent hour wishing they could have stayed longer as they wave you good night. Some, however, will sit rooted to the sofa until cockcrow—unless you do something. Don't worry about offending them; they are always insensitive. Yawning and stretching is a good start, followed by putting on your nightie. If they are still there when you come down, take out one of those bullhorns they use at marches, and announce, "Earth calling the Wilsons—it's time to go home!" That ought to do it.

❀ *"My vigor, vitality, and cheek repel me."*—Lady Nancy Astor ❀

How to
Pack the Perfect Picnic Basket

There can't have been many songwriters more successful than the prolific Jimmy Kennedy. What do you mean you've never heard of him? *If you go down to the woods today you're in for a big surprise.* That was one of his lines, from the million-selling *Teddy Bears' Picnic,* and he wrote numerous others you'll have heard of. Which leads me to my sermon for today: how to pack the perfect picnic basket. Naturally it's as easy as pie to pack an imperfect basket. Often things are missing: there's no knife to spread the butter, or there's no bottle opener for the beer, or there's no salt for the boiled eggs. So, if you'd like to do it properly, grab your basket because here's the inside know-how.

INSTRUCTIONS

1   Get yourself a decent receptacle to start off with. It doesn't have to be a handmade Victorian wicker thing with leather straps, but neither will half a dozen plastic shopping bags do.

2   Make a list of what you need first and set it all out so you can check it off, one item at a time, as it goes into the basket.

3   Don't go mad with the contents. The original Martha Stewart, Mrs. Beeton, bless her tongs, used to insist on a gigantic list of essentials, including a stick of horseradish, a little ice, some lump sugar, some pounded sugar, *four* teapots, and *three* corkscrews. She must have belonged to the militant wing of the party. Who carried all that impedimenta anyway—Mr. Beeton? No, keep it to a minimum, but don't omit anything vital. (Usually it's the salt that gets left behind, ruining the entire meal.)

4   Bring *enough* plates, cutlery, cups, and glasses.

5   Some sandwich bags are a good idea. You can mix things in them, drop apple cores in, and so on.

6 Food that doesn't need cutlery is good: sausages, boiled eggs, pickles, sandwiches, celery and carrots, brownies, chicken wings, tearable bread like focaccia or baguettes—oh! My mouth's watering already.

7 If you must take a can of something, for goodness' sake bring the can opener or your name will be mud (see salt above).

8 Don't forget the condiments: pepper, pickles, mustard, etc. These can turn a boring chicken leg, hot dog, or turkey club into a feast fit for a queen.

9 Salads must be robust. Thin lettuce, cucumber, and soft tomatoes can turn to mush on the way. I often combine the thickly sliced veggies in a big container and refine the chunks in situ, adding salad dressing on arrival.

10 Cheddar sweats like a stevedore when it gets warm. Try Stilton, which can survive the heat of a nuclear explosion.

11 For sweets, avoid jam and other very sticky, hard-to-manage sugary drippers because of the wasps: cupcakes and berries or other fruit are all OK, and you can dip almost anything into a bowl of whipped cream.

12   If you want cold drinks, put a few cans or plastic bottles in the freezer for an hour or so before you leave (some careful experiment required). By the time you arrive, they will be just right. Saves lugging ice around. I always take sugarless drinks: avoids the wasps and doesn't home in on my thighs either. Spritzers can be made on site and any kind of cold bubbles are good.

Finally, bring a few plastic shopping bags for the garbage. I don't know about you, but I always seem to produce a ton of garbage on my picnics. Here are a few of the other obvious things that sometimes get forgotten.

* *A decent blanket. There's nothing worse than lunch surrounded by cow pats and thistles.*
* *A couple of cushions*
* *Plenty of water*
* *A bottle opener for wine and beer (this is important!)*
* *A sharp knife (vital)*
* *Some handy wipes. These are a boon for impromptu dish wiping as well as hand and face cleaning.*
* *A roll of paper towels (gets used a lot)*
* *Paper or linen napkins*
* *Sun hats or a gigantic umbrella that will also keep the rain off*
* *THE SALT!*

❀ *"Picnic" comes from the French* pique-nique. ❀

How to
Curtsy

*J*ust in case you don't know, the word "curtsy" is a variation of "courtesy." The action itself is a formal greeting (made exclusively by girls and women) in which you bend your knees with one foot in front of the other and do a little bob, sometimes holding your skirt (doesn't look so good in jeans). It was once used by servants in front of their employers and by sugar-and-spice-type girls to grown-ups in suits but is used almost exclusively these days to show reverence toward members of the royal family.

Nonetheless, in these more egalitarian times, demonstrations of deference to mere authority are falling into disuse and the curtsy is on its last legs. Since 2003, for example, at the request of the Duke and Duchess of Kent, exhausted female tennis players have no longer been required to curtsy when they stagger off Wimbledon's Center Court. As necrophile Norman Bates says in *Psycho*, "One by one you drop the formalities."

But there again you never know when a curtsy is going to come in handy, for example, at one of those embassy affairs where liveried waiters are flourishing the ambassador's gilded plates, piled high with pyramids of those chocolate balls wrapped in foil. Or at your debutante party, of course.

INSTRUCTIONS

1   Unlike the "bob" curtsy, the quintessentially old-fashioned deep curtsy requires you to "slide back" on the inclined right foot, curling it behind and around the left, which remains static throughout.

2   Your sliding foot takes your weight, allowing you to sink gracefully, finally coming to rest, sitting on your bent right leg, arms falling to the side, and head lowered. This is a highly submissive and vulnerable pose.

3   When you are ready to stand, take your weight on your left foot, rising to your full height again. This deep curtsy is the basis of the

modern curtsies you will have seen or done, even the cheeky little ones.

A weird variation of this deep curtsy requires you to bend the knees outward, akimbo-style, instead of curling the right leg around the left. I've never tried this one but it sounds ungainly to me, as if you were lowering yourself perpendicularly on to a hippity-hop without the benefit of hands.

By the seventeenth century, a hierarchy of curtsies had developed indicating varying levels of deference and I have set out below the three main curtsy types.

THREE TYPES OF CURTSY

* *Curtsy en avant (literally "ahead")*: This one, used on entering a room, looks to me like the old servant's-bob curtsy, where you slide either foot to the front and then bend at the knees, body straight and weight equally distributed. You rise supporting your weight on the front foot.

* *Curtsy en arriere (literally "behind")*: Recommended for use on leaving a room, you step to the side and curtsy but with your weight supported on the back foot.

* *Curtsy en passant (in passing)*: Useful as a repeatable curtsy in a reception line. In this one you position yourself next to the person you are greeting, making a step on the left foot and half turn toward him or her. You then bend your knees, bringing the right foot forward. You rise with your weight on the same foot.

Or you could just say hello like a normal person.

❀ *The Texas Dip is an extreme Southern curtsy.* ❀

How to
Pass Off a Store-Bought Meal as Your Own

*T*his is the approach to take when passing off a store-bought meal as homemade. And it is a useful skill to have up your sleeve, just like cardiopulmonary resuscitation. Let us assume that you have spoiled a meal to the point that it is beyond saving. If it *can* be saved, see page 132: "How to rescue a meal that's gone wrong." Your guests are due in half an hour and you are frantic. But fear not, by using a little imagination you can save the day. The tips set out here may be used with carefully bought meals or with takeout. So wipe your tears—not on your apron, that would be unhygienic—and get to work. Remember: imagination is the key to success here.

INSTRUCTIONS

1   If you are panicking, stop.
2   Open the windows to get rid of the smoke.
3   Light a scented candle or some incense to mask the odor of nuclear conflagration.
4   Remove all traces of the disaster meal (take burnt remnants outside to garbage).
5   Scour the cupboards and freezer to find anything useable. Let's suppose you discover that you have little beyond a large bar of chocolate (hidden from your roommates), some fresh herbs, and a five-year-old frozen birthday cake, and a few vegetables.
6   Defrost the cake in the microwave. That's dessert.
7   While doing this, slowly fry an onion in butter. This smells delicious and is the first of your deceptions, since this onion will never be eaten. The purpose of this olfactory appetite-whetter is to seduce your guests' nostrils as they arrive.
8   Ring the *best* takeout place and order what you please. OK, it's

expensive and you don't get that thrill of culinary accomplishment, but beggars can't be choosers.

9   When it arrives *disguise it*:

*   *Remove* all packaging and transfer to nice serving dishes. Nobody will be fooled if you spoon it out of a foil carton.

*   *Always add something of your own*, for example, cherry tomatoes, cheese, fresh mushrooms and olives to the top of a pizza; fresh cream and a yogurt, cucumber and mint side dish to a curry; and longitudinally sliced spring onions to a Chinese meal.

*   *Herbs*: Whatever you are serving, strew plenty of fresh herbs all over the place.

*   *Curries*: Try cooking your own rice to go with a curry and serve it all sizzling from nice hot dishes.

*   *Some grated chocolate* added to a chocolate pudding that comes in the form of a powder out of a packet will turn it into a delicacy.

*   *Black Forest cake*: Disguise the factory processes by grating plenty of chocolate all over it, including on the plate. Very deceptive, that is.

10 Once your guests arrive, keep away from that microwave at all costs. Those beeps tell tales.

❀ *The Black Forest is a wooded mountain range in Baden-Württemberg.* ❀

How to
Entertain Unexpected Guests

*M*y Uncle Bob invited his best friend Jeff around for dinner and then forgot all about it until he saw him coming up the garden path. Leaping from his armchair, he ordered my auntie into the kitchen to improvise a meal. "But I haven't been shopping," she protested. "Never mind: do your best," he hissed as the bell rang. Bacon and eggs isn't much of a dinner if you've been expecting a spread, and when it was presented to him Jeff stared for a moment and then expostulated, "This isn't dinner. It's *breakfast*."

OK, there's a difference between forgotten and unexpected guests, but not much, in the sense that you've got to extemporize a bit. Here are some tips for dealing with the unexpected sort.

If they are guests you are happy to see:

* Make it clear what they can expect: if you're going out at 6, let them know.
* If you are busy when they turn up, try to involve them. Get them out in the garden with you or ask them to help you prepare the food.
* Never apologize for the mess. In fact, there's no need to apologize for anything—it's your home.
* Make sure they don't feel they have put you to huge trouble, unless they have.
* Put the coffee on right away.
* Don't keep thinking about the final episode of the costume drama that you've been waiting all week to watch. Keep the TV off!
* Always maintain emergency supplies in the house so you can make a throw-together meal at any time: soup, pasta, beans, and a few cans of interesting stuff. In fact, spaghetti with a jar of (emergency) sauce and some bits and bobs hurled in will make a feast in a flash. Especially if you unplug a bottle of wine at the same time. Frying an onion always produces a homey aroma and makes people feel welcome.
* If there are children in tow, do something exciting with them, such as playing a game. A good one is to see who can cram the most grapes under their lips and then whistle without laughing. There will be grapes on the floor, I'm afraid, so invite everyone to play outside. (Not in the main road, obviously.)
* If there's no food in the house, order takeout and suggest splitting the bill.
* Go for a long walk with the dog and catch up on your visitors' news. You definitely need to have a dog for this one, girls. Walking around with an empty leash makes you look too strange.

If they are unwanted guests, try the following:

* Pretend to be out. But don't get caught through the window, hiding behind the sofa. Very embarrassing.
* Ask them to help you drain the radiators.
* Serve them sardine custard with chopped eels and fish lips.
* Show them your lifetime's accumulation of vacation photos. Even the most hardened bores will find this too much to bear.
* Turn on the gas burners and go out. At least you'll be able to call the blackened ruins of your home your own, when you return.

❋ The Day the Earth Caught Fire *(1961) was directed by Val Guest.* ❋

How to
Pour Beer Properly

*U*nless you are a barmaid, the chances are that whenever you pour beer you will be doing it from a bottle or can. The technique for dispensing beer through a little tap from a barrel or cask is similar to the bottle method, but serving chilled carbonated lagers and keg beers in a pub requires a slightly different handling that I won't go into here.

The first thing to remember is that beer drinkers, like art critics and jazz enthusiasts, are divided into a number of hard-boiled factions each of which disagrees with and hates the others. Your beardy real ale drinker will happily swallow a warm pint that's as flat as a mill pond and cloudy—with bits in, but will insist on half an hour's debate about its manufacture. While your lager fan will demand a bright, clear icy cold drink with a good head on it—but not 5 inches of foam. Guinness aficionados, by contrast, are split into the bottle variety, who expect a room temperature drink with a brownish head of large bubbles that quickly dissipates, and the tap, keg, and fizz-gizmo-can lot who want a cold drink with an inch of almost white "cream" on top.

The method I've set out below is therefore a general technique that ought to help you do the job nicely for a range of beer-drinking types without making any of the basic mistakes, such as pouring three-quarters of froth, or putting a cask-conditioned bottle beer into a very cold fridge.

INSTRUCTIONS

1   Open the can or bottle. *If it is cold it will be more lively* than a warm drink and will therefore require more careful handling. Real ale and live beer (see below) should be served at room temperature, not fridge cold.

2   Anyway, hold the glass under the can or bottle and tilt its bottom up slightly. Touch the bottleneck or can to the lip of the glass and *slowly* elevate the can or bottle's bottom so that the liquid flows down the side of the glass rather than falling all the way to the foot. Doing it this way will prevent an excessive release of carbon dioxide bubbles, which will quickly fill the glass with froth. *Go slow.* This is the single most important beer-pouring rule.

3   If you are serving a pint in a pint glass, make sure you fill it right to the top so that the head, or meniscus if it's a stillish beer, sits above the rim. The only beer you don't have to do this with is Guinness. The head is considered part of the drink. Being served short measures absolutely infuriates quaffers in pubs and it's as well to bear this in mind even at home. You should always allow a lively beer to settle a bit and top it up to give a full pint. You will receive points for this.

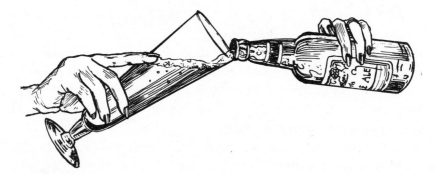

4   Guinness and other stouts are not as hard to pour as people imag-
     ine. The stuff in the can sometimes comes with a plastic gadget in
     it that will make it foam for you as you open it. Bottle Guinness
     should be poured like any other bottle beer and will have a similar
     sort of head—much less dense. So don't worry that you've done
     something wrong. You haven't.

5   *Bottle-conditioned* beer requires a particular technique because it is
     still live and fermenting in the bottle—you'll see the yeast sediment
     in there. There are two schools of thought: the Drinkers and the
     Leavers. If serving a Leaver, you should go *even slower* than you
     were already to avoid shaking up the sediment as you pour. And
     don't open a bottle that's just arrived from the supermarket. Keep an
     eye open as you near the last quarter of the bottle and the moment
     you see the first gray whisp of sediment, stop pouring and discard
     the dregs. This yeasty sediment is actually quite harmless. So if you
     are serving a sediment Drinker, pour as usual but as you reach the
     last eighth of the bottle swirl the liquid gently to mix the sediment
     into the beer. Then gently pour the cloudy remains into the glass.

6   It's always best to wear a dirndl when serving beer to a gentleman.

❀ *Some nineteen different varieties of Guinness are sold around the globe.* ❀

How to
Rescue a Meal
That's Gone Wrong

*D*o you remember when we all had much more time and much less
stuff; when plumbers earned *less* than teachers and hardly any of us
had second homes; when nobody worked such stupid hours and we all
had time to cook an evening meal? You don't? Well I'm not making it
up—there really was such a time.

Of course the advantages of *not* cooking dinner and getting takeout
are many, and the main one is that takeout is unlikely to go wrong. The

trouble with homemade is that, as often as not, what you hoped would be the perfect chocolate soufflé comes out of the oven all sunken and wretched. With this in mind I have prepared a few ideas for when it all goes wrong and you have guests. They cover generalized problems but are applicable in particular situations. With any luck, they should save your bacon.

CULINARY FIRST AID

* *Too lumpy*: If making gravy or sauce, keep a whisk by hand to get rid of lumps. Still lumpy? Pour through a strainer.
* *Too runny*: Mix cornstarch and cold water in a small cup and add to liquid a little at a time, stirring constantly. Not too fast, if the liquid is hot, because it will *suddenly* thicken, leaving you with a saucepan of "concrete" hanging from your wooden spoon. And be patient—don't add too much cornstarch or you'll end up serving your gravy in *slices*.
* *Too salty*: If it's soup or gravy, add more water. This will put you in the too-runny scenario so use the too-runny remedy. If it then gets too lumpy do the too-lumpy business. Don't go on all night like this or you'll have hundreds of gallons of unwanted sauce.
* *Burnt*: If it's a saucepan do not stir, but remove at once from the heat. You may be able to rescue the top few inches, but *taste* it. There's nothing more penetrating than the flavor of burnt polytetrafluoroethylene (Teflon). In any case, it's wise to turn the mess into a curry to hide the smack of carbonized aluminium.
* *Too spicy*: Boil up vegetables with no salt or flavoring and add this pulp to dilute the tang. A libation containing alcohol (vodka) or fat (milk) will dampen the ferocious chemical firestorm in the mouth. But don't serve water, which exacerbates the problem.
* *Overcooked meat or pie gone hard*: Make a thinish sauce and simply saturate the hardened foodstuff to disguise the problem. Hardened pastry is particularly amenable to the absorption process.

❁ *Clean burned pans by boiling sodium bicarbonate and water in them.* ❁

IV

Fun and Games

A Robust Guide to Leisure and Pleasure

Some say our national pastime is baseball. Not me.
It's gossip.

ERMA BOMBECK

How to
Ride an Ostrich

*H*ow the Queen of England ever learned to ride sidesaddle I shall never know. Have you *tried* it? I realize, of course, that it's a bit of a challenge to straddle a horse with a dress on—the Queen has the dress on, not the horse—but riding this way looks so asymmetrical. One thing's for sure: it isn't an elegant enough technique for Her Majesty should she ever decide to get on an ostrich.

Ostrich riding is a lively, if somewhat unpredictable, pastime suitable for any girl who can grip a handful of feathers while leaning back a bit. The Queen will find the chief advantage is that if (*when*) she falls off, her feet will already be so near the ground that she'll simply be able to step down—just so long as the bird is not going at full gallop. Ostriches can run at more than forty miles per hour, so once she's up to speed, the Queen will need to lean well back and counterbalance herself by sticking her knees well out in front. It's going to be touch and go in a crown and ermine robes. What she'll need to do is hitch her skirts up as she gets on and probably leave the crown on the sideboard in the kitchen. That will be safest.

Although getting off an ostrich is simplicity itself, getting on one is fraught with difficulty and is not something you can do yourself. Don't bury your head in the sand about this: two people are required to help you. For the Queen this might be the Duke of Edinburgh or Prince Philip or whatever he's called, if he's not doing anything, and somebody else.

MOUNTING THE OSTRICH

1   Someone (let's say Sarah Ferguson) puts a small paper bag over the ostrich's head to prevent giving it the willies, while another person (say Camilla Parker Bowles) keeps the bird still by hanging on to its tail. Watch out here because their powerful legs have two sharp-clawed toes on each foot and they bend their knees backwards so they can give you a hefty kick where you're not expecting it. (The ostriches, I mean; not Fergie and Camilla.) They are also

highly inquisitive and will peck the head of anybody who approaches them.

2 Ostriches are tall—half their total height is their neck—so stand on a milk crate or something to make mounting easier.

3 Luckily you don't need saddles, reins, stirrups, or ostrich brasses as you do with a horse. It's bareback riding: straddle the bird and tuck your knees right into the corner under each of the wings, which are long but sort of flappy and loose.

4 Grab hold of the bit of the ostrich's back where the wings meet the body and hang on.

RIDING

1 It's not so much riding as not falling off. As the bag is whipped off the ostrich's head and the tail is released, the creature will start to run, so lean back and bend your legs as the ostrich tries to throw you.

2 You will notice that as he picks up speed the ostrich will lift his wings for balance. Don't allow this to worry you because he can never take off; ostriches can't fly, remember. I say "he" but it might just as well be a she. You can tell from its color: males are black and white, females are brown.

3 Your hair is best protected by a hat that won't fly off. If it's long, braids or a bun are both ideal (see pages 219–223).

❈ *A typical ostrich carries two pounds of stones in its stomach.* ❈

How to
Forecast the Weather Like Your Grandma Used To

When I was a kid, there was a TV weatherman who was famous for a number of things including his lively jackets, nerdy hair, and Nostradamus-type meteorological prognostications such as, "Clouds bubbling up along the East Coast," and, "So there'll be plenty of sunshine in time for the races," and "Earlier on today, apparently, a woman called the studio and said she'd heard there was a hurricane on the way. Well, if you're watching, don't worry, there isn't." He said this immediately before the worst storm to hit our area for 200 years tore down our town trees, hurled trailers across roads, felled buildings, and killed eleven people.

Weather forecasters often seem to have trouble with their premonitions, even with the help of computers. I think we should go back to the old days when forecasts were done in verse, and a red sky at night invariably meant delighted shepherds.

My grandma used to hang seaweed outside her back door as a kind of weather teller. She told me she relied on it for her forecasts and knew that if the seaweed was dry the weather had been fair but if it was wet it had been raining. I realized quite early on that she was barking mad but liked her because of her fat arms, wooly pink sweater, and the boxes of chocolates she always turned up with. She had a number of other "weather tellers" around the house, too, and this is how to make my favorite of them.

WEATHER-TELLING MR. OSTRICH

Put a pinecone in a warm oven, removing it once it is dry enough that its scales open wide. It will now be highly sensitive to changes in atmospheric moisture: When the air is dry, and the weather likely to be fine, the scales will open wide. If unsettled weather is on the way, the scales will be partly closed. When rain is coming, the cone will be tightly shut.

REQUIRED
* *A pinecone*
* *A 2-inch square of corrugated cardboard*
* *A piece of poster board*
* *Pliable but stiff fuse wire*
* *Pliers*
* *Elmer's glue or modeling clay*
* *A sharp craft knife*
* *Watercolor paints*

INSTRUCTIONS

1   Start by twisting together three pieces of pliable wire, opening them out at one end to form the feet.

2   Stick the feet to a square of corrugated cardboard and allow to dry. This will allow you enough time to do your nails *and* have a cup of coffee.

3   Attach the feet to the pinecone body with some lumps of modeling clay (quicker) or Elmer's glue (stronger). Allow to dry.

4   Cut Mr. Ostrich's neck and head from a piece of poster board and, once decorated with a cheerful beaky smile and eyes, push the neck end into a slit in the base of the cone. Make the slit with the sharp craft knife but mind your fingers.

Mr. Ostrich makes a fantastic present for children and is as reliable as that TV weatherman I told you about.

❋ *In August 1849, a lump of ice 20 feet long fell on Ord in Scotland.* ❋

How to
Identify the Parts of a Horse

W hen it comes to identifying the parts of a horse, I presume we can all manage the head, ears, hoof, and tail. But what is the name for that part right on the top of his head, between the ears?

And where are the withers?

And what is the gaskin?

Well, one look at the "horse map" on the next page will turn you into an authority instantly.

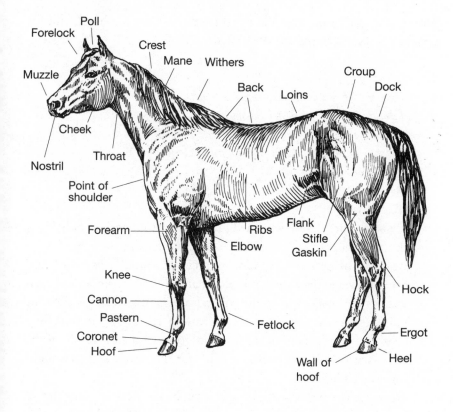

Forelock
Poll
Crest
Mane Withers
Muzzle
Back
Loins
Croup
Dock
Cheek
Throat
Nostril
Point of
shoulder
Forearm
Ribs
Elbow
Flank
Stifle
Gaskin
Knee
Hock
Cannon
Pastern
Fetlock
Coronet
Ergot
Hoof
Wall of
hoof
Heel

❁ *Camargue horses are born black but turn white as adults.* ❁

How to
Groom a Horse

M ost of us, I suppose, go through a horsey phase when we are young. I had posters of ponies on my wall at home but took them down when I became more interested in the lads at the stables, after a toothy gelding picked me up by the hair. Some of us, though, never grow out of the horsey phase.

Grooming is something you can do even if you only ever fall off horses; it is good isometric and spiritual exercise for the horse, and for you, too. So here's a guide to the basics.

REQUIRED
* *A currycomb: an oval rubber-tooth brush*
* *A dandy brush: a stiff-bristle brush*
* *A body brush: a soft-bristle brush*
* *A plastic mane comb (plastic comb, not plastic mane)*
* *A towel or rag*

INSTRUCTIONS

1 First tie your horse safely, then groom him from neck to tail, doing the starboard (right) and port (left) flanks in turn.

2 Begin by using the currycomb in a circular motion to loosen and bring to the surface dirt and dust that have settled under the hair. While you work, the comb will release natural oils, giving your horse's coat a healthy lustre. Take care of the bony bits though— back and shoulders in particular, and don't use a currycomb on the legs. Never do his face this way; it's far too rough and you might cause eye injuries.

3 Once you've finished with the currycomb, use the stiff dandy brush to "flick" the coat up so that the dirt comes away in light clouds. It's rather like a floor-brush action: flick, flick, flick.

4 When you have given the horse a thorough going over with the dandy brush, smooth down his hair with the soft-bristle body brush and sweep away final traces of mud and dust. The body brush stroke is quite unlike that of the dandy brush. Smooth the coat down flat in the direction of hair growth. This should produce an immaculate burnished appearance.

5 Now gently run the comb through the horse's mane. Like the tail, the mane can be delicate, so a plastic brush is best. If you want to braid the mane see the next section for full instructions.

6 Use the dandy brush for the tail. Be careful, though, because the tail hairs can break easily. Don't brush vigorously and don't use a comb.

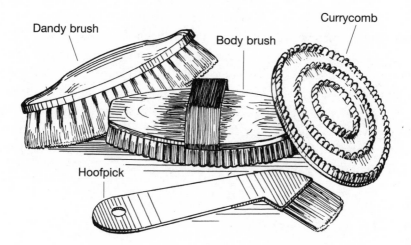

7   Finally, use a plain towel or rag to wipe over the horse's coat. This will bring up a luminous gleam. My Uncle Vivian always finished with a sheen-enhancing conditioner. But he used to polish his horse to such a brilliantly high gloss that riding became hazardous and he was always slipping off.

   ❀ *The longest recorded mane was 18 feet long. It was grown by a mare named Maude.* ❀

How to
Braid a Horse's Mane

The "pastern" is the part of the equine leg between the ergot and hoof, but in his dictionary Dr. Samuel Johnson defined it as "the *knee* of a horse." When a pestilential woman asked why he'd got it wrong, he replied, "Ignorance, Madam, ignorance," which was both witty and honest. By the way, if like me you thought that ergot was just a cereal fungus, then you might like to peruse the excellent horse map on page 141, where you'll discover all the bits of a horse helpfully labeled.

To braid good braids, you'll need a mane that is not too ragged and a horse who will stand still. It can be a fiddlesome business, so it is a good idea to wear a cotton stockman's coat or failing that an old quilted dressing gown so you can keep your scissors and thread in the pockets while you're working. Should your horse be fidgety, you can smooth things along by threading a separate needle for each braid and pinning them down the front. Take care not to break the hairs.

REQUIRED

* *A plastic mane comb*
* *A water brush (special horsey item)*
* *A pair of scissors with round ends*
* *Blunt darning needle with a large eye*
* *Some cotton thread, matching the mane*
* *A bag of rubber bands*

INSTRUCTIONS

1 Follow the grooming instructions on pages 141–143.
2 Using your fingers and the mane comb, divide the mane hair into equal clumps and put a rubber band around each.
3 Starting at the poll (see horse map, page 141), dampen each clump of hair with a water brush and lay it flat. These articles resemble the

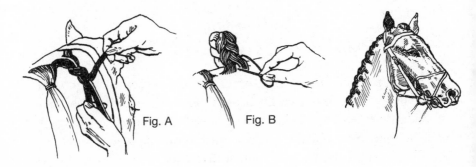

Fig. A   Fig. B

scrubbing brushes that the housewife of yesteryear used and are available from horsey suppliers.

4   Tie an 18-inch length of thread to the eye of the needle so it won't come off and get lost in the mane or on the ground if you drop it.

5   Start braiding from the ear end (I'm assuming you know how to braid; if not see pages 219–221), weaving the thread tidily into the braid as you go (Fig. A).

6   Braid as far as you can, then wrap the thread around the tuft and tie off with a half hitch (look, you'll just have to ask a sailor or look it up on the Internet or something; *I can't do everything*).

7   Pass the needle through the root of the mane, folding the braid in half and in half again.

8   Stick the needle back through the folded braid and the root and tie off by stitching through the braid a couple of times (Fig. B).

9   Finish by braiding the forelock.

❀ *Violin bows are made from wood and horsehair.* ❀

How to
Make a Garden in a Bottle

S hould you live in an apartment or have little time for tending a large garden, why not start a dwarf garden in a glass bottle? The bottle garden is a self-sufficient world that you can cultivate open or closed. Unlike the open variety, the lidded bottle garden retains moisture, and generally makes more of a demand on your time. The open garden is easier, and its plants will often grow up and out of the bottle, and hang attractively down the outside.

Open or closed, bottle gardening can become an absorbing interest, and a great relief from the strains of modern life. You are queen of this miniature universe and there is nothing nicer than to sit on a summer's evening and just watch your developing biosphere.

Required

* *A wide-necked decorative glass bottle, big enough to get your hand into*
* *Some ordinary houseplant compost*
* *A bag of fine alpine gravel, or similar (ask for advice at the garden center)*
* *A few miniature plants: anything decorative will do that won't grow too big and that can stand the moist environment*
* *For the ambitious, some long, thin gardening tools (you might have to improvise)*

The open garden

An open bottle garden, containing ground plants and maybe a few small animals such as earthworms, is suited to those with a flair for the architecture of small spaces but without the luxury of endless time.

Instructions

1   Line the bottom of your bottle with about 2 inches of gravel, to create drainage.

2   Evenly spread 2–3 inches of compost on top.

3   Plant your dwarf plants into the soil, spreading them around evenly. Even in a large bottle four or five plants will be plenty. Put the taller ones at the back or in the middle, and the shorter ones in front or around the outside.

4   Sprinkle a little more gravel on top of the compost. This acts as a mulch, preventing dehydration, and also sets off your plants attractively.

5   Keep your bottle garden in a well-lit place and water regularly. Be cautious, however, making sure you don't inundate the soil. A cupful three times a week is about right, depending on the ambient temperature and the season.

6   Replant your bottle garden twice a year so as to inhibit disease and to allow for the growth of your mini plants. Carefully pull them out and put them into little pots with some fertilizer. Clean out the

bottle thoroughly and replace your plants with new specimens. Tidy up the gravel surface.

There is no need to feed the plants in your bottle garden; there is enough nourishment in the compost to keep them going for their lifetime in the jar.

THE SEALED GARDEN

The sealed garden is best if you have a bit more time to spare and are prepared to create what is effectively a self-sustaining ecosystem. You will have to use the right sort of plants and take the time to find a few suitable animals to keep the thing going.

INSTRUCTIONS

The method is much the same as that for the open garden. Your sealed environment needs moist soil, a few plants, and some little animals like terrestrial isopods: worms, wood lice, and other small segmented creatures are the ones to look out for.

Your plants must be small and resistant to high levels of moisture—rotten roots is a common problem with a sealed garden—and they must be slow growers.

A sealed garden is happiest in a cool bright situation, *away from direct sunlight* so that Willy Worm and Wendy Woodlouse don't fry under the glass.

❀ *"Bonsai" means "tray planting" in Japanese.* ❀

How to
Do a Cartwheel

During my younger days I used to be quite acrobatic, and cartwheels were always my favorite. I remember doing a celebratory one in the bar after my exams, accidentally snapping a cigarette straight out of the mouth of an old man in a hat. He gave me such a look I just shrank.

Anyway, indoors is probably not the place for cartwheels so the instructions below are for outside only. Jeans are the thing to wear when you are cartwheeling. Flapping skirts not only spoil the aesthetics—and blind you by falling over your face—but lay you open to accusations of exhibitionism.

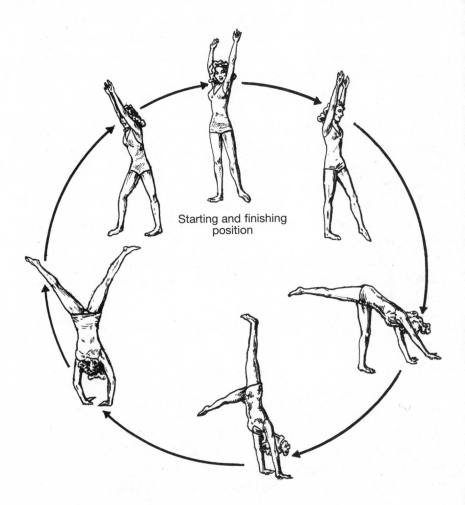

Starting and finishing position

Instructions

1 Empty your pockets.

2 Raise your arms to 10 and 2 o'clock as if acknowledging applause.

3 Step forward slightly with the left leg, your knee bent a little.

4 You can cartwheel left (left hand first) or right (right hand first), it's up to you.

5 Assuming you're going left, bend at the waist, reaching toward the ground with your left hand and kick your right leg into the air, up above your head.

6 Follow quickly with the right hand. As it touches the ground, your left leg should also have left the ground. Momentum and inertia provide the oomph as well as the stability in a cartwheel, so the slower you go, the less steady you will be. A good confident throw is what's needed to get you going.

7 Halfway through your cartwheel you will find yourself briefly in the straddle-handstand position. If you've tried a handstand, you'll know that it's hard to remain stable with legs pointing straight up. But it's easier in a cartwheel. With a bit of practice, a bit of speed, and *enough space* your legs should fly up.

8 Land with the right leg first, left leg next, finishing in the position you started, but with your right leg in front.

9 A good cartwheel requires rhythm and momentum. It's like the sails of a windmill: try thinking *hand, hand, foot, foot* as you go, moving in a straight line as if doing the cartwheel on a narrow bench. Try to keep your body *straight*. Most beginners do bent cartwheels, but practice helps cure this fault.

10 No need to rush, but don't be hesitant either: you've really got to *go for it*.

❀ *The Cartwheel Galaxy is 500 million light-years from Earth.* ❀

How to
Make a Snow Angel

*T*his climate change business is a real pest, what with palm trees growing on Mount Everest, sharks swimming around Iceland, and local
schoolchildren making snowmen out of nothing but rain.

But every now and again it does still snow. In fact, the mere dusting of
half an inch can close schools and factories, stop trains, and bring everything south of Washington, DC, to a grinding halt. So when it snows,
it's time to gird your loins, don your warmest gear, and make snow angels. What do you mean, you've never made a snow angel? Put on your
mittens at once and let's get out there.

You make one by lying on your back and sweeping your arms and legs

through the snow so that the heavenly being's wings and celestial habit are described on the ground.

INSTRUCTIONS

1   Dress warm, including hat and gloves.

2   Go out and find a pristine area of frosty or powdery snow. Wet snow doesn't work so well.

3   Fall gently backward and lie flat, arms by your side. (You should have previously checked for barely concealed jagged rocks and tent pegs.)

4   Now sweep your arms straight up so they touch your ears. Then sweep them down till they touch your sides again. Repeat the action a few times; you are making the wings.

5   Next, sweep your legs apart as far as they will go, and then together again. You're now creating the angelic habiliment.

6   Here's the tricky part: Get up without destroying your handiwork. A trail of boot marks and handprints all over your angel's holy garb spoils the aesthetics. A good way to get up neatly is to extend your arms and ask a friend at your feet to pull you up.

7   Survey the picture you've made. It looks exactly like an angel.

8   Take a picture with your cell phone and send it to everyone.

9   Go back inside for a mug of hot cocoa and a cookie.

❋ *Angels feature in Christianity, Islam, Judaism, and Zoroastrianism.* ❋

How to
Worm a Cat

When I began looking into this topic I was convinced that it ought to be possible to give a cat a worming pill without dragging the emaciated creature all the way down to the vet. Just as I was thinking that getting a cat *into* one of those baskets deserved a page to itself, I stumbled on an old document in my files that sets out in blunt terms the stark difficulty of the whole enterprise. The haunting quality of these instructions seemed truer to life than the bald directions on my packet of Wormola so I have written them down for you under the "Real World" heading below. May God have mercy on your soul.

How to give a cat a pill in an ideal world

1   Hold the cat's head firmly and open its mouth.
2   Put the pill at the back of its throat.
3   Hold its mouth shut and massage its throat until the cat swallows the pill.

If cat spits out a pill

1   Hide the pill in a lump of cheese.
2   Give the cat the pill in smoked fish to disguise horrid taste.
3   Coat it in peanut butter (the pill, not the cat).
4   If the cat just licks the peanut butter off the pill, crumble it up and sprinkle on food.

How to give a cat a pill in the real world

1   Cradle the cat in crook of your left arm, place your right forefinger and thumb either side of cat's mouth, and gently squeeze its cheeks. Pop the pill into its mouth and let the cat swallow.
2   Retrieve the pill from under TV and the cat from behind the sofa. Repeat step 1.
3   Recover the cat from the bedroom and discard the sodden pill. Pop out a new pill from the fancy foil dispenser. Cradle the cat in your left arm, holding its rear paws tightly with your left hand. Force the jaws open and push the pill to the back of the throat with your right forefinger. Hold its mouth shut for a count of ten.
4   Bathe bites with soothing unguent, then rescue the pill from under the bookshelf and the cat from the top of your dresser. Call a friend. Kneel on the floor, with the cat tightly between your knees. Grip its front and rear paws, ignoring the weird primeval growling from the cat. Get your friend to grip the head firmly with one

hand and force a ruler into the cat's mouth. Roll the pill down the ruler into the mouth and massage the cat's throat.

5   Tear the cat from your expensive curtains, get another pill, and sweep the shattered family heirlooms into the wastepaper basket. Run your scratched arms under a cold tap.

6   Wrap the cat in a large bath towel, with its head just visible. Ask someone else to lie on the cat and put the pill into the end of a drinking straw. Force the cat's mouth open with a pencil and blow the pill down the cat's throat.

7   Check the label to see if it's harmful to humans. Gargle with Scotch to take away the taste, while sponging the worst of the blood from the carpet.

8   Drag the cat from behind the washing machine and put it in the cupboard, closing the door on the cat's neck, but leave the head showing. Force the mouth open with a large spoon. Flick the pill down the throat with a rubber band.

9   Apply an ice pack to the welt on your cheek, and find the pill (again).

10   Call the fire department to get the cat down from the top of the poplar tree.

11   Tie the cat's front and rear paws with twine, like suckling pig. Bind them to a table leg. Don heavy-duty pruning gloves and a motor-cycle helmet. Push the pill into the cat's mouth followed by a large piece of steak. Holding the cat's head vertically, pour two pints of water into its throat to wash down.

12   Open a bottle of industrial-strength vodka. Bathe your wounds with half and drink the rest.

To give a dog a pill, wrap it in bacon.

❈ *Cat bites are rarer than dog bites but more prone to infection.* ❈

Understanding the Zodiac

The term "zodiac" is allegedly from the Greek meaning "circle of little animals." Zodiac signs are an infallible guide to one's disposition and likely future, but I don't believe in them because I'm Libra and Librans are very skeptical. The signs are set out below with their various attributes and characteristics:

Aquarius (the water bearer) January 20–February 18: Friendly but you never know what you will do next. Your lucky number is 4,226.6; your lucky tabloid is *The Star*; your lucky hand cream is Aveeno Intense Relief.

Pisces (the fish) February 20–March 20: Kind and sensitive but easily fooled. Your lucky road sign is "Slow Children"; your lucky news anchor is Brian Williams; your lucky canned soup is Campbell's 25 Percent Less Sodium Cream of Mushroom.

Aries (the ram) March 21–April 20: Born leaders who are easily irritated. You should avoid Virgos and Scorpios. Your lucky stone is sapphire; your lucky cereal is Special K; your lucky disease is necrotizing fasciitis.

Taurus (the bull) April 21–May 20: Patient and reliable but can be greedy. Steer clear of Libras. Your lucky stone is gravel; your lucky sandwich is "All-day Breakfast"; your lucky jargon is "blue-sky thinking."

Gemini (the twins) May 21–June 20: Lively but sometimes superficial. Your lucky stone is kidney; your lucky shop is Borders; your lucky disease is Hansen's (leprosy).

Cancer (the crab) June 21–July 20: Sympathetic but can be moody. You should avoid Aquarians. Your lucky sandwich is sun-dried tomatoes and mozzarella; your lucky jargon is "going forward"; your lucky airplane seat is 26F (next to the toilet *and* emergency exit).

Leo (the lion) July 21–August 21: Generous and creative but you always think you know best. Your lucky cheese is Stilton; your lucky disease is Sydenham's chorea; your lucky shop is Target.

Aquarius

Pisces

Aries

Taurus

Gemini

Cancer

Leo

Virgo

Libra

Scorpio

Sagittarius

Capricorn

Virgo (the virgin) August 22–September 22: A reliable, shy worrier, prone to hypochondria (you sound like a bundle of laughs, girl). Your lucky song is "Chirpy Chirpy Cheep Cheep"; your lucky philosophy is Logical Positivism; your lucky sandwich is shrimp and mayonnaise.

Libra (the scales) September 23–October 22: You don't like to rock the boat and can be a bit flirty. Avoid Taureans at all costs. Your lucky artist is William Blake; your lucky song is "Shaddup Your Face" by Joe Dolce; your lucky school subject is Driver's Ed.

Scorpio (the scorpion) October 23–November 22: Exciting and passionate but can become obsessed. Your lucky disease is neurofibromatosis; your lucky shop is Kmart; your lucky cleaning product is Mr. Clean.

Sagittarius (the archer) November 23–December 20: Optimistic and jolly but prone to social faux pas. Avoid Cancer. Your lucky composer is Leonard Bernstein; your lucky alternative medicine is urine therapy; your lucky novel is *À la Recherche du Temps Perdu*.

Capricorn (the sea goat) December 21–January 19: Ambitious and funny but a dreadful Scrooge. Avoid Gemini and Leo. Your lucky lingerie is French; your lucky sandwich is grilled cheese and ham; your lucky astronaut is Buzz Aldrin.

❦ *The calendar we use was decreed by Pope Gregory XIII in 1582.* ❦

How to
Play Hopscotch

There was this girl I remember at school named Gloria Oppenheimer, which was as good a name as anyone could ask for. She manifested the earliest and most magnificent mammarial exhibition of any of us, and, because of her initials (I *think*), she was known to every one as "Go!"

Anyway, years passed—as they say in books—and she became a simultaneous translator at the UN. Then one day she bumped into a man on the stairs in San Diego and ended up as an actor/director in/of—how shall I put it?—exotic films. She deserves a book all to herself, does Gloria. The thing was, though, that she had this phenomenal memory and knew more skipping and hopscotch songs than any of us.

There was the delightful (now politically out of favor):

> *My mother said*
> *I never should*
> *Play with the Gypsies in the wood.*
> *If I did*
> *She would say,*
> *"Naughty girl to disobey."*

This scanned and rhymed, but there was also a charmless lumpen one with technical problems, especially in line 2, that Gloria used to chant before throwing her stone:

> *I've got my favorite pebble,*
> *I'm going to get to go.*
> *I'm a hopscotch lover*
> *It's my turn to throw.*

Anyway, to come to the point, here are the rules of hopscotch.

THE GAME

Known all over the world, hopscotch began in Roman Britain when soldiers were made to run 100-foot-long military hopscotch courts in full uniform. The name is a mixture of "hop" meaning to hop (obviously) and *escocher*, a French word meaning to cut. No, I wasn't any the wiser either. In Germany they call it *templehupfen*, and *hinkelbaan* in the Low Countries. Which serves them right.

Each player has her own pebble or small stone, which marks her position throughout the game. The idea is to chase the stone through a chalk-drawn grid, with a mixture of hops and jumps. These grids vary slightly from country to country and even locally. The one in the illustration is fairly typical and resembles those we used at school. You mustn't touch the lines with

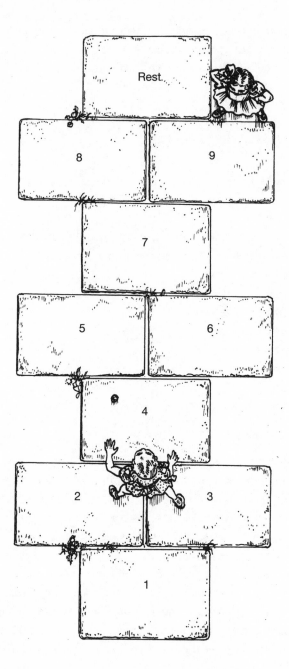

your stone or foot, or put down your hand to balance. The game is, there-fore, a mixture of chess, Twister, and sumo. The winner is the first girl to complete the course the requisite number of times.

PLAYING

1   Draw the grid and its numbers with a piece of chalk (see illustra-tion). My school was on a chalk cliff and lumps of the stuff were everywhere in the flowerbeds. We used them as stones, and for drawing the court, too.

2   Do rock, paper, scissors to decide who goes first.

3   Assuming you are first to go, start by throwing your stone into box 1. The aim is to get it to land in that box. If it does, you can begin the hopping business. This takes a bit of explaining. You may have only one foot in any numbered square. So you must balance on one leg in single numbered squares but may straddle double squares, alternat-ing your landing foot as you go. When you reach the "home" or "rest" square at the top you may land any way you wish. When ready, jump around and return, picking up your stone on the way. If it's in box 1 pick it up when your feet are in boxes 2 and 3. If suc-cessful you may now go on to box 2 and so on. If you foul by throw-ing the stone out of the intended box, land on a line, overbalance, miss a square, or forget to collect your stone, play passes to the next girl. Sometimes the rule is that any box containing a stone must be missed. Things can get quite exciting if there are more than three players.

I wonder what Gloria is up to these days.

❈ *Chalk is formed underwater from the bodies of marine organisms.* ❈

How to
Play Jacks

When my brother was a boy and I was a girl he played Tarzan and I played jacks. That was the law. My friend Lucy was an expert then and could play for hours. Now she lectures in dentistry and continues to play a mean game, using a set of polyurethane display teeth.

Jacks, sometimes called jackstones or onesies, is hundreds of years old and is based on the ancient game of fivestones that was played with five small pebbles, or sheep's knucklebones, in the days before My Little Pony and DVDs.

EQUIPMENT

Apart from the small rubber ball (usually terra-cotta colored), a set of jacks consists of between five and fifteen small, metal "asters," each consisting of a four-pointed cross, with "blobs" at its tips, positioned centrally about a blobless spinable axis. The playing field is almost always the tarmac of a playground, but the game works on a wood floor, too, or any other hard surface. The boundary is informal and is roughly an arm's length from the two players.

THE "PLAIN GAME"

After deciding who goes first, the competitors take turns to play. One turn involves scattering the jacks on the ground, then picking up the jacks (after a formula: see below) while bouncing and catching the ball. *Usually.* Of course you may already be shaking your head because you played it some other way. Indeed, the regional variations are many, and even in a single town there might be ten or fifteen different versions of the game, involving changes to the number of bounces, hands in use, number of jacks to be picked up in one turn, and so on. Occasionally the ball is bounced straight off the ground, or sometimes no bounce is allowed, just the upward throw (*tricky*). There may even be penalties for fouls such as accidentally nudging a jack that you are not picking up. These are often of the miss-a-turn type. In some games you are allowed

to separate two contiguous jacks by calling "kissing cousins!" while parting them with a finger poke. Game variations go by exotic names such as
double-bounce, eggs in the basket, and round the world.

Generally an escalating sequence of pick-ups is the rule, starting with
one (onesies) and moving up to fivesies—or more if you have more jacks.
In the U.S. variety of the game, a dozen or fifteen jacks is the regular
number. In most versions one hand only may be employed for bounces
and pick-ups, though the jacks are often put in, or on the back of, the re-
dundant hand, as they are collected. The girl to progress furthest is the
winner.

A WALK-THROUGH
This five-jacks variant of the game is called one-hand, one-bounce,
granny, or plain-game jacks. Other versions are based on this basic idea.
Let's assume you are to go first.

1 Broadcast the jacks on the ground.

2 Throw the ball up with the right hand.

3 With the same hand pick up a jack (this is onesies), letting the ball
bounce once.

4 Allow the ball to drop back into the right hand, which contains one
jack.

5 Pass the jack to the left hand, retaining the ball in the right.

6 Now repeat with one more jack, continuing in the same way until
all the jacks are collected. Twosies is the same as onesies, except
now you must grab, hold, and transfer two jacks at a time. *Note*:
With each game after onesies, there will be a remainder of jacks
smaller than the number you are supposed to pick up. Pick them up
in the same way, nonetheless, at the last bounce.

7 As soon as you fail to pick up the jack(s) or the correct number, or
the ball bounces more than once or rolls away or you commit some
other foul, your turn ends and your opponent takes over. If she
messes up, then the game comes back to you and you start again at
the number you failed on first time around.

SPECIMEN FOULS
* Failing to catch the ball
* Dropping jacks or ball
* Picking up the wrong number of jacks
* Touching other jacks
* Catching the ball too early or too late
* Using both hands or the wrong hand

Please don't play with plastic "safety" jacks; they are so light that they are almost impossible to pick up. They normally come with a monstrously unbouncy sinister plastic ball. These rubbishy space-age jacks are for dilettantes, amateurs, and Sunday players only.

❀ *The name Jack is from Jankin, a medieval diminutive of John (Hebrew).* ❀

How to
Read Tea Leaves

*T*he teabag is a modern miracle of convenience, but it has pretty much done in the art of tasseography, or tea leaf reading, though some practitioners are still to be found. Romance, health, work, and money are the life zones on which tasseographers tend to concentrate their focus, and tea leaf reading is the perfect diversion for any girl with eyes good enough to see the bottom of the vicar's teacup—whether for fun or profit. But you must use real loose tea; there's only so much predictive insight you can squeeze out of a cold teabag. Here are the basics.

INSTRUCTIONS
Take a cup containing tea dregs and vigorously swirl the detritus three times in a clockwise direction, allowing the tea leaves to slosh up and around the sides of the cup. When they have come to rest, peer sagaciously into the interior. It helps to wear big earrings.

The tea leaves should have settled in "swarms" on the cup's inner surface. These shapes are the symbols that you will read, and you should begin by looking for the simplest figures. The following forms have traditionally been associated with portent of different kinds.

* *Triangles*: a sign of good karma
* *Circles*: betoken success
* *Squares*: indicate the need for caution

You will probably also see letters—which refer to the names of friends or relations—numbers (connoting time), and frequently, human faces—smiles and frowns. Most of the shapes may look like nothing much at first, but the harder you peer the more likely they are to assume meaningful form: a tree, a horse, a serpent, Walter Mondale. Symbols near the rim are important, life-changing omens. Those on the sides of the cup are significant, but not earth-shattering. Figures on the bottom indicate change. Here are a few of the easiest to read, along with a guide to their interpretation:

Acorn: at the top—success; at the bottom—robust health
Anchor: rest, stability, constancy
Arrow: bad love news
Bell: unexpected news—good if near the top
Cabbage: jealousy; if speckled— jealousy at work
Cigar: new friends
Dish: trouble at home
Duck: money on the way
Elephant: wisdom and strength
Fan: romance
Fork: false flattery
Harp: love
Horn: prodigality

Horse's head: a lover
Insect: petty problems
Kangaroo: domestic harmony
Lamp: at the top—a banquet; on the side—secrets revealed
Man: near handle—a visitor
Mushroom: at the top—a move to the country
Octopus: danger
Ostrich: travel
Parasol: a new lover
Raven: bad news
Ring: at the top—an offer of marriage; if broken—broken engagement
Scissors: quarrels

Spider: work success
Thimble: change at home
Umbrella: aggravation
Vase: a friend in need
Wasp: stalled romance

Xylophone: I made that one up.
Nobody's ever seen a xylophone
in the leaves.
Zebra: overseas adventure

Sometimes it's hard to tell an octopus (danger) from a spider (work success) or a raven (bad news) from a duck (money on the way). I'm sorry, you're on your own here.

THE WHEN

Your subject's teacup is like a clock. Its handle, held at 9 o'clock, represents now, the time and place of the reading, with each quarter hour standing for a three-month period. For example, any shapes at 12 o'clock indicate happenings three months into the future, anything at 3 o'clock is six months down the road, and swirls at 6 o'clock represent doings in your subject's life nine months hence. By going around clockwise you can predict forthcoming happenings as much as a year into the future, and by subdividing the quarters you can make predictions for periods shorter than three months. But anything under a month is touch and go.

More tea, Vicar?

❀ *A zarf is an ornamental holder for a handleless cup.* ❀

How to
Water Ski

During the summer of 1922 , in what must be *the* sports brainwave of the twentieth century, eighteen-year-old Ralph Samuelson of Lake City, Minnesota, decided there was no reason why the principles of skiing on snow could not be applied to water.

And so it was that on June 28, with two barrel staves under his feet and being towed across the Mississippi River by his brother Ben, Ralph

Samuelson majestically failed to water ski, being instead dragged several yards before plunging impressively under the river surface.

Like all obsessives, however, he kept on going, replacing the barrel slats with a pair of proper snow skis. Now, swept along behind a motor boat powered by an enormous converted truck engine, he began to sniff the sweet smell of success, managing to stay on top of the water. Within days Ralph had invested in some leather straps and was refining his technique by leaning backward as he was whisked along, his ski tips slanted cheerfully upwards. From then on it was clear his new technique would take off, and today water skiing has become a glamorous sport beloved of svelte ladies and gentlemen in figure-hugging costumes, who zoom gracefully all over places like Lake Geneva.

SAFETY FIRST

Remember, *it takes three to ski*: one to drive the boat, one to do the skiing (you), and one to do nothing but watch you from the boat (the spotter); the last one is *very important*. The guy driving the boat is in charge of your safety so have a proper discussion beforehand to set out some rules. Plan where the boat will go and make sure everyone knows who is responsible for what. A tranquil surface is important, too. Waves are your enemy.

Other obvious safety matters include not doing it if you can't swim, getting a pro to take you through your first few attempts, not trying it in the public pool, and so on. You'll also improve safety if you use decent equipment. It's no good tying two ironing boards to your feet and hoping for the best.

TOP TEN TIPS

1 Wear a life jacket designed for water skiing and tighten the straps, which can whip you in the wind.
2 Remove all jewelry.
3 Use a tow rope at least 75 feet long.
4 Never wrap any part of the line around your body.
5 Keep away from the propeller. Always.

6   Have a spotter on board to take your signals and tell the driver if you fall.

7   Go over the hand signals before you get in the water.

8   Know the area. Your driver should avoid the shallows and the submerged shopping carts, but be aware of potential hazards yourself.

9   Pay attention to what other boaters are doing and give them a wide berth.

10   Don't ski in the dark or if you've been drinking. *Obviously.*

EIGHT SAFETY SIGNALS

1   Thumb up = *speed up*

2   Thumb down = *slow down*

3   Flat hand = *stop*

4   Cut throat = *I want to let go of the rope*

5   Finger point left and finger point right = *turn the boat in direction indicated*

6   Pat your head = *I want to return to the boat*

7   Make circle of thumb and forefinger = *OK* or *signal understood*

8   Hands clasped over head = *I'm OK* (after falling)

GET GOING

There's nothing complicated about any of this but it does require some practice, with guidance from a good instructor.

1   Get in the water and move well away from the boat before the engine is started.

2   Signal once you're ready to go.

3   As the boat slowly moves forward the line will tighten. When you give a thumb's up the boat will move off in a straight line with enough thrust to lift you up out of the water. Lean back and once you are up, signal to your spotter so that the boat's speed can be adjusted to your requirements. Then hang on and get the feel of things. You will fall over a lot; don't worry about it.

4   If (*when*) you fall, give the OK sign as soon as you safely can to let the crew know you are uninjured, so you can be picked up and get going again.

5   When you've fallen, hold a ski out of the water while you wait to be recovered. This makes you very visible to other craft.

6   The boat will come back and circle you slowly either to give you back the tow line or pick you up if you've had enough.

7   Wait for the engine to be switched off before you get aboard.

A FINAL WORD OF WARNING

The Newtonian forces at work while you water ski are pretty powerful and must be taken into account when you choose your bathing suit. It should be tight, robust, and very clingy round your bum. This is not vanity but self-preservation. My dear friend Veronica told me—and her story was backed up by the experiences of my good friend Helen—that she now always wears a wetsuit when water skiing. This change of attire followed a startling experience after she fell when water skiing in Canada. She told me she found herself being dragged along at speed—bottom first—and that the force of the incoming water was such that she was made the victim of an instantaneous, powerful, and unasked-for colonic irrigation. With friends like that, who needs enemas?

❀ *Lake Geneva is the second largest freshwater lake in Central Europe.* ❀

Bareback Riding for the Beginner

When my friend Laverne was young and foolhardy she visited North Africa. One day she was offered a ride in a jeep across one of their deserts on the condition that she take her own weight of water with her in a plastic container. Halfway across they went over a bump, breaking the axle, and, in slow motion, she saw the water bottles bounce up and come down again with such force that they split, pouring their water out of the bottom of the vehicle. She told me it was at this moment she realized she was a statistic.

After an hour in the tin oven, morbidly inventing headlines for the next day's papers, they were rescued when a jeep full of Germans miraculously appeared and took them back to relative civilization. While the axle was being repaired Laverne noticed a decrepit and emaciated mare standing in the shade, its ribs poking through its skin below the great dip in its back. Being Laverne, she decided to get on and was trotting along merrily when the old nag suddenly bolted. With foam flying from its yellow teeth, the wild-eyed horse galloped for half an hour across barren miles of semi-desert, while she clung on desperately to the mane. Finally it stuttered to a halt in the middle of nowhere and began gnawing a piece of cement. Laverne told me that this was how she learned to ride bareback.

For a less terrifying introduction to horseback riding without the benefit of saddle or stirrups, try the following:

1   Put on a helmet.

2   Choose the right horse. Avoid those that bounce you all over the place. A smooth gait is what you're after. A broad back and low withers will aid comfort (see horse map on page 141). If your horse has high or awkward withers, or if you keep slipping, try a bareback pad—rather like training wheels.

3   Ask an experienced rider to supervise your early efforts. If she walks with you, you can concentrate on not falling off. Fifteen minutes is enough for each practice session during the early stages. Even then you'll find that you need to sit down afterward, because your leg muscles will behave like Jell-O.

4   Practice someplace the horse is acquainted with. Not a field where fireworks are being tested, for example. And relax; don't fight the horse. If you move with it you'll balance better and the animal will be happier.

5   Look straight ahead, not down at the animal, or you may start to lose it, just as you do if you look at your feet while running down stairs. Don't ask me why.

6 If you *do* lose your balance, *don't use the reins* to regain your equilibrium; the horse will think you want it to do something, but it won't know what. Instead, grab hold of the mane.

7 If you can manage it, don't touch the horse's sides with your calves. This will force you to balance without relying on your legs. If you are used to stirrups, it will feel peculiar at first.

8 Don't dig your heels into the ribs to maintain balance because the horse will think this is a go-faster signal.

9 If you sense that you are about to fall, try an emergency dismount, which is actually easier without stirrups dangling in the way. If you do fall off, roll away from the horse's feet. A kick in your behind just adds insult to injury.

❀ *The world's smallest horse is Thumbelina—just 17 inches high.* ❀

How to
Row in Petticoats

Well, all right, petticoats are a bit old-fashioned, but how often has someone asked you to take the oars when you're not dressed for the task, in sequined cocktail dress and high heels? People expect the rower to grab hold of the oars with confidence and swarm across the lake so the dogs and children and picnic basket can be disembarked with dispatch and everyone can get on with their lives. What they do not want is you getting in a flap, spraying water over the party while rowing round in a huge circle so that you have to be humiliatingly towed to shore. I speak from shameful experience.

The remedy is to use a proper technique so that splashing is kept to a minimum and you are applying equal pressure to both oars. Your skirts and petticoats, should you have them on, can be quite comfortably tucked around your legs.

METHOD

1 Put on a life jacket. Takes about an hour with two people helping you.

2 Get in the boat so you are facing the blunt end. This can be quite a wobbly affair, which is why you put your life jacket on first. Sit down on the plank thing nearest the sharp end. (You row backward.)

3 Put the oars in the rowlocks, pronounced "rollocks" (don't blame me).

4 *Putting the oar in the water (the catch)*: Reach forward (nose over toes) with the arms straight, grasp the oars, and drop the blades into the water.

5 *Pulling the oar through the water (the drive)*: Lean back, pulling against the oars and pushing with your legs, keeping the shoulders square. Pull through the water. Don't dig too deep, and do not push down on the oars as you pull back or you'll lever them out of the water and fly backward in a flurry of droplets, banging your head on the sharp end.

6 *Taking the oar out (the finish)*: When the oar shafts are back as far as they will go, drop your shoulders and arms, allowing the blades to come out of the water.

7 *Get ready to do it again (the recovery)*: Feather the blade (turn it parallel to the water) and lean forward, pushing your arms out, so you are ready for the next pull stroke.

8 Start all over again.

Do not bend your wrists while rowing; keep your shoulders level and head up, using a smooth rhythmical stroke. Don't do it too much or you'll get shoulders like a linebacker.

❀ *In 1884, Tanneguy de Wogan rowed a paper canoe around France.* ❀

How to
Be the Perfect Cheerleader

W hen she was in college, my sister-in-law used to be a cheerleader. She told me it was jolly hard work getting all the girls to bounce up and down in time with each other, while smiling the rictus-cheerleader smile and singing the jolly cheerleader song:

We must, we must,
We must increase our bust!
The bigger, the better,
The tighter the sweater;
The boys depend on us!

This doggerel struck me as typical of the vacuous poesy of the Cheerleader School of lyricists. But as my atheistic friend Val says, Why deprive yourself of a good sing-song in church or at the game just because you don't believe the words?

Being a cheerleader requires a diverse range of skills, not least of which are stamina, good aerobic capacity, and robust cardiovascular health. A loud voice with plangent, distance-covering qualities is also desirable, along with a pair of strong legs. The list below gives you a few more tips.

* Smear a good inch of fake tan all over before donning your lurid "spankies" or "lollipops" (briefs). Those floodlights will otherwise wash all the color out of you.

* Long curly hair that bounces prettily is the best. Think '70s Olivia Newton-John and get hold of some curling tongs.

* Bright vermilion mouth-emphasizing lipstick is a must, as is a good thick black eyebrow pencil and heavy mascara. You are fighting the lights, don't forget.

* I haven't space here to go into the moves in detail—just follow the other girls. Many of the actions are derived from the jumping-up-and-down school of dance and are designed to accentuate your femininity in a way that will be noticeable by the crowd from where they are sitting. I don't wish to put it any more bluntly than that.

* Drink plenty of water.
* Smile, even when you are hot, tired, and want to go home and read.

To make your own pom-poms

1 Cut two doughnut-shaped circles out of cardboard about 1 foot in diameter.

2 Superimpose them and evenly wind several yards of scene-of-crime tape through the hole and around the doughnut, tying the end of one piece on to the next until you have a thickish layer.

3 Pass one blade of a pair of very sharp scissors between the cardboard doughnuts (through the tape), and slice right around the circumference, cutting through the tape (Fig. A).

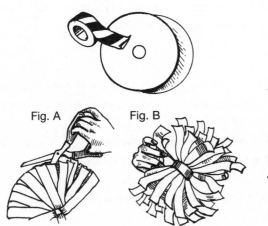

Fig. A   Fig. B

4 Tie a length of tape tightly round the middle, between the cardboard rings (Fig. B).

5 Snip the cardboard circles and remove, shaking out the finished pom-pom.

6 Add a handle.

❀ *Cheerleading started at Princeton University in the 1880s.* ❀

Karaoke Do's and Don'ts

*T*he Japanese word for "empty" is *karano*—*kara* for short—while "orchestra" is the English-derived *ōkesutora* or *oke*. Together these make the familiar word *karaoke*, or "empty orchestra." Here are some top karaoke tips. Unless you are a naturally good singer and confident performer, you should follow these rules religiously.

* Get up there as early as possible so that you are quickly forgotten and don't have to sit trembling for hours, waiting your ghastly turn.

* Brazen it out. If you can't sing, try to perform well. Noel Coward couldn't sing to save his life, but who could match his performance of "Mad Dogs and Englishmen"?

* If your voice is really horrid choose a tuneless shouty punk song.

* Duets are good: share the embarrassment and be generous with the blame.

* Personal lack of judgment of one's musical ability is in direct relation to the amount of alcohol coursing through the body. Never sing if drunk and don't mistake confidence for talent. You will regret it in the morning, and your audience will regret it now.

* Try to pick a crowd-pleaser that people will join in with. Foot-tapping catchy choruses will cover a multitude of sings.

* Avoid the following:

    "Stand by Your Man": Ladies who think they can sing, and can't, always pick this.

"Cabaret" as done by Liza Minnelli: Comparisons will be drawn to Liza, and you won't win.

"There's No Business Like Show Business" (à la Ethel Merman): Same as above.

"Wonderful World" as done by Louis Armstrong: You'll never reach those low notes.

* Don't fiddle or play cute games with the mike.
* Never play air guitar. You are not Eddie Van Halen.
* If you think you have star potential and want to go over big, practice at home first. Obvious really.

A FEW OTHER QUICK DO'S AND DON'TS

* Do use the introductory bars and the instrumental or dum-de-dum passages between the lyrics to introduce the number. Say something like, " 'Stardust' was made famous by Nat King Cole, and it is one of those sentimental songs that always brings tears to your eyes. It certainly will the way I perform it."
* Never give up mid-performance with a pathetic "Oh, I'm no good at this," or "Oh, silly me, I keep forgetting the words." In the entertainment business, the show must go on.
* Do try to find the proper key early on. There is nothing more ear-grindingly awful for a karaoke audience than having to sit there listening to your chromatic wanderings around the entire panoply of musical pitches, from Oriental to Accidental.

OTHER OPEN-MIKE OPPORTUNITIES

If you find yourself at a comedy club, microphone in hand, seize the day! To help you, here are a few common mistakes, with tips for avoiding them.

* Many beginners indulge in so-called HPM (high-peripheral movement). This is usually a sign of nerves and often includes such things as foot jiggling, excessive arm waving, and wild microphone movement. Keep that mike still unless you are moving it for a

theatrical reason, for instance, the hand-to-hand mike toss. It's not only that your voice keeps fading away; all the twitching drives the audience nuts.

* If you are doing impressions, for goodness' sake be up-to-date. Nobody's going to think much as you announce, "And now for my famous impression of TV's up-and-coming star, the one and only Lucille Ball." And don't forget that you need to exhibit an approximate *likeness*, at least in sound. This means rehearsal.

* Risqué jokes? This is part of the judging-your-audience exercise. A group of elderly church ladies will probably prefer something that steers well clear of swearing, politics, and the reproductive organs.

If you get a lackluster response or even boos, do not be rude, snotty, or, worst of all, a reverse heckler. Do try to bring them on board, but if you can't, leave the stage as gracefully as you can. And remember, it could have been worse. Performers at Scotland's notorious Glasgow Empire often said that if they liked you they didn't applaud, they let you *live*. A good rule is: if it's going badly, get off; if it's going well, get off. Wise words.

❀ *In 2007, North Korean authorities prohibited all karaoke bars.* ❀

Curling for Beginners

C urlers have gone completely out of fashion. I remember in wartime films how every housewife used to wear them in her hair as she did the laundry on a Saturday morning. I guess the passion-killing element did them in. Of course, "curlers" is also a word that describes those wacky people who curl. Curling is certainly a wonderful old sport; it began in sixteenth-century Scotland, where kilted highlanders with time on their hands whizzed stones called "loafies" across the frozen lochs.

Today the game is played by teams of four in professional indoor arenas, using highly polished forty-two-pound granite rocks and funny icebrooms. The field (sheet) is marked out on the ice and is some 150 by 14 feet in area. The ice is prepared by having water droplets sprayed onto its surface, and the consequent bumps are called "pebble," which, because of friction, cause the stone to turn in its path.

The object of the game is to slide the stone so that it stops at the far end of the sheet as close as possible to the center of a 12-foot-diameter bull's-eye called the "house" (see illustration). The opposition then tries to knock the first team's stones away from the target and occupy the space with their own—a sort of ice pétanque. The stones must land between the *hog line* (where you start) and the *back line* (behind the rings), and between the boards or out lines (the sides). Teams play alternately until each has thrown eight stones: two per player. The score is then worked out. Is this making *any sense?*

TEAMS

The names of the players are based on the order in which they throw. The lead usually plays first, then the second, then the third, and finally the skip. But not always, just to make things confusing.

* *Lead*: The lead, or first, throws the team's first two stones, and sweeps for the others.
* *Second*: The second throws the third and fourth stones and also sweeps for other players.
* *Third*: The third is the deputy, also called the mate. She throws the team's fifth and sixth stones, and usually sweeps for the second and the lead. She plays before the skip and holds her brush for the skip to aim at. The thirds are also responsible for working out the score between themselves.
* *Skip*: The skip is captain and plays the last two stones, which can often be decisive. She must therefore be the best player in the team. She holds the broom indicating where the other players must aim, but rarely does any sweeping. Typical!

So to recap: the lead throws first and second; the second, third and fourth; the third, fifth and sixth; and the skip last. I hope that's clear.

EQUIPMENT

* *Stones*: Specialist item not available from the corner store. Try an iron in an emergency.
* *Brushes*: Hog hair is most pleasing, but synthetic materials are preferable because they don't moult on the ice.
* *Shoes*: A "slippy" shoe on the left and a "sticky" shoe on the right. Honestly, I'm not making this up.
* *Apparel*: Dress warm, not in your bikini.

PLAY

Curling is always preceded by a handshake and the salutation: "Good curling!" Fair enough, I suppose.

1   Stand with the stone in your right hand, weight on your left foot (slippy sole) and right leg behind you. With your brush extended to your left, which helps you balance, deliver your stone by sliding it from the hack: the push-off plate.

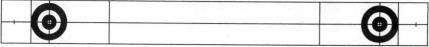

2   Aim at the brush held by the skip and as you let go give the stone a slight twist, which will cause it to bend its path. This is *not* why the game is called curling. It comes from a Scots word meaning to rumble—get the idea?

3   If the skip says so, anyone not doing anything follows your stone up the ice with her broom, sweeping *in front of it* like a goodun. This reduces friction, making it go faster, further, and straighter.

4   When all sixteen shots are played, the thirds decide who wins, and by how much. Every stone beating an opponent's is awarded one "shot." This concludes one "end." A standard game lasts for eight or ten ends.

5   There are many different shots allowed: stone budgers, bent ones, and everything, and the glossary is huge. Where they get the time beats me.

Or you could have a glass of something and watch a Doris Day film.

❈ *You can walk for as far as two miles during an eight-end match.* ❈

How to
Do the Cola Can Cancan

Who can forget La Goulue? What do you mean you've never heard of her? She was a cancan dancer, immortalized in the paintings of Toulouse Lautrec. He created several of her at the Moulin Rouge in Paris, contributing her raffish nineteenth-century charms to the bohemian milieu.

The cancan, as you are doubtless aware, is a vigorous high-kicking dance in two-four time, usually now done in chorus-line style. If you want to learn it, I think dance classes are your best bet; it's certainly beyond the humble purview of this book. But don't be downhearted, because I have something just as exciting, and even simpler, for you: the cola can cancan, which is suitable for performance at home, at college, or in the bar—or even for when you're feeling at home in the college bar. It is best done when you have a group of friends seated at a table, and a few cans of cola knocking about.

INSTRUCTIONS

1   Drink about two-thirds of a can of cola, leaving about one-third in the can. You will see that the can's underside has a circular ring below the taper, which facilitates stacking. Both the top and bottom of your can are thicker than the sides, and their reduced diameters allow a 15 percent saving in raw materials. When the can is upright it sits on this ring, but you are going to tilt it until it is balanced at a crazy-looking angle on the taper itself.

2   Take gentle hold of the can, without lifting it off the table, and tilt it to about 45 degrees, so that it is resting partly on the "ring" and partly on the side of the can, with the taper horizontal.

3   Release your grip but keep your fingers poised to prevent the can swinging too quickly from side to side. Once the liquid has stopped sloshing about you may remove your hand and the can will stay balanced. It looks weird, unnatural, and unstable, but it is in fact quite secure.

4   Push the can gently and it will swivel around in a charming and mysterious pirouette.

The reason the cola can cancan works when you drink some of the cola is that a new (low) center of gravity is created. A center of gravity, by the way, is a kind of "average" position for the weight of an object. Balance is possible only when an object's support is directly below its center of gravity. So don't expect this to work with a full, or indeed an empty, can. You will not be able to balance it and it will simply fall over, its center of gravity being too high. The lower an object's center of gravity is, the more stable it is. This is why it's hard to fall over when you are lying on the floor.

Because the cola is fluid and moves around, it retains its position relative to the can, even when you push it, and the center of gravity therefore stays in the same place.

If all this seems too dull to remember, you don't have to. What's more the display may be performed with a half-empty can of beer, which only adds to the fun.

❋ *In its first year, 1886, sales of Coca-Cola averaged nine a day.* ❋

How to
Identify Official State Flowers

*T*homas Hood wrote a poem called "Flowers," the first verse of which ends like this: "The cowslip is a country wench, / The violet is a nun; / But I will woo the dainty rose, / The queen of everyone." He might just as well have written: "The cowslip is an urban Ford, / The violet is a Honda; / But I will buy a Nissan rose, / And park her over yonder." It makes about as much sense. In fact, I think mine is such a good effort that I'll send it off to Hallmark.

Anyhow, I wanted to talk to you about the state flowers. If you take a look at the botanical notes below, you should soon be able to identify them all and understand a little of their personal idiosyncrasies.

1   *Alabama*: The camellia is the state flower of Alabama. A florid outgoing personality with shiny leaves. The pink blooms have a message, and the message is *I am a flower of the world!*

2   *Alaska*: The forget-me-not is almost the opposite personality type to the camellia. Small, quiet, diffident, but always chic. This pale blue flower takes pride in her appearance.

3   *Arizona*: When you meet a flowering saguaro cactus, you cannot but be charmed by her luscious pale pink blossom. Though this flower hints at a character forgiving of human foibles, you sense that there is more to her than meets the eye.

4   *Arkansas*: A delicate and pretty inflorescence with a sweet aroma, the apple blossom can be skittish at times and is prone to putting her foot down with a firm hand (as it were).

5   *California*: The California poppy has California written all over her.

Not literally, of course. A stunning orange, she speaks of a romantic and fiery Spanish undercurrent.

6 *Colorado*: The Rocky Mountain columbine is another tender flower, with blue petals, white petals, and yellow thingies—you know, those parts that stick out from the middle. A studious flower that scores straight A's.

7 *Connecticut*: Connecticut's state flower is the mountain laurel. Pink, cheerful, and clear-headed in a crisis. I'll bet the flower that blooms in the dreams of sleeping Connecticutters is often the mountain laurel.

8 *Delaware*: Peach blossom is another pink one. Delicate petals set off the more serious-looking floral interior. This ambitious flower harbors dreams of becoming a movie star. Will it happen? One can only wish her all the luck in the world.

9 *Florida*: The orange blossom is a star-shaped white flower of simplicity. She's has had a tune and a train named after her and that tells you something, I think. She hints at sunshine, but showers, too.

10 *Georgia*: The Cherokee rose resembles nothing so much as the sister of the orange blossom, but with larger, softer leaves. A flower of great mystery, she reads *Madame Bovary* in the original French.

11 *Hawaii*: For a state boasting such lively shirts, the ma'o hau hele (Hawaiian hibiscus) seems at first a demure flower, with her diffident yellow petals. But get out your ukulele and things soon heat up.

12 *Idaho*: The mock orange resembles the orange blossom even more than the Cherokee rose does, not only in appearance but also in her heavy sweet scent. First recorded by Meriwether Lewis, in 1804.

13 *Illinois*: The violet is intensely violet, with a blindingly white center. An aesthete, with a liking for the music of Zoltán Kodály and the architecture of Frank Lloyd Wright.

14 *Indiana*: The peony looks like a camellia that has been dancing all night. Bright pink petals with a ruffled, serrated look to their edges. This flower can often be found at the bar retelling stories of life in the fast lane.

15 *Iowa*: Iowa's wild prairie rose has an austere, spare, and simple beauty, rather like Katharine Hepburn in her younger days. A lover of fine literature.

16 *Kansas*: I bet there are other states that wish they'd put their names down for the sunflower before Kansas, but they didn't. Record-breakingly tall and beautiful, and a real moneymaker—oilwise. Rather too large for one's buttonhole, though.

17 *Kentucky*: Goldenrod is unmistakable: hundreds of tiny yellow flowers on droopy-looking stems. This flower looks good in a Chinese vase on a mahogany table. If you haven't got a mahogany table I don't know what to suggest.

18 *Louisiana*: Here's a confident flower: the magnolia. A magnolia tree looks magnificent when in bloom. The flowers don't stay for long but while they are there, it's a truly glorious spectacle.

19 *Maine*: The white pinecone and tassel is perhaps the most austere state "flower." A pinecone with a gummy aromatic resin is about as far from something like the rose as you could hope to get. Athletic in appearance and possibly good in the pentathlon.

20 *Maryland*: This is another flower that has a song named after it. The black-eyed susan is violently orange, with a jet-black blob in its center. A tremendously eye-catching flower.

21 *Massachusetts*: Also known as the mayflower, trailing arbutus is a delicate white flower with translucent petals. H. L. Mencken once identified a fellow from Cumberland Mountains, Tennessee, named Trailing Arbutus Vines. Aren't people funny?

22 *Michigan*: I knew it wouldn't be long before we ran out of popular flowers and the states started doubling up. Michigan shares the apple blossom with Arkansas, but no one seems to object. After all, it's greatly preferable to the stinkhorn.

23 *Minnesota*: The pink and white lady's slipper looks quite a bit like its name. The Minnesotans love lady's slippers. They grow to about 4 feet, inhabit swamps, and live about fifty years before they die. *The flowers*, not the Minnesotans.

24 *Mississippi*: Mississippi shares the magnolia with Louisiana. It makes perfect sense for two next-door states to enjoy the same appealing efflorescence and, who knows, maybe it minimizes their carbon footprint.

25 *Missouri*: The hawthorn is a prickly old tree and the blossom may seem an odd one to adopt, but its beautiful bunched white blooms are simply resplendent.

26 *Montana*: In Native American tradition, the sun changed the tears of a crying mother into the bitterroot so that she could feed her family. This state flower has a striking pink flower with sharp, radiating petals. A confident and friendly personality.

27 *Nebraska*: Goldenrod is yet another popular flower appropriated by more than one state—in this case Kentucky. But there's plenty of goldenrod to go around, so no one complains.

28 *Nevada*: The sagebrush is an aromatic woody shrub with small flowers spread along her branch tips. An unflagging soul who can take whatever you throw at her. An admirable quality.

29 *New Hampshire*: The purple lilac is native to England but was chosen to symbolize the hardy character of the men and women of the Granite State. Fair enough, I suppose. The small flowers grow in great big blowsy bunches.

30 *New Jersey*: Illinois, New Jersey, Rhode Island, and Wisconsin all chose the violet, but she comes in all kinds of variations, and the common meadow violet is the one New Jersey settled on. A very sensible flower.

31 *New Mexico*: The yucca flower is full of charm. A member of the lily family, she is sturdy as well as good-looking. Pale ivory flowers nicely complement the knifelike leaves. This flower knows what she wants, and she usually gets it.

32 *New York*: What can one say about the rose except that, in her multifarious manifestations she is beautiful, fragrant, and romantic? Once picked she lives but a short time, which is perhaps part of her great seductiveness.

33   *North Carolina*: The American dogwood's spring blossoms are most often white, although shades of pink are not uncommon. Another flower with a shrewd head on her shoulders.

34   *North Dakota*: North Dakota shares the wild prairie rose with Iowa. North Dakota's prairies are worth seeing, and next time you're passing through look out for the wild prairie rose. It's hard to miss in that panoramic flatness.

35   *Ohio*: The scarlet carnation is the perfect flower for the buttonhole. Her crinkled petals have a highly distinctive, not to say distinguished, look. An aristocratic flower for the woman about town.

36   *Oklahoma*: Oklahoma has three state flowers: the state floral emblem, mistletoe; the state wild flower, Indian blanket; and the official state flower, the Oklahoma rose. The ones I've seen are all red. Nothing wrong with that.

37   *Oregon*: The Oregon grape has hollylike foliage, blue berries suitable for cooking, and petite and compact yellow flowers. These flowers are very good at keeping secrets.

38   *Pennsylvania*: The mountain laurel is pink and geometrical looking, because of the dark anther tips, rather like a clock face. A good flower to be trapped in an elevator with. Overflowing with quiet authority.

39   *Rhode Island*: The violet again. There are some 500 species around the world. Most violets of the acaulescent species are zygomorphic with bilateral symmetry. So there!

40   *South Carolina*: Yellow jessamine is an indigenous tree-climber, producing a prodigality of yellow, funnel-shaped flowers that fill the evening air with an alluring fragrance.

41   *South Dakota*: The pasque (Easter) flower is the first flower of spring. White with pointy-looking petals and a fluffy yellow center, she heralds the dwindling of the winter gloom.

42   *Tennessee*: I once knew a girl named Iris. She had big hands. Sorry, I was distracted there for a moment. The iris is the state flower of Tennessee, and purple is the commonly accepted color. Luscious petals.

43   *Texas*: Big state, delicate flower. The bluebonnet, also known as buffalo clover or wolf flower, is a cheerful plant. Playful blue and white petals hint at a flower that prefers the company of ordinary mortals to that of aristocrats.

44   *Utah*: The sego lily has white, lilac, or yellow petals with a red and yellow fire-burst pattern in the middle. A striking flower that reminds one of a confident CEO with just a hint of humor in her demeanor.

45   *Vermont*: Red clover is not red; it is usually pink or faintly bluish, the petals clumped into a floral ball. If this flower were human, she would be a milkmaid rather than a high-paid executive.

46   *Virginia*: Shared with North Carolina, Virginia's state flower is American dogwood. There is something unmistakably sharp about her. No doubt she would be an admirable finance director for a growing business.

47   *Washington*: The coast rhododendron (*Rhododendron macrophyllum*) is a gorgeous pink extravagance with brown central flecks and upwardly curling pistils. A creature to stand back and admire.

48   *West Virginia*: Just to confuse you, West Virginia also chose the rhododendron. In this case, though, it's *Rhododendron maximum*. A delicate pink or white fleck-mottled bloom. Slightly more sedate than her cousin to the northwest.

49   *Wisconsin*: OK, we've got another violet: in this case, the wood violet, whose leaves are tasty and may be used in salads. Orson Welles was born in Wisconsin; I wonder if he ever ate any.

50   *Wyoming*: The Indian paintbrush is a scaldingly bright flower. But look again because the flowers are inconspicuous; it's the red bracts around them that chortle so loudly, in the manner of a used-car salesman.

❧ *The red fruit of the saguaro cactus is edible.* ❧

How to

Make a Halloween Jack-o'-Lantern

How delightful it is every October 31—known also as Halloween, All Hallows' Eve, or Snap Apple Night—to find three spookily dressed young rascals on the doorstep demanding money with menaces. "Trick or treat!" seems to me a classic dilemma: a choice between two options, both disagreeable. This tradition may be the result of England having for years coupled Halloween and Mischief Night (November 4), the time when youngsters played practical jokes on their neighbors: changing shop signs, whitewashing doors, and taking gates from their hinges. I suppose people didn't complain about boys removing their gates only because they didn't want them to take a fence. Sorry.

The Halloween pumpkin jack-o'-lantern is the archetypal symbol of this autumnal festival. Here's how to go about making one.

REQUIRED
* *A decent-size pumpkin*
* *A marker*
* *A sharp knife (watch your fingers)*
* *Some tea lights*

INSTRUCTIONS
1 Get yourself a decent-size pumpkin.
2 Draw a face on the outside.
3 Scalp the pumpkin so that you can get the seeds out. I prefer a clean, circular cut; others prefer a zigzag.
4 Scoop out the seeds and membrane with your bare hands. This is a sloppy old process much beloved of nieces and nephews. Don't throw away the seeds. Instead, separate them from the "string" (soul destroying) and put them on a baking tray. Sprinkle with salt and

bake slowly until crisp. They taste delicious, but take care not to burn them—I usually do.

5   Some 99 percent of pumpkins marketed domestically are used as Halloween jack-o'-lanterns. Nonetheless, the flesh is edible and is yummy stewed and served with butter.

6   Carefully cut the features you have drawn. For friendly, use round and upwardly curved lines. For mean, use sharp and downward-pointing lines.

7   A charming puking pumpkin may be made by cutting the mouth in the shape of a large hole and pulling the seeds and stringy gloop out through the orifice. It's a delightfully suggestive arrangement, much admired by boys.

8   Put a couple of tea lights inside, wait for it to get dark, and ignite the candles. You can put the top back on or not, depending on whether you do or don't like the smell of burnt pumpkin.

❋ *A serving of roasted pumpkin seeds contains about 285 calories.* ❋

How to
Make a Macramé Bikini

Macramé is a kind of needleless, hookless textile-making process that requires no heavy machinery, depending as it does upon knots. In this respect it differs from both knitting and weaving. The main macramé knots are the square knot and the full and double half hitches. Hemp is the material of choice; the ropey part, not the leaves, obviously, which are of no use at all and should be burnt.

Fancy ornamental macramé was once favoured as a pastime by jolly bell-bottomed sailors, between their roistering, sextant polishing, and shanties. They used it to decorate their bits and bobs about the boat and would spend hours bent intently over the hammock of Roger the cabin boy late at night, applying macramé embellishments to his auger crank before exhaustedly tossing themselves on to their bunks. Well, when your life consists of little more than rum, barnacles, and con-

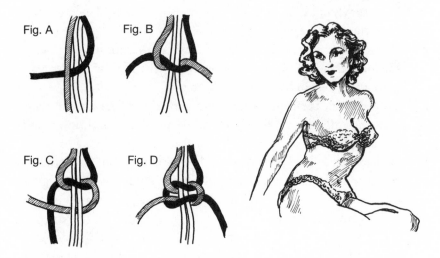

Fig. A   Fig. B   Fig. C   Fig. D

certina, you'll clutch at anything to invest your existence with a little gaiety.

It is recorded that seafarers would often compete to produce the most intricate macramé designs, and many cheery hours were occupied decorating their knife handles, bottles, and wife-beating sticks. No, not wife-beating sticks, I made that up. They would supplement their income by selling their artefacts at ports around the globe, and would, if generous, occasionally give a native girl one for nothing. It was in this way that the art of macramé was introduced into many cultures across the world. Along with the pox.

GETTING KNOTTED

To begin, get yourself four suitable threads of string, twine, or hemp cord. The general rule is to allow for a cord ten times the length of your finished article. The illustrations show the four filaments: one black, one shaded, and in the middle, two white. These two stay where they are as you make the knots. Those on the outside (shaded and black) do all the work.

Half knot

1 Bring the (black) filament on the right over the two middle (white) strands.

2 Bring it under the (shaded) strand on the left.

3 Bring the (shaded) left hand strand under the two white filaments (Fig. A) and up through the loop made by the white thread and the black one (Fig. B). Is this making any sense?

4 Tighten the knot by pulling gently on the shaded and black threads.

5 Repeat this knot over and over to make a helix or spiral (Fig. C).

6 Time for a glass of something.

Square knot

1 Make a half knot as above.

2 Bring the shaded filament, now on the right, behind the two white threads.

3 Pass it over the black thread on the left.

4 Place the black thread into the loop on the right by going over the white filaments and under the shaded (Fig. D).

5 Tighten the knot by gently pulling the black and the shaded.

Now it's time to make your bikini so off you go. What do you mean, you thought I'd be giving you instructions? Look, it's taken up a page to describe two simple knots; you'll just have to use your initiative. Or do what others do and make a macramé bracelet. Easy!

❀ *"Itsy Bitsy Teenie Weenie Yellow Polka Dot Bikini" was translated into Portuguese.* ❀

How to
Play Underwater Hockey

Underwater hockey or octopush was invented in 1954 by four divers from Southsea, England. It is a fast, non-contact pool-bottom game for two teams of six players, who try to score by pushing or flicking a plastic-coated three-pound lead puck into their opponents' goal with a very short buoyant stick held in one gloved hand. Although players are equipped with snorkels, most of the time they remain submerged.

REQUIRED
* *Mask*
* *Fins*
* *Snorkel*
* *Water polo–style cap (ear protection)*
* *Mouth guard (tooth protection)*
* *A tough glove (hand protection)*
* *A pusher (the stick)*
* *3 referees*

PLAY
Games consist of two halves, each of about ten minutes, with a short interval at halftime, during which ends are switched.

To begin, the referee places the puck in the middle, between the goals, and the teams wait in the water against their respective walls. Once the game has begun, players do their damnedest to score a goal without bashing into others. When a goal is scored, everyone returns to her wall to begin again. Simple, innit?

There are a number of fouls, from "hooking" an opponent with the stick to "obstruction": stopping the puck with a fin or a part of the body. Minor fouls incur an "advantage puck," whereby the fouling team is pushed back 3 yards from the puck, while possession passes to the opponents. For major penalties such as physical violence or really nasty sub-aqua bitchiness, nose thumbing, and hair pulling, referees may eject players.

Two water refs are in the pool in full kit, and a distinctive uniform, observing play at the pool bottom. One poolside ref tracks the time, keeps score, and calls fouls noticeable from the surface, such as failure to start a point from the end of the playing area. The poolside ref responds to hand signals given from the water refs to start and stop the game. Up to four substitutions are allowed during play.

It's not much of a spectator sport, unfortunately, unless you want to put on fins, snorkel, and mask, and get in with the players. And you can't expect a crowd of 300 in there, either; that would be silly and everyone's ice cream would melt.

❁ *4,000-year-old Egyptian drawings show men clearly playing hockey.* ❁

How to
Play the Harp

When I played the cello in the school orchestra there were always three girls left packing their instruments long after the piccolos and violins had gone home: Andrea Wernish on the kettle drums, who I think became a tax lawyer; Olive St. John on the doublebass (big nose); and Gail Vaughan Williams, who was alleged to be related to the late composer. Gail was both blonde and beautiful, and when she played she looked like an angel. Unfortunately her nonstop filthy swearing, spiteful bitchiness, and plant-wilting BO endeared her to nobody. But she did look good on the harp.

Because of its beautiful mellow sound, the harp is the ideal instrument for beginners and it's one of the few instruments that men don't seem very interested in. Just running your thumb down the open strings makes a lovely sound, and even simple beginner's tunes such as "A B March" and "Three Blind Mice" sound good. This is in contrast to beginner's French horn or violin, which will have the neighbors round with guns before you can say Bartók.

If you've tickled the ivories or played the organ then this is a good start to learning the harp. After all, the instrument is really just the insides of a piano turned sideways. If not, you are going to have to get used to reading two clefs at the same time and using both hands to make the notes. As a sort of signposting system all the F strings on a harp are black or blue and all the C strings are red or orange. That ought to stop you getting too far out of whack, though I don't remember ever seeing Marisa Robles staring at the strings and counting along.

INSTRUCTIONS

1   Cut your fingernails.

2   Position the harp between your knees and lean it back so that it rests on your right shoulder.

3   If you look down at your feet, you may see some pedals (probably seven). If you do, you are using a big concert harp. These pedals are not accelerators and brakes as some beginners think, and neither do they do the same job as the pedals on a piano, sustaining or dampening the notes; they are there for changing the pitch.

4   Start plucking. The only digit you don't use to play the harp is the little finger. You should know that the convention is that the thumb is numbered 1, index finger 2, middle is 3, and ring finger 4. You can vary the tonal quality by plucking with the fleshy part of your finger (warm and round tone) or the fingertip (brighter, louder), but not the nail.

5   Try to look the part, like Gail Vaughan Williams, by closing your eyes and letting your elbows rise and fall. Sway gently backward and forward as you play, keeping your movements smooth and elegant with an ethereal smile playing over your lips, and allowing your wrists to wobble about a bit.

That's all there is to it.

Look, if you were expecting to be able to play the Krumpholtz sonata after reading a five-point guide, then I'm sorry to disappoint you. You can only really cover the basics in a book like this.

❀ *Harpo Marx's real name was Adolph.* ❀

Twenty-Five Rules for Improving Your English

*H*ave you ever yearned to write a novel? Many people have, and there's certainly nothing wrong with literary ambition. The problem is that, unlike wannabe violinists, many wannabe novelists begin without having acquired the rudiments of their craft. Furthermore, in contrast to, say, Olympic swimmers who haven't bothered to learn to swim, they are not penalized by death; indeed a number of them go on to make good money from the book racket. Here's an example of the sort of thing I mean, cobbled together from several *real* efforts.

> Hank and Jenny had never met. They were like two hummingbirds who had also never met: exact opposites—she a ballerina who could rise gracefully *en pointe*, one slender leg extended behind her, like a dog at a fire hydrant, he as lame as a duck. Not the metaphorical lame duck, either, but a real duck that was actually lame, maybe from stepping on a land mine or something. He was as tall as a 6-foot-3-inch tree, with a hungry look—the kind you get from not eating for a while. She was short, her eyes two brown circles with big black dots in the center. They had first met by the pond in their suburban neighborhood that had picket fences resembling Nancy Kerrigan's teeth. A storm was brewing and they watched a little boat drifting across the water exactly the way a bowling ball wouldn't. Then the thunder began, ominous sounding, much like the sound of a thin sheet of

metal being shaken backstage during the storm scene in a play. The whole atmosphere had a surreal quality, like when you're on vacation in another city and *Jeopardy!* comes on at 7 p.m. instead of 7:30. Suddenly shots rang out, as shots are wont to do . . .

Better stop there. Now, there are several problems with this piece, including contradiction, tortured syntax, confusion of tenses, "gorged snake"–sentences, bathos, and an unequal struggle with similes. So for beginners at the novelist's trade, postulant journalists, and freshman wordsmiths of every stripe, here are my twenty-five rules for improving your English and avoiding a few of the beginners' mistakes.

Twenty-five rules for improving you're English

1 Use words correctly, irregardless of how others use them.
2 Be sure not to carelessly split infinitives.
3 Avoid clichés like the plague.
4 Use the apostrophe in it's proper place and not when its not needed.
5 Always avoid annoying alliteration.
6 Be more or less specific.
7 And don't start sentences with conjunctions.
8 Check for inadvertant spelling errors.
9 Parenthetical remarks (however relevant) are unnecessary (usually).
10 Verbing nouns weirds language.
11 No sentence fragments.
12 Contractions aren't necessary so don't use them.
13 Never generalize about anything.
14 Prepositions are bad words to end sentences with.
15 Verbs has to agree with their subjects.
16 Never use no double negatives.
17 Ampersands & abbreviations etc. are N.G.
18 Puns are for children, not groan readers.
19 Don't use a sesquipedalian word if a short one will do.
20 Check you're work for embarrassing homophones.

21 <u>Avoid exclamation marks.</u>
22 No underlining!
23 Capitals should NOT be used for emphasis.
24 Your work will be more effective if written in the active voice.
25 Eliminate all, unnecessary, commas.
26 Proofread carefully to see if you any words out.

If all these rules seem like too much, you could always just give up and go in for San Jose State University's Bulwer-Lytton Fiction Contest instead. This glorious annual celebration of bad writing is named after an English author and politician, best remembered today for such deathless prose as the following, from his pompous and constipated novel, *Paul Clifford* (1830):

> It was a dark and stormy night; the rain fell in torrents— except at occasional intervals, when it was checked by a violent gust of wind which swept up the streets (for it is in London that our scene lies), rattling along the housetops, and fiercely agitating the scanty flame of the lamps that struggled against the darkness.

Oh, dear.

❀ *In British English, an eggplant is called an "aubergine."* ❀

How to
Press Flowers

*T*he writer and comic actor Ronnie Barker once told me that he found the writing of an especially ingenious new lyric to a Gilbert and Sullivan song "tricky but satisfying." I remember his version of "Dear Little Buttercup" from *HMS Pinafore*, which finished: "Dear little Buttercup / lift your left buttock up / you've squashed my opera hat flat." I thought that homophone was so clever that I wondered why nobody had used it before. The artful rudery of Ronnie Barker—let alone the wit of the Savoy Operas—seems now to belong to an utterly bygone era, when gallantry was commonplace, when ladies still pressed flowers and swearing on television caused questions in parliament, when men were men and women were men dressed up.

So if you'd like to recreate that departed age and preserve a few of those smiling buttercups and the like with some old-fashioned flower pressing, here's the way to do it.

REQUIRED

* *2 heavy boards*
* *Several sheets of blotting paper*
* *A flower press (or car)*

INSTRUCTIONS

1   Get out there with your pruning shears and bring back a selection of flowers while they're in the pink. Thistles, cacti, and cauliflower don't press well, but any delicate native bloom should work nicely.

2   Put a board on the table and then put five layers of blotting paper on top.

3   Carefully lay your flowers on the paper, spreading out the petals.

4   Put another five sheets of paper on top and another collection of specimens on top of that, sandwiching as many layers as you like.

5   Transfer to your flower press. If you have no press, you can improvise by laying another board on top and finishing with a few items of heavy masonry. Or better still, drive a car up on to the board. Be safe, obviously.

6   Leave for thirty hours or so and then carefully remove your specimens and put between fresh paper.

7   Press for a further forty-eight hours.

You can display your flowers on boards yourself or have them professionally mounted and glazed, over a verse in copperplate hand, such as Robert Herrik's: "Gather ye rosebuds while ye may, / Old Time is still a-flying, / And this same flower that smiles to-day / To-morrow will be dying."

What could be more charming?

❀ *"Daisy" comes from "day's eye" (because it opens in the morning).* ❀

Mind-Blowing Mind Reading for Everyone

Once when I was on my way to a conference in New York City, I told my cabdriver that I was a clairvoyant and personality reader. "For example," I said, "I have a strong sense that you grew up in Minnesota but moved to New Jersey when you were a young man." He was amazed and agreed that this was right, so I continued. "My vibrations tell me that you like pineapples, and baseball, and French fries, but dislike *Gone With the Wind* and foreign food. You have two daughters: Elizabeth, who practices the violin till it drives you nuts, and Camille, who has a boyfriend who grunts at you all the time. You are married to Mary-Sue, who is learning Spanish and wishes she had done more with her life. You've been a cabdriver for sixteen years, you love the city but not the tourists, and you think the government is doing an OK job. Your name is Valdo and your birthday is December 24." The driver went crazy and asked me, "How the hell did you read my mind like that?" so I said, "You told me the whole story yesterday, when you drove me downtown."

The point of this tale is that people are so amazed when you do something seemingly supernatural that they don't stop to ask themselves, *What is going on here?* One way of cashing in on this is to do a thing called the Forer reading. What you do is ask your subject to write out a dream in her own handwriting, or simply ask for her zodiac sign. After a time (for "analysis") you give her a copy of the unique personality reading you have done.

Now, just for a moment, imagine that this is being done to you, and gauge the following personality reading for accuracy:

You have a need for other people to like and admire you, and yet you tend to be critical of yourself. While you have some personality weaknesses you are generally able to compensate for them. You have considerable unused capacity that you have not turned to your advantage. Disciplined and self-controlled on the outside, you tend to be worrisome and insecure on the inside. At times you have serious doubts as to whether you have made the right decision or done the right thing. You prefer a certain amount of change and variety and become dissatisfied when hemmed in by restrictions and limitations. You also pride yourself as an independent thinker and do not accept others' statements without satisfactory proof. But you have found it unwise to be too frank in revealing yourself to others. At times you are extroverted, affable, and sociable, while at other times you are introverted, wary, and reserved. Some of your aspirations tend to be rather unrealistic.

Most people find this a spookily accurate description of themselves, yet it is a made-up reading, the invention of psychologist Bertram R. Forer. You will see, if you examine it, that for each assertion, such as, "Disciplined and self-controlled on the outside," there is a countervailing statement, such as, "You tend to be worrisome and insecure on the inside." Now, most of us are a mixture of things and this personality reading covers all the bases. The declaration, "Some of your aspirations tend to be rather unrealistic," must be true of almost everyone. Obviously, specific details such as, "You have never tasted popcorn," or "Your boyfriend is named Trevor and had some dental work done last Tuesday," or "Those blue shoes you bought at J. C. Penney last October won't match your dress for Jill's wedding next week" would spell trouble. It's the generalized plausibility of the description that makes it persuasive, combined with the natural desire to believe this sort of thing. Try it out on a new acquaintance.

Even spookier

Before you read further, I'd like you to get ahold of a blank sheet of paper and a pencil. Done that? OK, read on.

Let's suppose that you asked a friend to make two simple drawings on a piece of paper and then had her seal the drawing in an envelope. Could you read her mind and accurately reproduce those drawings? Well, let's try an experiment.

I want you, without thinking too hard, to quickly draw two simple geometric shapes, one inside the other. Ready? Go!

Done? I will now try to read your mind.

I'm getting a circle, yes, inside a square. Or is it the square inside the circle? There are some confusing *triangular* lifewaves, but the circle-square idea is very strong.

How did I do? Did I get at least one shape right? Both? Let's make it more interesting. Turn the paper over and quickly draw, without too much thinking, two simple drawings of *any two things* you like. Go!

Done? OK, let me see if I can read your mind.

I see something to do with people, yes? Like a building or a house. Is that a person you've drawn? I vaguely sense water. Maybe that's something to do with a boat? Fish? I'm getting the impression of a tree or flower. Cats climb trees, is that what I see—a four-legged animal, a dog, a horse? At first I saw a circle like the sun. No, I think what I said is right.

How did I do? Did I get both drawings right? Or only one of them? Of all the millions of things you could have drawn, I probably got pretty close. If so, let me tell you that you can do the same thing by making use of what psychologists call "population stereotypes." These are objects of the sort that typically leap into most people's minds if they have to quickly come up with something.

If you ponder for a moment, you will realize that beyond the circle, square, and triangle, it's not easy to recall many geometric shapes in a hurry, and very few people will think to draw an elongated pentagonal cupola inside a stellated cubicuboctahedron. The circle, square, and triangle are generally thought of in *that* order, and you can increase your chances of success by hurrying your subject a little.

When you are giving your reading, be suitably vague. You might say, "Is that a circle I see?" If you get a frown, move on: "No, I think a square?" until you get a smile of encouragement. This is called fishing for information. By asking for *two* shapes, you make it more likely that you will get at least *one* right.

But how about asking your subject to make two drawings of absolutely anything she pleases? Well, the same principle applies. Very few people will have time to draw—or want to draw—an alpenstock or a full-swage steel raceway rod end bearing. In fact, the most common drawings tend to come up a lot and the order in which they appear is remarkably reliable:

1   *House/building*
2   *Stick figure*
3   *Boat*
4   *Tree*
5   *Cat*
6   *Face*
7   *Fish*
8   *Flower*
9   *Sun*
10 *Dog/horse*

If you group things together in one vague guess, such as "Something to do with people?" and get a no, that is hugely useful information, allowing you to leap straight to number 4, the tree, which is the same thing as a flower for the purposes of your guess. Animals may also be lumped together; a fish and a boat likewise, if you mention water first.

After a little practice with friends, you will find that you get lots of unasked-for help. For example, people will subtly nod or smile, or carelessly flash their drawings at you, so take advantage. If you give your victim a *long* pencil, you can often get a clue to what it is she is drawing by watching the movements of the blunt end. As you can see, this mind-reading lark calls for a certain amount of multitasking, so it shouldn't present *you* with any big problems.

❀ *The original yellow of taxicabs was selected because it is the easiest color to spot.* ❀

How to

Play Chinese Roulette

*T*here is little evidence that anyone has ever actually played such a foolhardy game as Russian roulette, but it is generally described in literature as a recreation for six players, a revolver, and a bullet. The rules are that the first player inserts the bullet into a chamber and spins the cylinder. The gun then passes to the player on the left, who puts it to his or her temple and pulls the trigger. If it doesn't go bang, it is passed around until it *does*. Chinese roulette is exactly the same except that it is played with candies instead of a loaded revolver. It is therefore safer, if somewhat more fattening. Here are the rules.

REQUIRED

* *6 wrapped candies*
* *6 warped players*
* *A list of forfeits*
* *A pencil and paper*

INSTRUCTIONS

The six candies represent the imaginary revolver chambers. To "load the gun," the first player goes somewhere quiet and marks a black spot in the middle of a small square of paper. She then unwraps a piece of candy (taffy, chocolate, and gum will all do) and inserts the black spot before carefully rewrapping it so that it is indistinguishable from the others. She now puts the six candies into a dish and rejoins the other five players, passing the dish to the player on her left, who takes a candy and unwraps it. If it is "empty" she has survived. She eats the candy and passes the dish to her left.

Eventually someone will get the black spot, at which point things stop and she is given a forfeit off the list.

A FEW SUGGESTED FORFEITS

* *Persuade a stranger to buy you a drink (easy).*
* *Remove an item of underwear without leaving the room (tricky).*
* *Persuade a man in uniform to remove his jacket and tie (hard).*
* *Remove the left shoe from a man whose name begins with a particular letter and fill it with potato chips (very hard).*

A NOTE ON THE ODDS

If you want to increase your chances in Chinese roulette, an understanding of the odds will help. It looks as if you wouldn't want to be the sixth player because player number 1 has only a one in six chance (17%) of getting the black spot, player 2 a one in five chance (20%), player 3 a one in four chance (25%), player 4 a one in three chance (33.33%), player 5 a one in two chance (50/50) until player 6 who has a one in one chance of the black spot (100%). But this is not quite right.

Put it slightly differently and you'll see that player 1 has a five in six chance of survival, roughly 83 percent. But player 6 also has a five in six chance because each player before her might get the black spot, and one of them probably will. So, whether you play first (less chance of getting the black spot) or last (more chance of someone else getting it first), you have the same odds, an 83 percent chance of survival.

If you do go last you can watch your odds going down. With five players to go, your chances of survival are a cheerful 80 percent; with four to go, it's respectable odds of 75 percent; with three, a not-bad 66.67 percent; and even when there are only two remaining players, your odds are still even or 50/50, which is a lot better than any game you can play in the casino. Nonetheless, if everyone's had a turn and survived, and you find yourself last, I'm afraid the 83 percent chance you started with will have dropped to 0 percent. Put another way, it's 100 percent probable that you have lost. One advantage of Chinese roulette over the Russian sort, though, is that even the unlucky one can play again.

❀ *When added, the 36 numbers on a roulette wheel equal a spooky 666.* ❀

Skipping Games You Thought You'd Forgotten

S kipping games are as old as the hills. We used to spend hours at school jumping in and out of the whirling rope and I had a little puppy, his name was Tiny Tim; I put him in the bathtub to see if he could swim. He drank all the water; he ate a bar of soap—the next thing you know he had a bubble in his throat. In came the doctor; in came the nurse; in came the lady with the alligator purse. Sorry, I got completely caught up in a reverie there. How many girls even know what an alligator purse is these days, I wonder? Anyway, here is a guide to some of our finest skipping lore.

SOME SKIPPING TERMS EXPLAINED

* *Under the moon or front door*: Running into a revolving rope that rises away from the skipper as it hits the ground.
* *Over the moon or back door*: Running into a rope that rises toward the skipper.
* *Rope-rotation speed terms*: salt = slow; mustard = medium; vinegar = fast; pepper = very fast.
* *Keep the kettle boiling*: Skippers line up to jump into the rope, which maintains a steady rhythm. The rope should never be "empty."

RUN-AROUND (REQUIRES AT LEAST FIVE SKIPPERS)

The skippers split into two groups, forming a line on either side of the spinning rope. They now run in through the "front door," jumping once and leaving from the same side. They then run round the rope turner, go to the end of the line on the other side, and repeat the business.

FIVE, FOUR, THREE, TWO, ONE

This is an elimination game that gets harder as players drop out. On the first round each skipper enters the front door and leaves by the back door, running around the rope turner back to her place while everyone shouts: "Five, four, three, two, one." Skippers must jump as indicated. A hesitation or a miss means expulsion. All skippers have a go before a second round is begun. Here's how it goes (the italics represent the *jump*):

> First round: *Five*, four, *three*, two, *one*.
> Second round: *Four*, three, *two*, one.
> Third round: *Three*, two, *one*.
> Fourth round: *Two*, one.
> Fifth round: *One* and *one* and *one*, etc.

I LIKE COFFEE, I LIKE TEA

> I like coffee, I like tea,
> I like Matilda [more likely Britney or Madison, these days] in with me.

The nominee joins the skipper so that two are now skipping.

> One, two, three, *change places*, seven, eight, nine, *change places*, etc.

On the command "change places" the two change places until someone messes up. Keep score as you go along.

I'M A LITTLE BUMPER CAR

> I'm a little bumper car, number 48.
> I went round the coooooooooooorner,

Here the skipper jumps out, runs round the rope and rope turners, and then jumps back in while the chanters maintain their cry of "coooooooooooorner."

> And slammed on my brakes.
> A policeman caught me,
> And put me in jail.

How many bottles of ginger ale?
Ten, twenty, thirty, etc.

The rope is turned faster and faster until the skipper messes up or the whistle goes and you troop in for math. And, no, I don't know what the ginger ale business is all about either.

❈ *"Ten minutes' skipping is as good for you as a forty-five-minute run."* ❈

How to
Ride a Hippity-Hop in a Miniskirt

The 1970s seemed like Limbo when we were in them, but now everybody looks back through rose-tinted spectacles and says how wonderful it was to sit on a wall all day, bored rigid in purple flares—the *only* item of clothing ever to be refused by the Salvation Army on grounds of taste. Just count yourself lucky you're too young to remember them (if you are).

Amongst the stupid products available during the '70s was a device for flipping your LPs forward one at a time so you could select one (made by K-tel). This saved you having to use your finger. Then there was the legendary Brush-O-Matic, also made by K-tel, which—wait for it—brushed your clothes. All the boys rode bicycles called "Choppers," which had dangerous-looking gears situated between the seat and the handlebars, and all the girls bounced up and down on hippity-hops, huge inflatable orange balloons adorned with a silly face.

Hippity-hops, aka space hoppers, were fun, if slightly unladylike. We even had some at school, which we were encouraged to ride by Miss Snellgrove during warm-ups in PE. Miss Snellgrove was a gym mistress of such obviously Sapphic tendencies that we presumed she was really just hoping for a flash of bare thigh. She wore boots, I remember, had hair like Leonard Nimoy, smoked a pipe, and though her first name was Monica, insisted on being called Bernard. *I'm not making this up.* Anyway, you can still find hippity-hops here and there so here's the way to ride one in a miniskirt, based on the Snellgrove technique.

SNELLGROVE METHOD

1 *Lingerie choice*: Balance good looks with good coverage (just in case).

2 Straddle your hopper with feet on the ground in front to stabilize you, and the handle between your legs. Handles come in two forms: (A) twin horns and (B) a sort of spade handle. The latter will better conceal your undies.

3 Give a couple of gentle bounces to get a feel of the spring potential.

4 Leap into the air keeping the hopper between your legs, but instead of landing on your feet lift them up by bending your knees, landing instead on the hippity-hop's big round bum.

5 Place your feet back on the ground moments after you land and spring off for the next bounce.

6 Change direction by pushing off harder with your right foot (to turn left) and left to turn right.

7 *Always bounce with the wind behind you.* I've seen the skirts of careless girls simply blown inside out.

❀ *K-tel was founded in the 1960s in Winnipeg, Manitoba.* ❀

How to
Swing Upside-Down on a Trapeze

When I was young I used to have a wonderful book called *The Circus Comes to Town*. The pictures were so evocative that when the circus really did come to town I begged my parents to take me. The big top, the dashing ringmaster and hilarious clowns, the lions and tigers and gaudy elephants, the sawdust, the roar of the crowd—you know, all the stuff. Well, we ended up at a hideous municipal building—a malodorous aircraft hangar of a place—to witness Charlie Cairoli the famous unfunny Franco-British clown ending his career. There were no lions, no sawdust, and no big top. I do, however, remember a troupe of trapeze artists in sparkling costumes, but I may have transplanted them into my memory from their exciting page in *The Circus Comes to Town*.

Anyway, in case you decide, after all, not to work in a call center but to become a magnificent woman on the flying trapeze instead, here are the basics. *Please* use a safety net.

HANGING BY YOUR KNEES

1   Grab the bar with both hands and start swinging until you have a bit of momentum going.

2   When you're ready, pull up your knees between your chest and the bar. Slide your feet over the bar so that it finishes behind your bent knees. Bring your heels close to your thighs. Maintain a good swing as you do this, if you possibly can.

3   Keeping your knees tightly bent, let go with your hands and uncurl your body as gracefully as possible, letting your arms fall toward the floor.

4   Keep swinging by alternately arching your back and throwing your arms forward.

BEING CAUGHT BY A MAN

1 Facing away from each other, you must now swing toward each
   other very carefully. Timing is of the essence: you must meet at the
   highest point of your swings. Don't go too fast or you'll both crack
   your heads open.

2 As the person being caught, you have the responsibility of helping
   the catcher. Arch your back with your head thrown back and your
   arms above you in a rigid pose like Superwoman.

3 With your head thrown all the way back, you'll see everything
   back-to-front and upside-down. Just as you are getting used to this
   crazy view you will become aware of a man in a leotard (your partner) hurtling toward you unstoppably, like a demolition ball on the
   end of a chain. As soon as you feel him grab your wrists, release

your knees so that your trapeze is freed, swinging away "empty." You will now be dangling—and swinging—dramatically from the arms of your catcher, high above the crowd.

4   If he misses or drops you, try to land in a safety net rather than on a concrete floor, which can be somewhat unforgiving.

❀ *The French acrobat Jules Léotard invented the leotard.* ❀

V

Knock 'Em Dead

Be Blindingly Beautiful

I have flabby thighs, but fortunately my stomach covers them.

JOAN RIVERS

A Quick Guide to Proper Deportment

When he was a little boy, my friend Antonio was made to eat spaghetti while balancing the *Dizionario Enciclopedico Italiano* on his head. Now he has beautiful manners, deports himself with élan, and hardly ever pinches girls' bottoms.

In years gone by, deportment was a big thing in the United States, too, especially for young ladies—a whole industry revolved around it and you wouldn't be seen dead in the street without pearls. This was the time when Swiss finishing schools and charm establishments for girls would groom debutantes-to-be in the niceties of polite manners, etiquette, and posture, when elocution lessons were de rigueur for those unlucky enough to have been born common but who wished to improve their lot. When I was growing up, our own version of the Italian encyclopedia trick was to get a young lady, coifed and gowned, to promenade in front of her peers without the hardback edition of the *Collins Book of Birds* falling off her noddle.

Anyhow, here is a quick rundown of the basics. I've devoted another whole section to the proper way to get out of a car without showing your skivvies (see page 31). Otherwise, these pointers are pretty straightforward and easy to grasp.

BEARING

Posture is vital to get right. Shuffling around in a plastic rain hat and grandma coat with a Wal-Mart shopping bag in each hand is guaranteed to make you look bad, but compound it by slumping forward and staring at your feet, and you'll never impress the duke.

The general principle is to stand erect: shoulders back, stomach in, buttocks in, back and neck straight but not rigid. Ears, shoulders, hips, knees, and ankles should be of columnar straightness. A plumb line hung from your earlobe should pass right through the middle of your ankle.

See page 22 for advice on high heels, which will help you stand straight.

CONDUCT

1   Don't eat with your elbows on the table. Your mom was right.

2   When eating soup, tip bowl and spoon *away* from yourself.

3   Affect confidence and look people in the eye when you speak to them.

4   Don't point with your finger—not because it's rude but because it is masculine. Use your whole hand or incline your head in the intended direction. Imitate the way the women do it on the weather forecast.

5   An instruction from 1845 still applies today: *Never scratch your head, pick your teeth, clean your nails, or worst of all, pick your nose in company; all these things are disgusting. Spit as little as possible—and never upon the floor.* That last is particularly important. If there's one golden rule, more important than all the others put together, it's *that* one.

❀ *Burping is also known as belching, ructus, or eructation.* ❀

How to
Give Yourself a Brazilian Wax

N amed after the country where it originated, the Brazilian wax is an especially thorough bikini wax, informally known as the "G-wax" or plain "Brazilian." It differs from the common or garden-variety bikini wax in that practically all the hair is removed from the pubic and bumular area, with just a narrow strip being left behind, like a wisteria blossom over the front door. It's important not to confuse the Brazilian with the so-called Hollywood, Sphynx, or smoothie, which is a total slash-and-burn wax.

Arab, Turkish, and Persian women as well as Albanian and Mediterranean ladies have been waxing like gooduns for centuries, and there is now even a male version called the "boyzilian" or, charmingly, "back, crack, and sack." The ancients used sugar-based waxes for their waxes, but you will be using a wax-based wax.

You can purchase kits all over the place, which use either hard or soft wax. With soft wax, a muslin or cotton strip is pressed firmly on top of

the wax and pulled off once it has cooled. The hard-
wax technique requires no strips—you just
hang on to the hardened (still pliable) wax
and pull. Whereas soft wax can be sticky
and leave behind a residue, hard wax
will not do this and is therefore gen-
tler and less painful, gripping the hair
without adhering to the skin.

The first time you do a Brazilian
wax, take a couple of painkillers
half an hour before. This will ease
things a little. Some waxees report
mild post-wax "Brazilian itch" (or
"Britch"), but it's otherwise an innocuous
process. Remember though: never reapply wax to an already waxed area.
Ouch!

Here's the way to create the perfect bikini wax in the privacy of your
home, and at a fraction of the cost of a salon visit. Start at the front and
move toward the back, not forgetting to leave a little landing strip, as described. You'll need to adopt all sorts of odd positions to get at everything, but do not be tempted to cut corners by using gaffer tape. The
results can be unsightly.

All right then, girls, good luck!

REQUIRED
* *Store-bought bikini waxing kit (hard wax recommended)*
* *A microwave oven*
* *A few wooden or plastic spatulas (not kitchen size—smallish)*

INSTRUCTIONS
1   Take a shower and trim the hair. You only need about ¼ inch for
    the wax to grab hold of.
2   Heat the (hard) wax in the microwave according to the instruc-
    tions. Stir until it's thick and honeylike, but don't allow it to get too

hot or you'll hurt yourself. Test the temperature with a finger before you put any of it on to your bikini area.

3   Using a spatula, apply a thick layer of wax in the direction of hair growth and allow it to cool for half a minute or so, until it is still pliable—follow the instructions on the label.

4   Now for the moment of truth: hold the skin taut and pull the wax away in one swift motion against the direction of growth, thus tearing the hairs out by their roots. Oh dear, just thinking about it makes your eyes water, doesn't it.

5   Immediately apply firm pressure to the waxed area with fingers or palm so as to lift off any remaining particles of wax.

6   Finally, tweeze out any stray hairs.

7   Once you've finished, spread a soothing lotion over waxed areas.

Waxing should take between twenty and thirty minutes and will last up to two months before stubble appears, allowing you to wear a minimalistic bikini without having to worry about taking a comb along to the beach. In this respect it's better than shaving, which will have you scratching like a squirrel within a couple of hours.

❈ *Brazil is the fifth largest country in the world.* ❈

How to
Make a Little Black Dress Out of a Garbage Bag

The little black dress was invented by Coco Chanel in 1926 and has been fantastically popular for more than eighty years. Asked once by journalists about her creation, Ms. Chanel commented, "Scheherazade is easy. The little black dress is hard." This reminds me of one of those quotes they put on final exams and then say, "Discuss," leaving you stunned and speechless owing to the utter vacuity of the material.

The LBD is always flattering and suits almost any occasion or venue, from cocktail party to casino. It can be worn by anyone, knowing no social, style, or size boundaries, and like all the classics its secret is simplicity. It can be serious, chic, *and* sexy, and will outlast all your trendy frocks without itself ever going out of style. You can even add jewelry, from pearls to plastic and it will still look good. To fashion one from a garbage bag in an emergency, just follow these simple steps.

REQUIRED
* *2 large, black garbage bags*
* *Scotch tape*
* *Sharp scissors*
* *Gaffer tape*

INSTRUCTIONS
1   Turn one bag bottom-up and cut a hole in the middle, large enough for your head to fit through.

2   Cut the front artistically into a scoop or V-neck. Keep your cuts smooth and flowing; you want a clean line, not lots of little snippy snips.

3   Cut armholes at each side to produce the classic sleeveless sheath. The holes should be large enough to allow your arms to slip through comfortably without cutting off the circulation and turning them white and cold. For the busy woman, those bags with the black handles at the sides are a godsend, providing ready-made neckline and armholes. All you need to do is cut the bottom out for your legs. But beware of bags with a white plastic drawstring, which are neither useful nor attractive.

4   Decorate the shoulder seam with a wide 6-inch strip cut from another garbage bag. Tie into a small bow at each shoulder. *Note*: Less is more. When it comes to bows think Jackie Kennedy, not Minnie Pearl.

5   Nip the dress in at the waist with a couple of lengths of doubled-over bag taped together to form a belt. This is easier if you have it on at the time. Don't attempt to approach the project like a tailor with a bit of chalk. You can't chalk a shiny garbage bag.

6   The dress should be knee length. For the hemline there is a choice of classy finishes:
    (A) a straight slit up one side or up the back.
    (B) tapered length, higher at the front than the back or higher on one side than the other.

For that supermodel look, cut a hole for your head as above then split the bag down each side seam from the shoulder (use a sharp knife or scissors. You don't want a raggedy old tear). Place the dress over your head, and securely tape the seams closed at the side, using strips of gaffer tape in an accent color (maybe matching your handbag or lipstick). This will produce a flesh-revealing gap—so make sure you put the tape on such that you cover all the parts you'd prefer to keep under wraps.

*   Keep legs bare or wear sheer stockings.
*   Add classic earrings, and maybe a minimal silver or gold necklace or some pearls. The little black dress is made for teaming with your accessories.
*   Do not iron.

ACCESSORIES

You've done the difficult part now and the world is your oyster, or at least your clam. So here are a few ideas for accessories, starting with the simplest:

Belt: Take a long 3- or 4-inch-wide strip and double it over, securing with Scotch tape. Now, with the tape on the *inside*, bring the ends around your waist to the front and, keeping it simple, trim off the raggedy bits and tape the terminals down. A buckle can be easily made from the lid of a small square food container, such as the white plastic ones with Mr. Tupper's patented "burping seal."

Hat: I recommend simply snipping off the corner so that you get a conical piece just big enough to go on your head, crease pointing forward, of course. A few stuck-on plastic grapes add a touch of elegance that's hard to beat. You'll look just like Eleanor Roosevelt.

Purse: This is perhaps trickiest of all. You'll certainly have enough for a voluminous container if, like my grandma, you like to carry with you everything you might ever conceivably need, marooned on a desert island for thirty years. The best way to approach this is to cut a horizontal piece from the bottom of the bag and divide this in two vertically. Tape the open vertical seam closed and add a couple of straps (see belt instructions above). For security, you can make a closing flap by cutting another piece to fit and taping it into position. Don't put any melons or other heavy objects in the bag or the straps will be off before you can say "Botheration!" and your makeup and possessions will be broadcast across the sidewalk.

CLOTHING ITEMS *NOT* TO MAKE FROM A GARBAGE BAG

Garbage bag shoes are utilitarian and un-pretty, they look like big black balloons, and they make *you* look like Minnie Mouse. Pants are capaciously flowing, but not very breathable. There is one item of clothing, though, that you must *never* try to make from a garbage bag, and that is a pair of panties. It's just like wearing a greenhouse: the steam and condensation are simply intolerable, and the noise you make as you walk has to be heard to be believed.

❀ *Coco Chanel's real name was Gabrielle.* ❀

How to
Braid Your Hair:
The Plait Ordinaire

*T*he braid, or plait, has never really gone out of style. If it was good enough for Cleopatra, it should be good enough for anyone.

In case you've never braided your own hair, here's a guide. It's easiest to get the hang of this by trying it out on someone else first.

REQUIRED
* *Ouchless hair elastics*
* *Hairbrush*

* *A hair clip to secure layers and stray strands (a bulldog clip will do in an emergency)*

INSTRUCTIONS

Once you get a rhythm going, the plait ordinaire is easy. Your hair should be fairly long (or what's to braid?), and dry.

1 Brush your hair to remove tangles. Takes about five hours.
2 Sweep it back into the nape and divide into three equal clumps (Fig. A).
3 Take two clumps in your left hand (separated by a finger), and the third in your right. Bring your right hand over the top of the middle bunch and pass the right hand clump to your left hand, while passing the middle clump to your right hand. (Does that even begin to make sense?) You should now have two bunches in your left hand again, only they're different bunches than when you started (Fig. B).
4 Cross the outside clump in your left hand over the new middle clump. You can use your right hand to grab this and bring it over, leaving two bunches in your right hand (Fig. C). (Get the idea?)

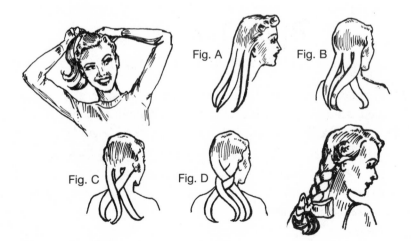

Fig. A

Fig. B

Fig. C

Fig. D

5   Pass the outside right bunch, over the middle.

6   You should now be looking at something resembling a plait. If you are looking at what looks like an explosion in a horsehair sofa factory, something's gone wrong. Anyway, let's presume you're doing OK. Keep crossing right over center and then left over center (Fig. D). This is the key to understanding the braid.

7   When you run out of hair, tie it off or secure with an elastic: a nice one, not one of those worm-colored things the postman dropped on the path.

The plait ordinaire is good for creating curls if you sleep with the braid in.

❊ *Two of Cleopatra's several husbands were her brothers.* ❊

How to
French Braid:
The Plait Français

Bodybuilding competitions for women began with such galas as the *Miss Physique* show, which looked to me like an old-fashioned bikini contest with added protein. But as the years rolled on, the iron was increasingly pumped by bodybuilding women until their biceps sprang out like Cornish pasties, their tummies rippled, and some of them became hard to tell from Arnold Schwarzenegger before he became an intellectual and went into politics.

The reason I mention this is that the plait Français (sometimes known as the French braid) requires the elevation of your arms for absolutely ages and is utterly exhausting. All the blood flows out of your hands and the limbs begin to ache wearily; after a bit they start to wave around of their own accord like reeds in a pond, and finally they wither and drop, numb and lifeless, often falling heavily on your head and knocking your glasses off. But are you going to be so easily put off, or are you ready to join the ranks of bionic women, Miss Physique, and the

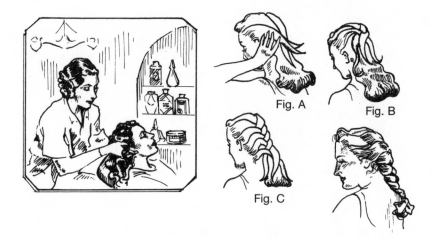

Fig. A

Fig. B

Fig. C

steely plaiters of purpose, and put your hair up in the plait Français? Oh good, that's what I hoped you'd say.

The main difference between the plait ordinaire (see previous entry) and the plait Français is that, rather than just three strands of hair, more hair is introduced to the braid as you proceed. If you are doing it on yourself, remember that stamina is required.

INSTRUCTIONS

1   Separate the front part of your hair (including the sides) from the hair at the rear, pull the separated hair back to the crown, and divide it into three equal clumps (Fig. A).

2   To start, do a quick left-over-center, right-over-center (as in the plait ordinaire). Don't bother being neat when you are learning (Fig. B). Most early efforts look like the work of one of those blind basket weavers the first time they try it. Once you're into your stride, you can begin to concentrate on maintaining tension and clump size, and things will begin to tidy themselves up a bit.

3   As you continue, add extra hair taken *from directly underneath each new section* that is about to be crossed over. Pick up the same amount each time. Use your little finger to separate the clumps.

This will let you hold the main hair firmly while you pick up the new hair. Your plait will follow the curve of the head as you go (Fig. C).

4　Keep on until you reach the nape and you've used up all the hair.

5　Finish with a regular braid and secure with an elastic.

❊ *The main component of hair is keratin, just like fingernails.* ❊

How to
Put Your Hair in a Bun

W hen I was young and foolish I used to think that ladies who wore their hair in a bun had to be at least sixty and possibly German. Maybe it was something to do with the word "bun": sort of auntyish and brown, redolent of knitting needles, tweed skirts, and long gray Sunday afternoons destitute of interest, activity, or anything except the perfume of dust, old meats, and denture cream. It seemed to me the look to avoid.

Then one day I saw a tall gazelle-like young woman slinking down the street in a most alluring way that I kind of wanted to emulate. She had—I found it hard to believe—her hair in a bun. As I watched her disappear around the corner she withdrew from her tress a long pin, and shook down the hair all over her shoulders, like Sophia Loren in some film or other. *Aha*, I thought, *buns can be cool.*

If you'd like to try it, here are the instructions. You'll be really pleased to learn that you don't need to be neat when you're making a bun. A sort of wanton messed-up look is much better. Your hair, though, must be longer than shoulder-length.

INSTRUCTIONS

1　Finger-rake your hair back into a ponytail at the nape of your neck. This will give you a reckless, casual girl-about-town look. If you're after that prim-librarian-who-nevertheless-goes-wild-after-hours look then brush, for a neater effect. Secure with an elastic.

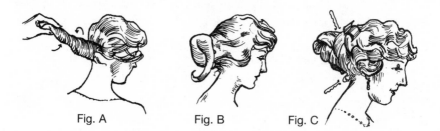

Fig. A   Fig. B   Fig. C

2   Twist the tail until the hair begins to bind and stiffen, recoiling on itself (Fig. A).

3   You can encourage a messy finish now if you pull a few short strands from near the ends of the ponytail.

4   Wrap the tail around on itself in the nape to make the bun (Fig. B).

5   Poke the end under the original covered band and then fix with a hairpin or grip. Don't use a clothespin; it looks bad (Fig. C).

You can vary the look, and still turn heads, by sweeping the hair up into a bun at the rear from a low side parting or making a bun of just the crown of your hair and leaving the rest dangling seductively.

❋ *The Chelsea bun was created in the eighteenth century at the Chelsea Bun House.* ❋

How to
Make an Ice Cube Necklace

*D*id you hear about the guy on the *Titanic*, who said to the barman, "I know I ordered ice but this is *ridiculous*"? Well, what with this climate-change business it's a wonder there's any ice still to be had. Nonetheless, should you be able to lay your hands on a cube or two, here's a delightfully simple and pretty trick you can do to wow your friends. It's suitable for performing in a lively bar or restaurant, or at the domestic dinner table when the conversation evaporates.

REQUIRED

* *A necklace-length piece of string*
* *A glass of ice*
* *A little salt*

INSTRUCTIONS

1   Remove four or five ice cubes from your glass and position them close together in a neat line on the tablecloth in front of you.

2   Wet the string by dipping it in your glass and lay it across the tops of the ice cubes, leaving two trailing ends.

3   Ask someone to pass the salt, and sprinkle it liberally over the ice cubes.

4   Now for the suspense. Wait for ten seconds or so, then lift the string by its ends and the ice cubes will hang from it like gigantic rough diamonds, stuck fast.

5   Arrange it around the neck of a willing friend, tying it in back, and say, "*Cool* necklace!" They'll think you're *so* amusing.

Why does it happen? Good question. In case you're interested, liquid water solidifies (freezes) at 32°F but sprinkling salt on an ice cube lowers its freezing point to well below 32°F (don't ask why) and the ice therefore melts. The melting water then washes away some of the salt and the freezing point rises again such that the water refreezes, binding the string between the two ice layers.

The trick isn't exactly impromptu, because you need to carry the string in your purse, but once you've practiced a couple of times, you'll be able to cause a bit of a stir with it. I even saw a friend of mine do it with a long man's shoelace—a long *lace* that is, not a long man; do try to keep up.

❀ *A soccer ball–size lump of ice fell on Aurora, Nebraska, on June 22, 2003.* ❀

How to
Pluck Your Eyebrows

*A*s Ariel says in *The Tempest*, "Where the bee plucks, there pluck I," and who can blame him? There's something singularly architectural about a plucked eyebrow that neither mascara nor subcutaneous Botox can match. A really artistic pluck will draw attention to your eyes, just like a good picture frame, emphasizing and "enlarging" the peepers and delineating the bone structure of your brow line. Heavy-duty plucking will be required to subjugate a vigorous brow-bush or divide a unibrow. But while a touch of elegance or neatness is fine, don't go mad. The biggest mistake is to pluck to near baldness or to leave two insectoid "antennae" over your eyes. Eyebrows can take months to regrow so go careful; leave more than a paltry scribble there on the outcrop. Here's the way the experts do it.

REQUIRED
* *Eyebrow pencil*
* *Proper angled eyebrow tweezers*

INSTRUCTIONS
1 You need good lighting. Full sun is best, so sit near a window. Don't sit 1 inch from the mirror all the time. Lean back every now and again to have a look at your whole face and the general effect.
2 Wash your eyebrows with soap. This will make them thicker and easier to grasp.
3 Plan. Decide the shape you want and draw a guideline on your eyebrows, using an eyebrow pencil. The eyebrow should start at a point in line with the inner corner of your eye. Good rules of thumb are to make them thicker in the middle, and taper them in an elegant swoop to a point on the outside edge. Pluck a smooth, attractive arch, the highest point of which you can estimate by visualizing a line running from the corner of your nose at its junction with your cheek, through the centre of your pupil. Your brows will look most

attractive if they extend a little beyond the corner of each eye. The space in between should be not less than an eye's width. Have a look at the models in your favorite magazine and copy theirs. (Not Marilyn Manson.)

4   Use a pair of proper eyebrow tweezers. Doing it with pliers is bound to end in tears, and pluck hairs from *below* your brow, not from above.

5   Pull the skin tight at the temple and begin plucking in the middle of the eyebrow. Move toward the outer end, plucking only one hair at a time. Return to the middle and pluck toward the nose. Do a little bit of each eyebrow at a time. That way you'll get a balanced appearance instead of one big fat one and one skinny little one.

6   Finally, rub your newly nudified brows with some cotton balls dipped in an astringent such as witch hazel.

❀ *The oldest known tweezers date from the third century BCE.* ❀

How to
Lose Six Pounds in Six Hours

M aybe you've got an impending weekly weigh-in at the diet club or someone's sprung a blind date on you for tonight and you simply *must* get into those jeans that, at the best of times, require you to lie on the floor and writhe into them while two friends with pliers stand by ready to close the zip. If that's the case, here's the answer.

LEVEL ONE

*   *Sit in a sauna (often good for a pound or two).*
*   *Take diuretics (dandelion or nettle tea).*
*   *Cut hair short.*
*   *Dress light: no belt (obviously); wear diaphanous dress.*

LEVEL TWO

* *Leave glasses off.*
* *Wear cheap air-filled flip-flops instead of those huge great heavy sandals.*
* *Remove all jewelry, including tiny earrings, nose piercing, and wedding ring.*
* *Cut hair extremely short.*
* *Give blood (an armful weighs quite a lot). Refuse juice and cookies!*
* *Swap big undies for tiny thongs, crotchless panties, or net bikini bottoms.*
* *Go braless.*

LEVEL THREE (DESPERATE LAST-FEW-OUNCE MEASURES)

* *Cut or bite toe- and fingernails way down.*
* *Pluck eyebrows.*
* *Shave legs.*
* *Do a Brazilian wax (see page 214).*
* *Turn up in G-string (or go commando), and bare feet.*
* *Remove makeup.*
* *Blow nose.*
* *Pick scabs.*
* *Clean ears.*
* *Shave any remaining body hair.*
* *Read something sad and have a good cry.*
* *Shave head.*
* *Exfoliate—twice.*
* *Squeeze pimples.*
* *File hard skin from bottom of feet.*
* *Spit.*
* *Breath out last lungful of air before getting on the scales—tiny droplets of water vapor escaping may just tip the scales in your favor.*

Failing all these, have your legs amputated.

❀ *The parent company of Weight Watchers is H. J. Heinz.* ❀

How to
Buy the Right Size Bra

When I was chatting to the Queen of England recently I told her about the problem her female subjects sometimes have in getting hold of a bra that fits properly. You know, one that doesn't drive you mad by digging in like an elastic band round a raw sausage and extruding great squashy pads of fat. But it was no use; she couldn't hear me up on that balcony.

Despite her wry comment that, "I have to be seen to be believed," the Queen actually gets the best advice going when it comes to braland. I know this because in 1960, while she was granting Somalia its independence, she bestowed on Rigby & Peller—the famous Knightsbridge bra firm—the Royal Warrant of Appointment, making them her official "corsetieres" and augmenting her own role as Britain's titular head.

SIZING

Rigby & Peller say that some 80 percent of the women who come to them for an expert fitting are wearing bras that don't fit, which *I* could have told them. You should see my red one with the raggedy straps: it's like being in a straitjacket. They recommend getting the thing properly fitted, and they also believe that a tape measure leaves a great deal to be desired when calculating bra size. Because so much hangs on the measurements and because we are all different—with a limitless diversity of body shapes—a tape measure can be only a crude guide.

It cannot be overstated that having your bra professionally fitted is by far the best way to do it. Women change shape and size over time, sometimes dramatically, so you should have a proper fitting regularly. Try on a range of styles from different brands: you'll find that some cuts will fit you better than others.

WORKING OUT WHAT FITS YOUR BITS

1   To make life difficult, there is no such thing as a definitive bra size. The size varies along with the style and fabric.

2   To put on a new bra, bend over and lower your ladies into the cups. Then stand up and wriggle about a bit in the old-fashioned way, tucking in anything that's still hanging out.

3   Fasten the bra on the loosest hooks to start with—so long as the band is snug. It will loosen up with wearing, washing, and wriggling. As it does so you can go tighter. If you have a plump back, three hooks are better than two.

4   Bras should be *hand washed*. Never tumble dry or hang on a radiator.

5   The band should lie snugly against the narrowest part of your back, in the middle, and level with the bra front. If the fit is correct you should be able to run your finger along the inside without having to saw it off to get it out again.

6   Try on your bra under a tight-fitting top. You should look smooth and curvy. If you look like a bag of jackfruit, something's wrong.

7   Underwires should curve comfortably around your breasts. They should never cut in. To test whether it is doing its job properly, put the bra on and push against the wire. If it yields softly, it is resting on your breast, so try a larger cup size. If it feels hard, it is lying against the chest wall, which is where you want it.

8   Move around in your new bra and lift your arms over your head. It shouldn't ride up, spill anything out, stop providing support, or get all out of whack.

9   Common problems include the "bulging tire" effect that comes from too tight a band, and the "hot cross bun" effect that comes from too small a cup.

10   If your breasts are spilling out the front, or your silhouette is lumpen, or you're falling out of the bottom of an underwire, try a bra with a smaller back and larger cups.

11   If the bra is loose round the edges, try a smaller cup size.

12   If the band is riding up your back or if your straps are cutting in, try a smaller back size.

13 If the underwire is digging in below your armpit, try a bigger cup size.

14 If you have large breasts, non-stretch straps will provide a more dependable hold.

15 If your size goes up and down (this is common), get a bra with some stretch in it. If you have large fluctuations, get yourself some bras of different sizes.

16 Try a variety of bras for miscellaneous outfits and occasions: seamless, strapless, sports . . .

Finally, please remember that these are only tips and guidelines. The main point to keep in mind is that DIY in this department is unlikely to work for you. In fact, you will probably make a complete mess of things. So fling away that tape measure and go and get a proper fitting from the professionals. You'll be glad you did.

❀ *Mae West spent two hours a day rubbing cold cream onto her breasts.* ❀

How to
Do the Pencil Test

Until his retirement, my Uncle Bob was a salesman for a stationery company. In his spare time he was also an expert snooker player, winning numerous trophies. When I was a teenager he used to take me along to pubs and snooker halls around the country to help him carry his cues, and it was during a tournament lull in a musty village hall that he first introduced me to the history of the pencil. I remember him telling me that the earliest pencils were produced in Keswick round about 1558 but that it was the Italians who developed the wooden "holder."

Uncle Bob told me that owing to the preponderance of pencils in his house his second wife had become obsessed with the pencil test and that she used to stand for hours in front of her bedroom mirror, appraising her performance over and over and over. If you haven't heard about—or tried—the pencil test, here is your chance to try it. It's a simple test designed to discover the condition and pertness of the female bust, and you can do it on, and for, yourself at a moment's notice.

REQUIRED
A pencil. The best pencils for the purpose are of smooth uncoated wood. Painted pencils have a greater predisposition to "cling," thus skewing results.

INSTRUCTIONS
1   Go upstairs (if you have an upstairs) and make sure you will not be disturbed.
2   Take your clothes off and stand in front of a full-length mirror.
3   Place a wooden pencil horizontally under your breast of preference at its junction with the chest.
4   Stand still.

RESULTS ANALYSIS
A correctly positioned pencil that nonetheless falls is an indicator of top-quality upwardly pointing glands. Either the bra-wearing stage has not yet been reached (you must be young), or you are in extra fine fettle pertness-wise. If the pencil is held in place by the weight of the breast and does not fall (no jiggling allowed), then you have failed the test. However, this *should not* be seen as a critique of physique—possibly quite the reverse. Jayne Mansfield was a pencil-test failer of the first order if ever I saw one and she was a centerfold girl. Nonetheless, it is important to note that if the pencil can be removed only by pulling with both hands and rolling about on the floor, then a really good uplifting bra is in order, and should be *on* order.

THE VERTICAL OR MAE WEST TEST
This one is for the ambitious.

Put on your most alluring bra and insert a pencil vertically into the cleavage. If it is held without falling, the cleavage is perfect.

❈ *The world's biggest pencil, on display in Malaysia, is 65 feet long.* ❈

How to
Shave Your Legs Properly

During the Elizabethan age, a shaved forehead and eyebrows were all the rage and, together with her gorgeous long black teeth, Queen Elizabeth I sported a famously high forehead, which she may have shaved to accommodate those tall wigs. I don't know what her legs looked like because they were always under her skirts plugged into a pair of fine silk stockings, which in 1560 she liked "so well, because they are pleasant, fine and delicate, that henceforth I will wear no more cloth stockings." But I have the feeling that Liz's lallies were unshaved and looked a bit like a man's in tights.

The modern trend for bald legs and armpits really took off in the May 1915 edition of *Harper's Bazaar*, which pictured a model with hairless underarms in a sleeveless evening gown. By the 1920s razor companies were running campaigns to persuade flappers that hirsuteness was unfeminine and over successive decades, with rising hemlines and increasingly visible lower limbs, women reached more and more for the razor. During World War II, a shortage of nylons led to young ladies shaving their legs so as to facilitate the simulation of stocking seams by nifty use of the eyebrow pencil.

In olden days, a glimpse of stocking was looked on as something shocking, now, heaven knows, the sky's the limit and the celebrity trend for waxing anything that moves has resulted in the nowadays commonplace "Brazilian" (partial) and "Hollywood" (total) below-the-belt depilation.

But let's stick to old-fashioned legs for the moment. There are a few tips that will make the shaving experience nicer for you, though I can't promise that a man in a Ferrari will instantaneously whisk you off to a romantic dinner the moment you've finished. Indeed, I'm reminded of Deana Carter's lugubrious country song "Did I Shave My Legs for This?" But never mind, we might as well be hopeful, so here are the vitals.

1   Use a really good razor. Go for the big brands.
2   Exfoliate before shaving: exfoliation—the removal of dead skin—can prevent ingrowing hairs. It also makes your pins *look* better.
3   Soak your legs for at least three minutes before shaving: water softens the hair.
4   Use a proper thick shaving gel or foam (men's works as well as women's). Soap is insufficiently lubricious, but hair conditioner will do the job nicely.
5   Rinse your razor after each stroke.
6   Change your razor often.
7   Work from the ankles up for the closest shave unless your skin is irritated by shaving, in which case shave in the direction of hair growth.
8   Shave slowly, there's no hurry.
9   Watch out around your ankles, it's easy to nick yourself. Styptic pencil!
10   Always moisturize afterward.

❀ *The leg's interosseous membrane separates its front and back muscles* ❀

How to
Give Yourself
a French Manicure

The observation that a man's index finger is generally shorter than his ring finger, and that the reverse is true for a woman, was first recorded in the nineteenth century. Recent research has also suggested that finger ratio can be an indicator of aggression. The bigger the gap between a short index and a long ring finger, the more aggressive (*read* masculine). And it is certainly true that short stubby fingers covered in oil and holding a ratchet look masculine, and long, slim well-manicured ones appear feminine.

The instructions in this section will tell you how to achieve the acme of elegant home manicure, and long-looking fingers, without having to take out a mortgage at the salon—just the cost of your nail polish.

Women have been doing their nails for at least 5,000 years, according to something I read somewhere, but the origin of the "French manicure" is a bit hazy. "French" is one of those appellations beloved of advertisers and marketing people because it gives a flavor of sophisticated chic to everything from kissing to fries. No surprises then that the cosmetics company Orly first registered the trademark "Original French Manicure" for a home manicure kit in 1978, and that the "Frenchie" is one of the most asked for manicures in the salons of today.

The thing that sets the French manicure apart is the milky white tip to the nail, which, in combination with the characteristic "nude" pink bit, emphasizes its length.

To complete your own perfect French manicure, just follow the steps below. But make sure your nails are in a decent state before you start. Be honest: if you are an incorrigible nail-biter you might do best investigating the fakery at the salon. And if you are a harpist or work in the potting shed all day then long nails are just a pest; better read another page.

Whatever you do, please *practice* your Frenchie before going out on a date with a new gentleman. You don't want to raise your glass with fingers that look as if Jackson Pollock's been painting them.

REQUIRED
* *White nail polish*
* *Clear or "nude" nail polish*
* *A cuticle stick*
* *Nail scissors (or clippers)*
* *A nail file and fine emory board*
* *Self-adhesive stationer's hole reinforcers*

INSTRUCTIONS

1   Before you start painting your nails, remove any old nail polish, using ordinary nail polish remover and a cotton ball.

2   Wash your hands and soak your fingers in a bowl of warm water for a while to allow the skin and nails to soften up a little (if they prune you've gone too far), then give them a thorough dry.

3   Using a cuticle stick, or something else designed for the purpose, gently push back the cuticles so they are neatly in line.

4   Carefully trim and shape your nails with scissors, clippers, nail file, and fine emory board. Then give them a quick rinse and dry.

5   Now for the tricky part. Paint the tip of each nail with white nail polish. You need a confident and purposeful movement from a steady hand. It can be tricky, but here's a brilliant dodge: peel off one of your hole reinforcers and tear it in half. Stick this to the end of your nail such that it provides a mathematically perfect radius guide to the curve. Paint the white in the little gap at the end of the nail and then wave your hand around and blow on it a bit in the usual way until the polish becomes tacky. Depending on the polish's opacity, you may need another coat, but let the first dry or you'll be in a right old mess. Carefully peel off the sticker and *presto!* a nice crisp edge.

6   Once all your white tips are done, paint the whole nail with a clear or translucent pale pink "nude" color. Don't do it all splodgy—about three strokes is all you need. The first straight down the middle, the next two down the sides. Then leave well enough alone. The brushwork will look a bit Impressionist for a while, but it gradually blears into a smooth finish. You may find you need a couple of coats, but don't keep trying to fiddle with it; you'll ruin it and have to start all over again. It's usually now that a man will wander in asking you to hold a wet fishing net or carboniferous piece of exhaust pipe. Don't. Neither should you be tempted to start scrubbing the doorstep or cleaning the dust bunnies from under your bed. Watch a bit of mindless TV or something instead and wait until the polish is good and dry.

Once everything's hardened, apply a clear final coat to protect your glamorous French manicure. You can improve its durability by painting on a new topcoat each night. You can't keep this up forever though or you'll have horrible scabrous nails an inch thick.

❀ *Fingernails are made of a tough protein called keratin.* ❀

The Imelda Marcos Guide to Shoes

During the 1992 Republican National Convention, Pat Robertson treated everyone to the benefit of his intellectual thoughtfulness. "The feminist agenda," he announced, "encourages women to leave their husbands, kill their children, practice witchcraft, destroy capitalism, and become lesbians." Some felt he was going a bit far, and in 2006, in a defiant bid to show Mr. Robertson what feminists are really like, the 77-year-old Imelda Marcos—former first lady of the Philippines—launched a range of jewelry, bags, and sneakers, which she selflessly christened the Imelda Collection. The Imelda Collection's very pink and possibly not-all-that-feminist website says: "It is from the detritus of her colorful life, from the flotsam and jetsam of her own dramas, that Imelda makes jewelry." Oh, yuck me sideways! Aren't people funny?

Anyway, to get back to the real world for a moment, here's a guide to shoes that Imelda would have killed for if she'd known about it before the arrival of the bunion years. See what you think.

TOP TIPS

* Go shopping for shoes at the end of the day, when your feet are slightly larger. Otherwise your new shoes will only fit you in the morning.
* Try on both shoes if your feet are different sizes. (Common sense, surely.)
* Have your feet properly measured once a year. That's not your

boyfriend and you rolling around giggling with a ruler after a couple of Camparis.

* Wear tights when buying shoes that you will be wearing with tights. You wouldn't think it would make a difference but it does.

* For leather shoes, it's best to polish them while they are still soft and warm from wearing.

* If your shoes get wet, do not dry them over heat; they will get really hard. Allow them to dry slowly, and stuff some newspaper inside to prevent shrinkage.

* Rotate your shoes. Not while you're walking, of course. I mean don't wear the same pair many days in succession.

* Keep your footwear smelling sweet by putting an orange peel inside them overnight. Or you can drip some lavender or lemongrass oil on a tissue and leave it in the shoes overnight.

* To freshen up old suede shoes, steam them over the kettle. Don't cook your hand.

* Keep unworn boots stuffed with newspaper. Unworn shoes benefit from a shoe tree.

* After a short walk on salted pavements in the winter your leather shoes can be spotted and stained. Mix 1 tablespoon vinegar with a cup of water and just wipe the marks off.

* Canvas shoes look new again with the application of some carpet shampoo.

* If you think your feet look too big, try wearing high heels with chunky wedges. Pointy toes make your feet look longer, and feet in light shoes look bigger than in dark—so avoid. Detailing and flounces will make your feet more petite, so get out your feathers, your patent leathers, your beads and buckles and bows!

❀ *Imelda comes from the German words for "entire" and "battle."* ❀

Alpha Woman

Boldly Go Where Angels Fear to Tread

I am Catwoman. Hear me roar.

CATWOMAN

Belly Dancing for the Complete Novice

*T*here's a mystical allure to belly dancing that you just don't get with clogging or pole dancing, and the whole thing is steeped in history. There are even a few Persian miniatures dating back to the twelfth century depicting Middle Eastern terpsichore of this kind. The basic steps consist of a series of sensuous circular motions of one part of the body or another, such as the characteristic slow hula hoop action of the hips and the cheeky pelvic tilt. The side-to-side "Hindu head" and back-and-forward "chicken head" are distinctive, too, along with hip snaps, shimmies, and a move that sounds like a pub: the Turkish Arms. For the more adept there is the balancing of baskets and swords, not forgetting the rich variety of unusual demonstrations with the exposed belly button. Let's be honest though, I don't have space here to turn you into a Mata Hari overnight, but with a few rudiments under your belt you should be able to give a good performance on the kitchen tiles or bedroom carpet.

COSTUME

First you must dress the part. You'll need two or three yards of chiffon or silk or something, for your veil. Ethnic bangles are a must, and you'll need to get hold of one of those tiny hats like a sequined bun to put on top of your head. A gorgeous, metallic pearly bra with dangling coins will give you that desirable full-headlamp effect, and a skimpy pair of bejeweled trousers, slit to expose the full leg and in a slinky material, is de rigueur. I tried using a pair of my brother's Speedos covered in glitter, with a bit of old net curtain tucked in, but it left something to be desired allure-wise.

You'll also need two sets of zils, those tiny finger cymbals, attached to the thumb and middle finger of each hand with a bit of elastic. Much of this stuff can be got at specialist suppliers, or you can improvise, depending on your level of ambition and what's in your wardrobe and on your dressing table. Long hair is better than short if you want to look authentic, as is a great deal of very black eyeliner.

A WORD ON NIPPLE TASSELS

Strictly speaking, nipple tassels have no place in traditional belly dancing, but with the rise in popularity of so-called exotic dancing they can,
I believe, be legitimately regarded as a related accoutrement. Nipple tassels come in two parts: the little conical caps, more properly referred to
as "pasties," and the tassels themselves, thus allowing impoverished bur-
lesque dancers the economy of just a single pair of tassels for attachment
to a variety of pasties.

Attaching the pasties is as much art as science, and the preferred adhesive is theatrical spirit gum. This is the stuff that actors stick their fake
moustaches on with, providing a firm hold and being kind to flesh. My
own experiments with Cowgum and gaffer tape resulted, it is true, in reliable adhesion but sounded on removal something akin to half a yard of
tearing calico and made my eyes water like anything.

Once you've got the little darlings on, you need to practise the twirling.
There are two main techniques for this. The first is to put your hands behind your head and bob up and down. The tassels should soon start to
spin, and you'll notice that they both twirl into the center. If you wish to
get them rotating in the same direction, you must vary your technique by
bending forward with your hands on your knees. Now rub your palms up
and down your thighs, alternately left and right, standing up slowly at the
same time. I confess that there is a problem with both these techniques
and that is that they are pretty lacking in glamour—particularly the first,
which makes you look as if you're sprinting for a bus without the benefit
of mammarial support. One alternative is to try raising your arms, left
then right. You should then be able to provoke a good spin—in opposite
directions—while retaining your poise.

SOME SIMPLE BELLY DANCING MOVES

* *Basic belly dance position*: Stand with your abdomen held in and your
  chest high. Your head should be up. Extend your arms in front of
  your chest as if embracing a phone booth, keeping a gap of a foot or
  so between your hands, and put out your left leg as if you were
  stepping forward. Support yourself mainly on your right leg, the

knee of which should be slightly bent. The left hip (the one with your extended leg attached to it) is the hip with which you will be leading the wiggling.

* *Horizontal hip thrust*: Move your hips backward and forward while twisting at the waist. This is not an up-and-down movement; think washing machine on rinse rather than hippity-hop. Hold your legs and upper body relatively static while you push your left hip forward and right hip back, then reverse the move: right hip forward, left hip back.

* *Pelvic tilt*: Possibly the most seductive belly dance move. From the basic position, bring your left leg back parallel to the right and push your buttocks forward and upward such that the base of your pelvis is lifted in the direction of the arrow (Fig. A). Reverse the move, causing your buttocks to stick out again (Fig. B). Combine the slants with a bend of the knees in the following way. Do three slants in a row, lowering yourself a little more with each tilt by further bending the knees, then unbend. Repeat the move a few times. But for goodness' sake do it sensitively, girls, or you'll look less like Salomé than a lady of the night. You can vary the speed of this move according to the musical pulse. Do not be put off by the 9/8 time

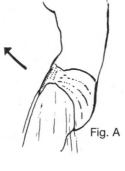

Fig. A   Fig. B

signature, just count it like this: 1, 2/3, 4/5, 6/7, 8/9, and so on. In the mystic Orient, mothers rock their babies to beats like this.

* *Shoulder thrust*: A very easy but slinky move. Push your left shoulder forward and the right backward, then reverse. Try to avoid giving an impression of Les Dawson in drag, making himself comfy. Slow and luscious is the thing to aim for.

* *Belly roll*: A great abdominal exercise, this one. First push your belly out—not too far or you'll look like Buddha. Then pull your belly in and hold this position as you lift your chest. Drop the rib cage and push your belly out again. It's in and out, a bit like the hokey-pokey but without shaking it all about. If you can manage a belly flutter (a vibration of the diaphragm), then go for it.

* *Veil removal*: What you basically do in this move is swoop your arms alternately in a large figure eight, pulling the veil free as you do so. It's a bit like patting your head and rubbing your tummy, I'm afraid, so if it all goes wrong don't be disheartened. If you *do* get the hang of it you can combine it with any of the moves above.

Nothing could be simpler.

❀ *The First International Belly Dance Congress was in the UK in 2007.* ❀

How to
Look Glamorous in a Sidecar

Maybe you're too young to remember sidecars, which have gone the way of washboards and petticoats. A sidecar was a kind of rigid bullet-shaped bubble just large enough to contain a girlfriend, which was attached to the port (left) side of a motorbike, supported on the road-side at the back by its own little wheel. Traveling in a sidecar in wet weather, you could pull over your head a perambulator-type hood with a plastic window at the front and sort of steam yourself into oblivion as you hurtled down a lane, alley, or twitten, toward some fun.

Nowadays a few remaining sidecars are still to be seen zooming about, transporting girlfriends wrapped in warm blankets. They are referred to as "outfits" by the dedicated band of enthusiasts who drive them. Communication with the driver is at last possible via a microphone, which is an improvement on the old days when you had to wait till your boyfriend decided to stop before you could speak to him, no matter how desperate you were.

If you find yourself pressed into a sudden sidecar caper, you should wear close-fitting clothes: jeans and a tight windproof jacket are recommended. Sneakers or something equally serviceable will be needed on your feet. You'll also require a motorcycle helmet and maybe goggles, too, to stop your eyes from streaming like geysers. If you have long hair, tie it back securely or you will emerge with a hairdo like a horizontal witch's broom. Also, the seat can be a bit uncomfortable after about thirty miles—a comfy cushion helps a bit.

Come to think of it, I don't think it *is* possible to look glamorous in a sidecar. No, all in all and on second thoughts, maybe it would be as much fun to put on some music, light some candles, and sit down with a Sidecar cocktail instead. Here's how to make one.

INGREDIENTS
* *2 ounces brandy*
* *1 ounce lemon juice*
* *1 ounce Cointreau*

INSTRUCTIONS
1 Combine the ingredients in a mixing jug with plenty of ice.
2 Stir and strain into a glass with a sugar-coated rim.
3 Drink.

Yes, that's a better idea.

❊ *Cointreau was first produced in 1849.* ❊

How to
Pretend You Are Still in the Office When You're Really at the Bar

Once upon a time I worked for a convivial boss who would announce at 11:57: "Well, I'm off for a burger and a pint," and would disappear for hours, returning at about 3:55, just in time for coffee fetched by his discreet and long-suffering secretary. He used to have regular "haircuts" during the day, too, and would often come back smelling strongly of pomade—at least I *think* it was pomade. *Shame* was not in his vocabulary.

Nowadays, many of us work in open-plan corporate-style offices for puritanical bosses who regard anyone who actually *goes out* for lunch as a sort of brazen recalcitrant determined to bring down the company by brash and willful ineptitude, foot-dragging, malcontentment, and bureaucratic sabotage.

If that rings a bell with you, and you are one of those people who thinks she deserves some slack occasionally—especially after working two weekends in a row, unthanked—then this procedure is for you. It sets out exactly how to look as if you are still in the office when you are— in fact—deeply installed at the pub or fine restaurant of your choosing, and another drink on its way from the bar in the hands of a good friend.

METHOD

The key to success here is to make your absence look temporary and short term. You need to establish and operate a two-coat/two-handbag/two-phone system: a fake one for the auditors and another for your surreptitious use. The way you operate the scam will become clear from the points below.

1   Keep a spare coat permanently in readiness on the back of someone else's door on another floor. Leave your usual coat (the one you

wore to work) hanging on the back of your chair when you sneak out, now wearing the standby coat. Contrasting colors will throw people off the scent if they happen to catch sight of you in the street.

2   Leave your chair turned at an angle to the desk so that you seem to have gotten up suddenly.

3   Leave your dummy cell phone very visibly on the desk. This naughty phone can be an old one; it doesn't even need to be working. Obviously, nobody ever leaves the office without her cell phone. But switch it off in case anyone tries calling or texting you and it doesn't make a noise: a bit of a giveaway.

4   Leave a notepad on the desk with a half-finished list on it.

5   Leave a pen on the notepad; the cap should be left *off*.

6   An open bottle of water and a sandwich with a bite out of it (very persuasive) should be sitting prominently by your computer.

7   Leave a decoy email on the screen with a half-finished sentence, such as: "I'm just gathering the last bits from people so I can sort out your important . . ."

8   Leave your dummy handbag somewhere visible: at the foot of a filing cabinet is good. This should appear to contain all your vital stuff: makeup, purse, hairbrush, book, and so on, but is a fake. You have sneaked your real bag out with you.

9   Immediately before stealing away, make yourself a mug of boiling hot black coffee and leave it on your desk, with the spoon still in it. It should be a large thick mug because that will allow the liquid to cool more slowly. The longer it steams, the more recent your departure will appear.

10   Ask any friendly colleagues who may be aggressively asked where you are by the boss to respond, "Oh, I think Finance [or HR or Sales or whatever] asked to see her." Don't forget the "I think." It's a lifesaver. *Note*: Nobody should ever *volunteer* information.

11   On your return, dump coat and bag in the usual hiding place and visit the ladies' room to fix your windswept or ratty-wet hair. While you are about it, warm your frozen pink cheeks with the hand dryer.

12   Use a strong perfume to mask any oppressive alcoholic miasma that clings to you, and pop in an extra-strong breath mint to camouflage the vino-flavored breath.

13   Only the complete beginner eats garlic while on a sneaky long lunch. Avoid!

14   Be subtle about your timing. Work through the usual lunch hour, asking loud pointless questions of everybody and generally drawing attention to yourself. Then slink out at 2:40. Much less obvious than going out at lunchtime.

15   When you swish back into the office *holding a piece of paper covered in numbers*, say in a loud voice, "God, I am absolutely *starving*."

16   Don't be tempted to work late. All that does is reveal a guilty conscience. When you do leave, say, "I'm simply not staying late *again*—it's getting ridiculous."

Don't make the mistake of a sometime colleague of mine who badly misjudged the intake of the falling-down liquid one lunchtime, allowing it to pass the point at which it could be safely masked. Instead of claiming a sudden attack of the vapors and going straight home—the recommended emergency procedure—she returned to the office and sat in an empty meeting room, groaning loudly into a wastepaper basket that she hugged on her lap. We got her out in the end, supported on the arms of two long-suffering officemates.

At the movies: Suppose you decide to nip out craftily to see that classic of 1980s Swedish cinema, Ingmar Bergman's *Fanny and Alexander*. Well, don't run before you can walk, because this movie lasts an astonishing five hours and twenty minutes. My popcorn went soggy. No, start small and work your way up, because if you're missing for five-hour stretches, even the most clueless boss is going to realize something's afoot. Begin with short films, such as those lovely little Pixar animations. Try leaving a suitable truthful excuse such as, "Gone to sit in a darkened room for a few minutes," on a sticky note on your computer.

At the mall: The danger of on-the-clock time-wasting at the mall is that you may be observed by vigilant (nosy) colleagues on their lunch break or doing something legitimate such as purchasing emergency stationery. The answer: take a leaf out of their book. Put on one of those yellow hard hats and carry a striped pole and you can walk all over the mall, have a coffee, meet friends, and do your shopping without arousing the slightest suspicion from workmates who happen to be there, too. Don't make the beginner's mistake of wandering back into the office with your hard hat and stripy pole, though, or the game will be up.

At the spa: The hard thing about coming back from the spa is that you are likely to be abnormally relaxed and glowing, quite the opposite of your regular frazzled look of daily despair that office life brings to your face. So before you re-enter the office, drink a large espresso and run up and down the fire stairs. Then you can come back in looking as crazed as you usually do. I'm sorry if this has undone your expensive work at the spa, but sometimes you have to choose: you can't have everything you want in life, or at least not all at once.

❋ *People photocopying their anatomy is said to cause 23 percent of copier faults.* ❋

How to
Go Over Niagara Falls in a Barrel

You know that feeling you sometimes get, when life is driving you crazy with its boring tediousness, and the weekend prospect is a barren one of joyless knitting patterns, dirty dishes, and desolate grocery shopping? Well, the French have a word for this, *ennui*, and we've had enough of it, haven't we! The time has come to strike back, to kick against this oppressive monotony, to reclaim those thrills and excitements that are our right! Yes, it's time to go over Niagara Falls in a barrel!

The first person to go over Niagara Falls in a barrel was a woman, 63-year-old retired schoolteacher Annie Edson Taylor, who claimed (unpersuasively) to be only 43. This was 1901 and Annie, at something of a loose end, thought that this stunt would make her rich and famous. So she got hold of a long, thin pickle barrel and put in an anvil for ballast. On October 24, her birthday, she strapped herself to pillows and climbed inside (*with her cat*). Then, watched from the bank by a doubtful audience, she went over the falls.

Minutes later, Annie was pulled from her barrel with only a small cut to her head. She never made any money from the amazing feat, but she'd started a craze. Ten years later, a fellow named Bobby Leach went over in a steel barrel and also survived the plunge, dying, in a very boring way, many years later after slipping on an orange peel.

But there have been noteworthy failures, too. In 1920, Englishman Charles G. Stephens *tied himself* to the anvil inside his barrel. All that remained after his plunge were a few broken staves and his tattooed right arm. In 1930, a Greek waiter named George L. Statakis became trapped for many hours behind the falls and suffocated. His three hours' air supply was enough, though, for his good-luck turtle to survive. In 1995, using a more modern approach, the reverberantly named Robert Overacker put on a parachute and rode a Jet Ski over the edge to publicize the cause of the homeless. His chute failed to open and, as he plummeted to his death, he found himself promoting only the benefits of better parachutes.

INSTRUCTIONS

Naturally, you want to succeed in your attempt so you need to understand a few things first. The Niagara Falls are actually three falls, and the only survivable one is the so-called Horseshoe Falls. The plunge itself, variously described as "a skydiver's free fall" or "dropping in an elevator without a cable," is, of course, the safe part of the exercise. It's the landing that's dangerous. The Niagara River pours hundreds of thousands of gallons over the Horseshoe Falls every second and it's a 170-foot drop to the water below.

Even though more than half the daredevils who go over the falls in a barrel survive, the chances are pretty high that you will hurt yourself. You are, for example, likely to receive a brain injury from the rapid deceleration when you land. There is also the obvious danger of being smashed to pieces on the rocks and/or being pummelled to death by the water. There's drowning of course, and suffocation, if you find yourself trapped behind the falling water. So how do you survive?

There are various theories, including obvious ones about having a stout, water-resistant container that will *absorb* energy instead of transmitting it to your body. Some people have used giant ball-like contraptions, while others have protected their barrels with solid foam. There are four main survival ideas, but I'm not sure how good the evidence is for any of them.

1   *Use the "water cone"*: This "protective cushion" is supposed to exist at the foot of the falls and is said to soften the blow as you land. Hmmm.

2   *Bodysurf*: This is for those people who wish to practice first without a barrel. "Riding" the water as a bodysurfer does is said to allow you to "slide" over the falls rather than falling straight down and splattering on the concrete-hard water surface. Let me know how you get on with this one.

3   *Be put in near the brink*: The idea behind this one is that if your barrel goes into the water upstream you will accelerate as you approach the edge, making the exercise more hazardous. There's no evidence I could find that this is significant. You'll just have to try it.

4   *Be lucky*: This is the best one in my view. Prayer, crossing your fingers, and being kind to animals are all said to improve your chances.

Finally, I should point out that going over the Niagara Falls on purpose is not only likely to introduce you to your maker fairly quickly, it is also expensively illegal. So don't try it! (As if you would.)

❀ *An elephant is 70 percent water.* ❀

How to
Walk on Stilts

S tilt walking is an ancient art that you can get on top of with just half an hour's practice. And some stilts, of course. At the turn of the twentieth century, walking on stilts was reported to be "the very latest fashionable amusement of the 'new woman' in London . . . Just why girls should not walk on stilts or engage in any similar sport no one yet has given a satisfactory answer." Precisely! So here's how.

PREPARATION

* Let's face it, you are going to fall over occasionally, so learn to fall properly by "curving" inward slightly and landing on a broad area of your body, such as your shoulders. Protective clothes are a good idea when you first start (knee pads, hard hat, etc.). Don't start off in your ball gown and high heels.
* The "height" of stilts refers to the distance from the foot plate to the ground. A good height for beginners is between 1 foot and 2½ feet. This is an ideal height for indoor stilting as well. A sort of logarithmic vertigo-multiplication factor comes into play as you go up in height. You feel enormously higher up on 4-foot stilts than you do on 2-foot stilts. Beyond 3 feet you begin to lose contact with people down on the ground, but the huge increase in visual impact and audience appreciation is worth it, especially once you've got your special velvet trousers on and some twinkly makeup.
* Stilts easily sink into soft ground and you can find yourself stuck like a scarecrow, so choose a firm, even surface to walk on.
* Practicing beside a high wall or in an alley allows you to "bounce" off the side if you lose your balance and increases your confidence.
* Practice with a spotter who can support your weight and catch you if you wobble.
* Once you are a confident stilter you'll need to choose some attractive clothes. Long, wide velvet trousers that cover the stilts look good with a sequinned top and some glitter on your cheeks.

* The stilts (and clothes) can be found at specialty suppliers. Consider renting before you buy.
* Baked-bean-can stilts with strings tied to them in place of poles are a cheap alternative. You hold the string loops in your hands and walk along on the tin cans. Unladylike and unimpressive in equal measure. Avoid.

DOWN TO BUSINESS

1 Grasp one stilt in each hand, put your left foot on to the foot plate of the left stilt, and lift yourself up straight. Lean against the wall or ask your spotter to prop you up.

2 Put your right foot on to the foot plate of the second stilt and straighten up into classic stilt position. Balancing on stilts without walking is rather akin to balancing an umbrella or broom handle on an extended finger. It has the same sort of constant-adjustment feel to it.

3 Practice lifting alternate legs (in the same spot) to get used to the crazy sensations. Once you feel relatively confident, start taking your first steps and keep on going—the forward momentum will help you to keep your balance. Take slow, short steps at first to avoid doing a split, which, unlike the balletic version, is unattractive, what with the screaming and those long poles going in all directions.

4 Pick the stilts up high as you go or you'll find yourself tripping on bumps and declivities in the road. A sort of robot march is the effect you are after. OK, at first you'll look like the Tin Man in *The Wizard of Oz*, but things will quickly improve.

5 That's really all there is to it. You can progress to taller stilts as you become more accomplished.

❀ *Hitchcock's* Vertigo *is ninth on the American Film Institute's list of great American movies.* ❀

How to
Launch a Ship

*T*here aren't many things as exciting as the launch of one of those enormous ocean liners, where some fancy personage, often in a silly hat, smashes a bottle of Champagne against the hull, with the stirring invocation, "May God bless her and all who sail in her."

Ship launching dates back to the ancient rituals of long ago, such as the immolation of two oxen as Noah readied the Ark for flotation. These sacrifices developed over the years into a ceremony politely asking the gods to safeguard ship and crew from the perils of the sea. For a long time, wine was poured onto the ship from a silver "standing cup," but this gave way, first to a bottle of wine and then to Champagne. In recent years all U.S. Navy ship-launchers have been female, and female members of the British Royal Family also seem to spend much of their time launching ships.

The failure of the bottle to break is thought to be an omen of bad luck. For example, on April 27, 2000, Princess Anne—the one who looks like a horse—failed to smash her bottle over the bow of a $400 million British passenger liner named *Aurora*. It is interesting to note that the ship broke down almost immediately and had to limp back unceremoniously to port for repairs. A plague of misfortunes then followed, the most notable of which was the infection of 600 helpless passengers with the highly contagious and unattractive norovirus, leading to an onboard epidemic of diarrhea and vomiting, and culminating in an international bust up when the ship was refused entry to Spanish ports.

In the States, launching ceremonies are based on the European tradition, and this is what you should do if you wish to launch a ship yourself.

INSTRUCTIONS

1   Be a prominent female, preferably aristocratic, and, if at all possible, First Lady. The first First Lady to act as a ship's sponsor was Mrs. Calvin Coolidge. (Actually, she was launching an *airship*.)

2   Choose your outfit. Think Madeleine Albright, not Madonna. If you can't *be* patrician you must *look* it, so get a hat. Something like a pillbox, which won't blow away in the wind.

3   Find a ship that needs launching. Call up the U.S. Navy; they're bound to have a list somewhere.

4   Choose your "christening liquid." When Mrs. Herbert Hoover launched *Akron* (another airship) in 1931, Prohibition was still in force, so instead, the First Lady pulled a cord that opened a hatch, releasing a flock of pigeons. Bottled river and seawater have both been used over the years in place of Champagne.

5   Practice your bottle-smashing skills with some cheap Champagne, a rope, and the side of a brick house.

6   Write and memorize your speech. This needn't require much paper. A typical speech might go: "I name this ship, *Whatever*. May God bless her and all who sail in her."

7   Finally, if the Champagne bottle doesn't break, just smile aristocratically. Don't keep bashing it on the hull, swearing under your breath; it looks bad.

❋ *The pressure in a bottle of Champagne is three times that in a car tire.* ❋

How to
Slide Down a Fireman's Pole

*T*hose music hall comics produced some long-lasting jokes—not good maybe, but durable. I was in the Cask and Glass the other day when I overheard the following: "Is anything worn beneath the kilt? No, it's all in full working order." That must have been old a hundred years ago.

What is it about a man in a kilt? Or a marching band of pipers in kilts? It makes me go wobbly all over: all those buckles and knives and pipes and bright colors and huge great fuzzy hats. There's something about uniforms that provocatively emphasizes the masculine characteristics of the wearer, which appeals. And you can take your pick, from soldiers and sailors, from pilots and policemen, from storm troopers, and even from traffic wardens. But I reckon near the top of the list must be the fireman in uniform.

So I wondered, would it be possible to persuade a fireman to show me how to slide down his pole? I'd already read that the first firemen's poles were introduced in the time of horse-drawn fire engines, when firemen lived above the stables. I had also noted that a spokesman for a British firehouse boasts the longest pole in Europe—some 40 feet of it. Good lord, sir, that's a huge one!

The trouble is that firemen's poles have recently come under the health and safety microscope with reports of poles being omitted from a new West Country fire station because of the danger that firemen might suffer "chafing to the thighs." I would like to put it on record that I hereby volunteer to massage soothing ointments into the thighs of any fireman suffering intercrural distress. Just contact the publisher.

In the end I managed to speak to a very helpful senior fire officer and would like to record my thanks to senior fireman Clive Eustice for his help with this one. I would *like* to thank him but all he said was:

> You wrap your legs round the pole at the ankles and that's about it, to be honest. Your hands are used only to balance, but you can do it without them. The speed of decent is controlled by the legs, although most poles aren't long enough to worry about that—just wrap and drop!

So in light of the paucity of the information provided, and the news that members of the public aren't allowed to slide down firemen's poles, I am withholding my thanks. If you have better luck than I did in trying to slide down a fireman's pole, I'd be pleased to hear your story.

❀ *A flame is a self-sustaining, oxidizing chemical reaction that produces energy.* ❀

How to
Wolf Whistle

*T*here was a mistress at my school named Miss Dexter. She was known to us all, naturally enough, as Sinister Dexter, which we thought frightfully clever. But actually this was unfair as well as inaccurate, because Miss Dexter was the antithesis of sinister, resembling, as she did, Dame Margaret Rutherford in the role of Miss Whitchurch in *The Happiest Days of Your Life* (1950). Anyway, the thing was that she could whistle like a sailor and was able to call us in from the school boundary with an earsplitting shriek that would have given the "Orange Blossom Special" a run for its money.

Of course, we girls used to practice like anything to get a good whistle going like Miss Dexter's, and there were two main schools of thought when it came to technique: the finger-whistlers and the non-finger. I belonged to the finger sorority, but I confess that neither group was much good, able to produce only a sort of osculatory sucking-wheeze, reminiscent of the sounds made by the black ooze of the great Grimpen Mire as it swallowed another horse.

Well, the other day, my sister-in-law Marianne was around for lunch with my Auntie Sarah and me, and we discovered that *she* could whistle like a factory at five. What is more, after just a few minutes, my Auntie Sarah found that she was able to do it, too. Though I struggled for ages, I failed, letting the side down badly. Nonetheless, in case you want to have a go, in a blow (literally) for sex equality, here are the definitive instructions, based on my sister-in-law's technique, so that next time you're passing a bunch of good-looking construction workers you can get in first.

The mechanics

1   Hold your fingers in the position shown on the next page: thumb resting on the curled middle and ring finger.

2   Open your mouth and touch the tips of your thumb and middle finger to the tip of your tongue.

3   Push your tongue back into your mouth like
    an accordion. You have now created a nar-
    row channel inside your mouth and a small
    exit hole. By blowing forcefully through the
    gap—though probably not as hard as you
    think—you should start to hear occa-
    sional whistly sounds. Don't overdo it—
    it's easy to become light-headed.

4   Practice is the key to success so do not be
    deterred by failure; keep at it while you are
    in the bath, watching TV, in bed, and so on. After a while it will
    suddenly happen and you'll be whistling like an old pro. Don't try to
    learn it in church, though, because the noise—when it finally
    comes—is absolutely deafening and you'll simply blast the congre-
    gation off their pews.

5   As you gradually refine your technique, you'll discover that you can
    do the good-old *wheep-wheeoow* wolf whistle as well as the
    wheeoow-wheep that Miss Dexter used to call us in from the play-
    ground, all those years ago. Whatever happened to her, I wonder?

❀ *The wolf shares a common ancestry with the domestic dog.* ❀

How to
Turn Down a Rotten Marriage Proposal

O ne of the problems of being a young lady, of course, is boys and
    knowing how to handle them. It's something I think you learn on
the job—if you'll pardon the unfortunate idiom. Like choosing cushions,
rejection is one of those things that is largely the responsibility of the female, and it can take a while to learn how to do it with grace and charm.

Suppose some gentleman of whom you are fond, but no more, suddenly presents you with an engagement ring at dinner or goes down on

one knee, what are you going to do? First of all, *never* say yes if you don't really mean it or you'll end up like Nancy Astor, who remarked, "I married beneath me; all women do."

Here is the proper way. I'm assuming that you are a *lady* and not some scabby toothless gal for whom a "Naaaaah!" between cigarette puffs will be sufficient. And unless it's one of those creepy stalker types, text messages and emails are plainly unsuitable.

INSTRUCTIONS

1   Be honest but kind. Don't say, "Harry, you are nice but I don't like you and would *never* marry you, because of your effeminate, passive demeanor and those skinny chicken legs, and your low-level job with Airfix, and your lack of a sense of humor, and your awful mother, and your BO." Instead make it crystal clear in polite terms that, though you like him, you *do not want to marry him*.

2   Don't apologize.

3   If he keeps up a protest about how you were made for each other, use the broken-record technique: repeat that though you like him you definitely don't want to marry him. If the message doesn't get through after repetition, you are beating a dead horse. Go on to the following points.

4   If you find an engagement ring in your pudding at a restaurant, just swallow it.

5   Explain that marriage to anyone is not your cup of tea at the moment. Notice the clever use of words?

6   Ask your father to refuse permission for your hand (and the rest of you).

7   Claim lesbianism.

8   For the man who is still not receiving, rent a billboard in Times Square with the bald message: "Earth calling Harry Bloggs. Get it into your fat head: Mavis Davis does not want to, and WILL NEVER, marry you!"

❀ *Zsa Zsa Gábor has been married nine times.* ❀

How to
Escape the Second Date

There are many reasons a relationship might go stale and I'm not going into them all here. The point is, though, that sometimes the second date suddenly seems about as desirable as watching a post mortem. So here are a few ideas that will allow you to slip your collar the next time you want to escape a date.

The creeping realization that things are bad often comes upon you while you are already on a date, and this can be a good time to make your action plan live. I'm assuming that you really don't like him and never want to see him again, so there's no place here for mild evasions and excuses: you've got to go in for the kill. Use the freelancer's technique of never saying no to a job. Instead get him to turn *you* down. The way to do this is to make yourself completely un-dateable by being totally embarrassing or vile.

INSTRUCTIONS

* If you're already out on a date, blow your nose on the tablecloth.
* Drink too much and start shouting.
* Pinch every male bottom in sight (waiters are good).
* Order the most expensive dish on the menu with Champagne and then leave it.
* Develop a maniacal laugh and a strange twitch.
* Wink at the men and order them all drinks on his card.
* Demand that he choose there and then between you and his mother or between you and sports.
* Wear a knee-length tweed skirt and knee-highs.
* Stop shaving your legs.
* Stop washing your hair.
* Smear on your makeup disgustingly.
* Become embarrassingly opinionated.
* Take up Churchillian cigars.

* Stop brushing your teeth.
* Wear a track suit with a filthy slogan on it.
* Stop changing your clothes.
* Begin loud and very public burping.
* Call his friends and arrange dates with them all.
* Never just stand him up. That would be unladylike.

❀ Date palms take about seven years to bear fruit. ❀

How to
Jump in Line at the Ladies' Room

Have you ever seen men lining up for the restroom? No, I thought not. But how often have you rounded the corner in the restaurant, airport, or pub only to find a five-mile snake of women shuffling uncomfortably toward their purpose? *Exactly.* My Uncle Bob says it proves that men are good finishers as well as good starters, but I have this theory that there should just be twice as many ladies' toilets as men's. Until that happy day, here are a few ideas for shameless line jumping for those moments when desperate measures are called for.

* Get very close to the person at the front and ask in a dribbly voice, "Do you mind if I go in? I think I'm going to be sick again." They will push you ahead with alacrity.
* Pretend to be foreign: just push in waving your arms and shouting incomprehensibly.
* Carry a bicycle bell and ring at people as you push in. This adds a mysterious authority to your brazen conduct.
* Avoid busy times (the end of a movie, the end of wedding toasts, immediately post coffee and dessert at a dinner).
* Borrow a child and ask her to jump up and down urgently. Give knowing looks as you sail through the line.

* Carry a stethoscope and brandish it with a brisk, "Excuse me, I'm a doctor." They'll let you through every time.

* Put on some yellow coveralls (foresight required) and tell the crowd you're the cleaner. It's a bit of a nuisance dragging that "Cleaning in Progress" sign around with you all the time, but it pays off when you need it.

* In the theater or concert hall, get up and out before the encore or curtain call.

* Go in the bushes. Simple, old-fashioned, effective, and reduces your carbon footprint.

* Men's toilets are always an option. In fact, they are the best option. My friend Laverne never hesitates to use the men's room. As she emerged one day from the men's room in a busy pub near the Central Criminal Court, a man exiting ahead of her turned and said in a loud voice, "Thank you, that was very refreshing." She never batted an eye.

❀ *World Toilet Day is celebrated around the world every November 19.* ❀

How to
Juggle Wolves

Alfred Hitchcock turned out a whole string of successful films during the 1950s, and *Rear Window* (1954) is among the best. At one point the protagonist Jeff (James Stewart) is watching a young lady from his apartment window as she entertains a group of men in her apartment across the way. He remarks to his glamorous friend Lisa (Grace Kelly), "She's like a queen bee with her pick of the drones," to which she retorts, "I'd say she's doing a woman's hardest job: juggling wolves." If that rings bells with you, here are a few hints and tips for making wolf juggling a little easier.

METHOD

1   Resist their blandishments by remaining in control.

2   Make sure each wolf lives in a different town and is from a different social circle. And, if possible, is a speaker of a different language.

3   Choose different character types so they are unlikely to meet or know one other. In other words, not three racing drivers or ear-nose-and-throat surgeons from the same town.

4   Don't tell anyone what you're up to (especially bitter, dateless friends). If you are a practiced wolf juggler you will know that socializing with any of them among your friends is a bad idea. Why encourage competition?

5   Be sure to wash off one man's aftershave before meeting up with the next one.

6   Spread yourself out over Thanksgiving and Christmas (Christmas Eve, Christmas morning, and Christmas dinner). And buy each one the same present; it makes it simple to remember.

7   Tell your second-favorite man that you always spend Valentine's night in with your mother, reading the poems of Amy Dickinson.

8   Choose men with the same first name so that whispered nothings or sleep talking do not get you into trouble. There are few embarrassments more embarrassing than murmuring, "Oh *Hank*..." and having Maurice prod you in the side with the demand for an explanation.

9   If you adopt the previous tactic, for gawd's sake don't text the wrong one, confirming a date. You'll have all kinds of explaining to do, unless you'd like to find out how amenable they both are to a sort of ménage à trois—to put it politely.

10 Make sure your men never phone you at work or the cat will be out of the bag before you can say "gossipy Gertrude."

11 Juggling more than three wolves is too stressful and the advantages are outweighed by the amount of effort required on your part to keep four or more on a rolling boil. If a new man does start to beep on your radar, torpedo one of the others before taking things further.

❊ *"So many men, so little time."*—*Mae West* ❊

How to
Pull Off a Man's Shirt in a Twinkling

One of the most barefaced swindles ever conceived, the Shirt Steal was a favorite of the finest music-hall double acts of yesteryear. It's one of the funniest bits of stage business you'll ever see, and unlike an escape from a straitjacket inside a padlocked mailbag, it's a parlor trick very suitable for a lady. Here is my own postmodernist version, appropriate for close quarters and ideal for the office party or family function.

THE EFFECT
Following some cheerful belly dancing (see page 241) or the singing of a sentimental song or two, you ask a distinguished-looking gentleman if he will help you with a little experiment. As he comes forward to a smattering of polite applause you comment on his smart clothes and ask if you may borrow his necktie. Unwilling to appear churlish, he says yes. You now loosen the tie and slide it off slowly and seductively. This should provoke an expectant murmur, which will be suddenly checked as you whip out a wicked-looking pair of garden shears or kitchen scissors.

Ignoring the look of frank alarm on your gentleman's features you announce in a loud but somewhat uncertain voice, "The Cut and Restored Tie is a very difficult trick for a lady. And it often goes wrong." At this point your assistant snatches back his tie and begins rolling it up. You look hurt and remark, "Well, that's OK, I'll use your shirt then," and seizing his shirt by the collar you suddenly yank it off, right over his head, leaving him standing there bare-chested in just his jacket, with his hair all up on end.

PREPARATION
Your assistant, as your audience may have twigged by now, is really a stooge. The best subjects for this jape are middle-aged professional-looking gentlemen. Uncles and other male relations can often be roped

in, as can complete strangers if you flutter your eyelashes a bit. They seem to enjoy both the limelight and the subterfuge. Maybe some of them also enjoy having their clothes boldly torn off in public by a lady, but let's not go into that.

A little preparation is required, of course; so not too long before the performance the two of you need to slip away unseen to set things up. Once you are somewhere private, ask your confederate to remove his jacket, shirt, and tie. Be clear in advance about why you are asking him to do this; you don't want things to develop in untoward ways. On the other hand, if he's all gorgeous, there's no point in cutting off your nose to spite your face . . .

Anyway, back to business. Drape the shirt over his shoulders and do up the second and third buttons at the front. Dangle the sleeves down his arms and ask him to grasp the cuffs securely while he puts on the jacket. Once it's on, arrange the cuffs around his wrists but leave them unbuttoned. Draw the lower part of the shirt around behind him, tucking it under the back of his jacket, which you button up in front.

Next ask your accomplice to put on and tighten his tie but leave the top button undone. Now poke the tie neatly under the front of the jacket and, so long as he doesn't move about too much, things should appear quite normal. It is unfair to leave a man like this for anything longer than a few minutes so don't wait an age before you begin the performance.

PERFORMANCE

Follow the instructions set out above and when it comes to the point where you finally pull off the shirt, turn your assistant to face you with his arms relaxed at his side. Quickly undo the second and third buttons of his shirt and firmly grasp the back of the collar with both hands. In one swift movement, pull the shirt over his head and off. He will have to bend forward and hold still as you do this. The sleeves of the shirt often resist but a steady and firm tug does the trick. Try to make it smooth, though—clinging on for dear life as your assistant writhes about with you in a humiliating tug-of-war spoils the effect.

As the shirt comes off, you will hear a roar of approval from your spectators, along with a few whistles if your assistant has a whistle-worthy chest. Before the hooting subsides, shake your man's hand and return his shirt. If your audience has realized that he is a confederate it will only add to their enjoyment, so make the most of it. Ask for a round of applause for such a good sport and take a moment to bathe in the reflected glory.

❧ *Detachable shirt collars were invented in* 1827 *in Troy, New York.* ❧

How to
Meet Your Ex's New Girlfriend

Once, as the guest of an old beau, I attended a wedding reception where I was seated with some of his other exes. I say "some" but in fact there were eleven of us, occupying two huge tables. And what a lively lot we were; the laughter was simply raucous, provoked chiefly by our swapping of stories about this particular gentleman's—how shall I put it?—*foibles*. Yes, that's it. We all felt a bit sorry for the bride that day, partly because of the sheer number of us, to all of whom she had to be introduced, but also because we each knew what was in store for the poor girl.

Meeting your ex's new flame is always a slightly weird and often tense occasion. Will she be prettier, cleverer, wealthier, more charming, sexier—with a superlative hourglass figure? Will she have breeding, brains, and beauty? Is she, in short, a willowy Nordic princess who is a professional model and pin-up with degrees from Oxbridge, Harvard, and the Sorbonne? Secretly, of course, you hope she will be a witless, lumpen ne'er-do-well, with flies buzzing round her toothless head. Unfortunately, she is usually a lovely girl of great charm and intelligence. Which is only to be expected really. After all, your ex has good taste: that's why he chose you. But that doesn't stop you feeling feelings of *unfavorable* comparison the whole time.

Anyway it's time to gird your loins. Prepare for the worst but hope for the best, and take whatever comes. Here are a few tips:

* Always start off with grace and style (stay on guard, though, just in case).
* When you meet her, make sure it's on your own terms. If at all possible, you should have your new partner hanging on your arm (or hire an escort).
* It's sometimes better if your new man doesn't know that this fellow is your ex. The subtle effect of this is to make your old flame and his new girlfriend feel insignificant when you airily introduce them, damning them with faint praise to the man on your arm—and getting her name and details a bit wrong in the process.
* Never look as if you've tried too hard, but make sure your hair is good and that you're looking nice—and as tall as possible. (See how to descend a staircase in high heels, page 22).

If you harbor feelings of revenge:

* Turn up with a filthy (clear) plastic bag containing horrible images downloaded from disgusting websites featuring elderly grannies and animals, several pairs of grubby women's undergarments, a cheap wig, a Scout's uniform, and a few dirty compacted handkerchiefs. Announce, "Oh, you left some things behind."
* Then send your floridly gay friend over to greet him with, "Where did you disappear to last night, you naughty, naughty girl?"
* If meeting number 1 goes especially badly, arrange meeting number 2 for the back of an airplane, one mile up just before her first sky dive. Take scissors.

❀ *At red-carpet events, Hollywood execs are kept apart by trained assistants.* ❀

How to
Hide a File in a Cake

S uppose your man has been fitted up by a grass and had his collar felt
by the rozzers who then verballed him, saying he sang like a canary
after "falling down the stairs." Now the beak has banged him up with a
load of nonces and mean screws so it's up to you to spring him. Do you
have a clue what I'm talking about? Because I don't. The old file-in-the-
cake-trick is the way to go. This is what you must do . . . (Crossfade to
long shot of prison. Exterior. Night.)

INGREDIENTS
* *8 ounce superfine sugar*
* *8 ounce butter (soft)*
* *8 ounce self-rising flour*
* *4 eggs, beaten*
* *1 tsp baking powder*
* *2 tbsp milk*

FILLING
* *Whipped cream*
* *A jar of good raspberry jam*
* *Confectioners' sugar (for the top)*
* *A small but sturdy file*

INSTRUCTIONS
1 Heat oven to 375°F.
2 Butter two 8-inch cake pans and line with wax paper.
3 Beat ingredients (except for jam, cream, and confectioners' sugar) to
  a smooth consistency so that it drops off the spoon.
4 Dilute with water if it's too thick.
5 Divide the mixture between the cake pans and drop the file into
  one of them. Smooth off the surface and bake for about 20 minutes

or until golden. The one with the file may cook slightly faster as the metal heats up inside. When done, the cake should spring back if you depress its surface.

6   Turn out the pans and cool the cakes on a rack. You will clearly see the file shape on the base of one of them, where it's sunk to the bottom. Turn this one flat-side down.

7   For the filling, spread the jam generously over the bottom cake.

8   Spread cream over the other (the one with the file in it) and carefully position on top. Dust with a little confectioners' sugar. Martha Stewart would probably do this through a doily to make a pretty pattern.

Take the cake along to the prison on your next conjugal visit and cross your fingers.

❂ *Robert Stroud, "the Birdman of Alcatraz," spent seventeen years on "the Rock."* ❂

How to
Seduce a Man

*T*he thing you need to understand about men is that they are not like you when it comes to selecting a mate. For a woman, a man must pass a number of implicit tests before he will be considered suitable. Among the physical hoops he must jump through are height (tall better), masculinity (aggressiveness, strong jaw, large nose, strong forehead, wide shoulders, shorter index finger than third finger), and power (high-earning job, status symbols: for example, expensive car, house, watch, and clothes).

But these good-mating or "Tarzan" indices must be counterbalanced by good fathering skills. So qualities such as humor, sensitivity, strategic thinking, playfulness, charm, and being brainy will also count.

In contrast, a man just wants the prettiest girl he can find right now. Of the three famous qualities—brains, breeding, and beauty—that a girl is supposed to require so as to get on, beauty heads the list; a beautiful checkout girl will be more desirable to a man than a plain princess. Being smart and polished will help, of course, as will serving up a delicious dinner, but those women who say the way to a man's heart is through his stomach are really aiming too high. The physical qualities a man responds to are not really to do with being thin, though. Tall is good, as is an hourglass figure, which transmits the message: *I can have babies and feed them*, but what really pulls men, beyond the first suck of Neanderthal attraction, is a positive temperament. Men greatly prefer enthusiastic, cheerful, adventurous women, even if they do not look like Marilyn Monroe (*who does?*). Confidence is a huge aphrodisiac for a man, so if you are exciting and upbeat rather than negative, moany, critical, and lugubrious you already have a huge advantage in the seduction stakes and an inbuilt capacity to outlast the gormless Barbie dolls, whose attraction withers for many men, once they open their mouths to speak.

Seduction: a list
Here are a few things you can do to help along what is already not a difficult job. Think Mrs. Robinson in *The Graduate*.

* Wear things that emphasize your best parts. Legs, boobs, neck, arms, abdomen. If you're lucky enough to be good all over, conceal some of it.
* Get close to him.
* Pay him proper attention. Listen attentively and look into his eyes. If his pupils are dilated, you know you are having an effect. Either that or you are down a mine.
* Look at his mouth while he speaks. Don't gape; move in a triangle between eyes and lips.
* Lean toward him while licking your lips. Be subtle about it; you don't want to look as if you've just eaten a bucket of the Colonel's fried chicken.
* Play with your hair.
* Stroke your thigh.

✳ Whisper a question to him.

✳ Touch him. Grab his watch to check the time; push him playfully when he says something amusing; accidentally bump your knee up against him; lean up against him; tuck a loose hair behind his ear.

✳ If sitting, cross and uncross your legs (men find this extremely alluring, especially if you have long legs and a short skirt).

✳ Ask him to blow on your neck. Any excuse will do.

✳ Ask him to help you undo your top shirt button or attach your necklace. Is he drooling yet?

✳ Tell him you are cold and ask him to warm your hands.

✳ Men are very visual creatures. Tell him you are thinking about buying a swimsuit and ask him which type he thinks would best suit you.

✳ Dip your finger in your ice cream and offer it to him to taste. Are his cheeks flushing? If so, you're doing OK.

✳ Grasp his knee then slowly advance up his thigh, squeezing as you go, but stop before you get to the shorts line.

✳ Talk about vaguely erotic—or frankly erotic—things. One of my friends always talks about her Brazilian wax to men she's interested in. Their tongues just fall out.

✳ Sit playfully on his lap (this is an absolute killer for chaps. Especially if you wriggle about a bit). You may well notice an effect. That's all I'm saying . . .

✳ If he asks you back to his place, make sure you don't end up like the James Thurber cartoon, where the man is saying to the lady, "You wait here and I'll bring the etchings down." Bad result.

❀ *In* The Graduate, *Anne Bancroft was just six years older than Dustin Hoffman.* ❀

How to
Write a "Dear John" Letter

Oh gawd! How are you going to break off this romantic relationship compassionately? Sometimes the best way is an old-fashioned good-bye letter, especially if the man is at a distance. So sit yourself down with pen, paper, wastepaper basket, and a glass of water (not wine), and start your first draft. You'll do several versions, let me tell you. Here are some tips for avoiding a few of the beginner's mistakes:

1   Don't do it on the computer. Nobody wants to receive a printout, and it need hardly be said that an email or text message saying, "You're dumped!" is simply not good enough from a lady. So use a pen, and be nice.

2   Don't start your letter "Dear John . . . ," unless you normally start that way. Begin with just his name, "John . . ." and write in your usual style: not intimate in tone but friendly and kind.

3   Many men reread their Dear John letters over and over. It helps the news sink in, so for goodness' sake be careful what you write.

4   Avoid blunt criticisms of his faults. Remarks such as "Your ears are not only hairy inside, but completely uneven and much too big," or "You look like a sack of cauliflowers in bed," may be true but are unnecessarily unkind. Spite is undignified; magnanimity should be the order of the day. And you do not want a thoughtless remark that you cannot un-speak to haunt you down the years. Certainly don't make unflattering comparisons such as "Aziz in Accounts really knows how to make a lady feel special," or "Your legs look so spindly next to Gary's next door."

5   Nor should you say things such as "You've stopped buying me flowers," or "You used to be much more athletic," because he might believe that a change in his behavior can patch things up. It can't, or you wouldn't be writing a Dear John letter.

6   Be clear and unambiguous in your message. Tell him plainly that

you are ending the relationship, and do this straight away. Don't leave it till after some news about how your grandma's hat was sat on by Mrs. Winterbottom.

7   Admit that the decision has been a hard one for you to make (if it has), and that in writing you have had to marshal all your courage and resolve.

8   Say that the relationship has not been right for some time and tell him frankly that you are not right for each other. These are useful clichés that allow for fault on both sides, and they underline the finality of your decision. He will doubtless recognize the truth in what you say, and see that you have made up your mind.

9   Let's be honest, you are probably not a saint yourself, and it might help to admit this to him. Don't though, whatever you do, pour out a long confession of your serial infidelity, containing lurid details of the magnificent threesomes in his flat with the lead guitarist and drummer of the Sex Pests while he was doing his voluntary work with the underprivileged. It will just cause him unnecessary pain.

10   Be exclusively positive about him and wish him well for the future. This lets him know that, although you don't want to continue the romantic relationship, you have not completely written him off as a human being, and that you still respect him and hold him in some regard as a man. You do, don't you?

11   It is best not to suggest staying friends or being "just friends." This seldom works and can be a torturous encumbrance for him. A clean amputation heals quicker.

12   Stay amiable in your sign-off. Use your first name. There's no need for "Yours faithfully" but don't use the word "love" either or put little kisses. You'll just undo all your hard work and confuse the hell out of him.

13   Once you've written your letter, *set it aside for a few days* to let the body heat go out of it. Before you send it, read it again critically to make sure you have said exactly what you mean. It can be a very difficult thing to do.

REPLIES

What if you receive a reply? Well, it's up to you now; I can't run your whole life for you. With any luck, he will have understood and you will be spared the experience of a friend of mine who wrote a Dear John letter to her soldier boyfriend and received in reply a parcel containing a photograph of herself along with a whole load of pictures of other girls—the sisters, girlfriends, and cousins of other members of his platoon, she guessed. A short note on the back of her original letter read: "Dear Amy, I forget which one is you. Just take your picture out and send back the rest. Cheers, Adam."

❦ *The quill pen was introduced around 700 CE.* ❦

Index

Bunty Cutler was not born in Paris, France, where her father wasn't a celebrated diplomat. She did not graduate first in her Bryn Mawr College class and did not then receive a prestigious Rhodes Scholarship to Oxford University, where she didn't undertake a doctorate in evidence-based epistemological reliabilism. After Oxford, Bunty never worked for the United Nations in Frankfurt, Germany, where she didn't write a celebrated biography of Albert Schweitzer in her spare time. After not returning home, she held no influential positions at NBC, before not becoming Assistant Literary Editor of *The New Yorker*. She did not then surprise everyone by launching herself on a successful career as the author of a string of bestselling cookbooks. She is not married with two children and doesn't live in a charming beachfront home in Barnstable, Massachusetts, where she never enjoys walking her dogs and playing the piano. Bunty does not have homes in London, Los Angeles, Manhattan, and Nice, where she hasn't written two acclaimed postmodernist novels. Her much-anticipated autobiography is not shortly to be published.